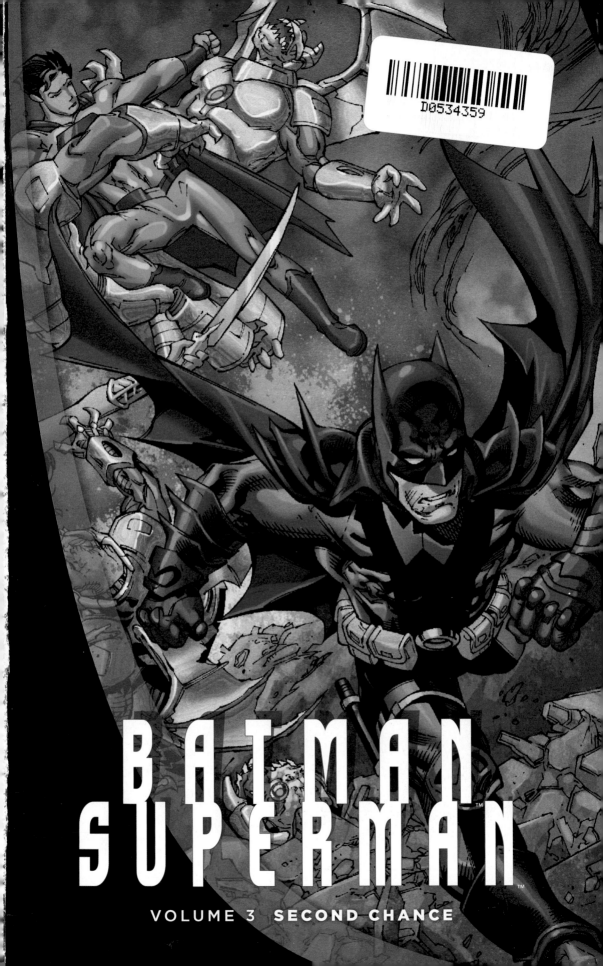

BATMAN™
SUPERMAN™

VOLUME 3 SECOND CHANCE

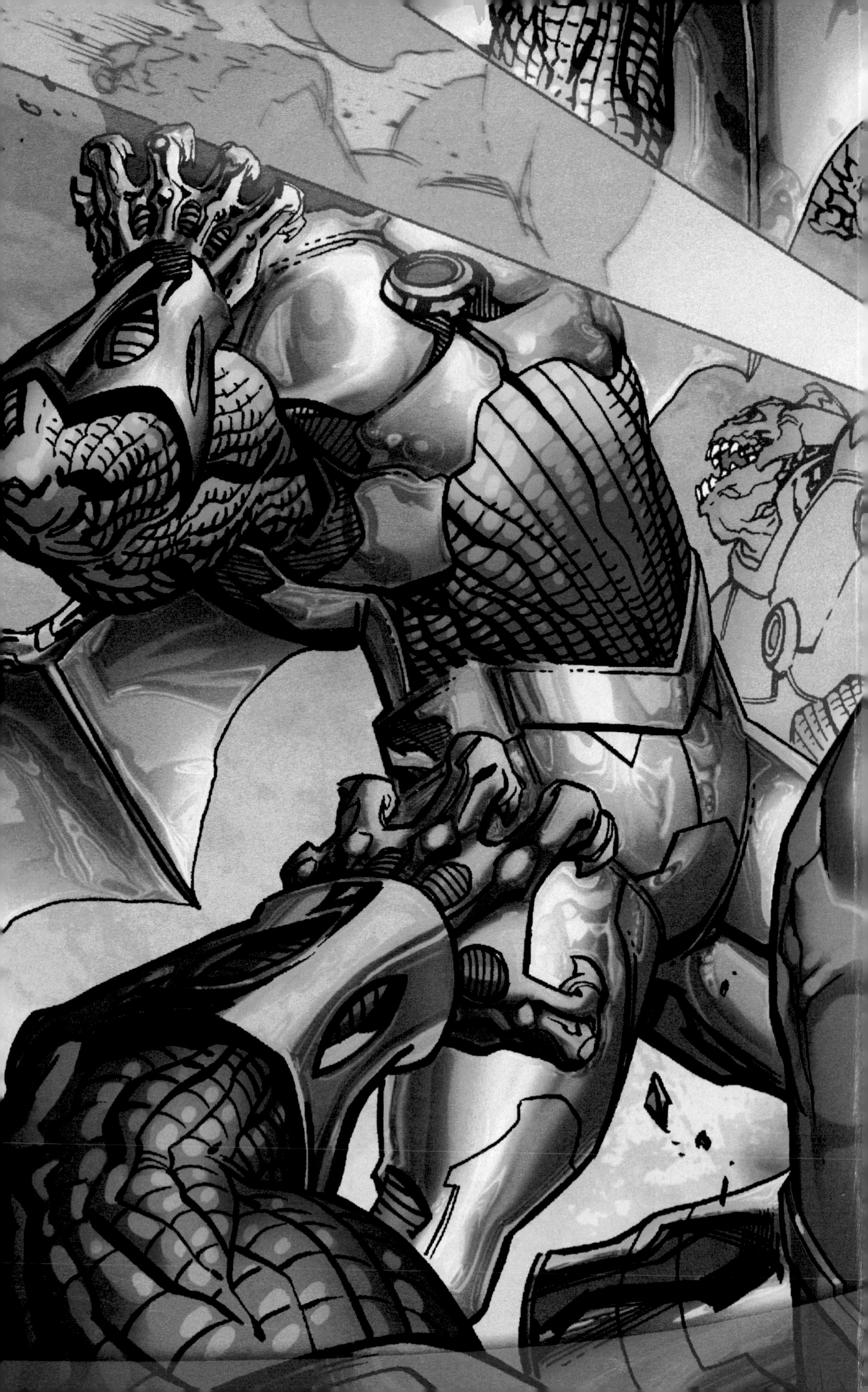

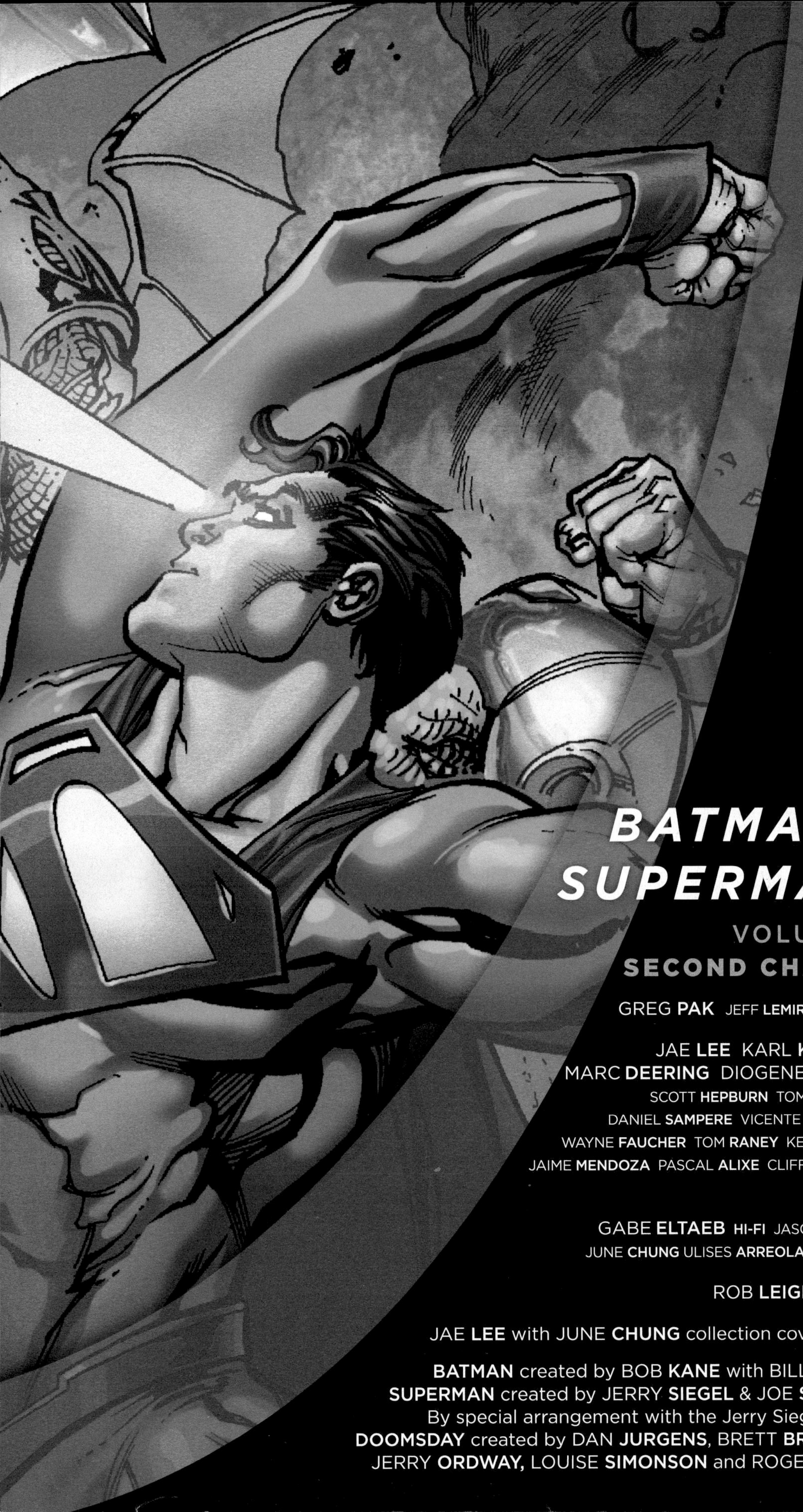

BATMAN/ SUPERMAN

VOLUME 3

SECOND CHANCE

GREG **PAK** JEFF **LEMIRE** writers

JAE **LEE** KARL **KERSCHL**
MARC **DEERING** DIOGENES **NEVES**
SCOTT **HEPBURN** TOM **DERENICK**
DANIEL **SAMPERE** VICENTE **CIFUENTES**
WAYNE **FAUCHER** TOM **RANEY** KEN **LASHLEY**
JAIME **MENDOZA** PASCAL **ALIXE** CLIFF **RICHARDS**
artists

GABE **ELTAEB** **HI-FI** JASON **WRIGHT**
JUNE **CHUNG** ULISES **ARREOLA** colorists

ROB **LEIGH** letterer

JAE **LEE** with JUNE **CHUNG** collection cover artists

BATMAN created by BOB **KANE** with BILL **FINGER**
SUPERMAN created by JERRY **SIEGEL** & JOE **SHUSTER**
By special arrangement with the Jerry Siegel family
DOOMSDAY created by DAN **JURGENS**, BRETT **BREEDING,**
JERRY **ORDWAY,** LOUISE **SIMONSON** and ROGER **STERN**

EDDIE BERGANZA Editor – Original Series RICKEY PURDIN Associate Editor – Original Series
ANTHONY MARQUES JEREMY BENT Assistant Editors – Original Series
JEB WOODARD Group Editor – Collected Editions LIZ ERICKSON Editor – Collected Edition
ROBBIE BIEDERMAN Publication Design

BOB HARRAS Senior VP – Editor-in-Chief, DC Comics

DIANE NELSON President DAN DIDIO and JIM LEE Co-Publishers GEOFF JOHNS Chief Creative Officer
AMIT DESAI Senior VP – Marketing & Global Franchise Management NAIRI GARDINER Senior VP – Finance
SAM ADES VP – Digital Marketing BOBBIE CHASE VP –Talent Development
MARK CHIARELLO Senior VP – Art, Design & Collected Editions JOHN CUNNINGHAM VP – Content Strategy
ANNE DEPIES VP – Strategy Planning & Reporting DON FALLETTI VP – Manufacturing Operations
LAWRENCE GANEM VP – Editorial Administration & Talent Relations ALISON GILL Senior VP – Manufacturing & Operations
HANK KANALZ Senior VP – Editorial Strategy & Administration JAY KOGAN VP – Legal Affairs
DEREK MADDALENA Senior VP – Sales & Business DevelopmentJACK MAHAN VP – Business Affairs
DAN MIRON VP – Sales Planning & Trade Development NICK NAPOLITANO VP – Manufacturing Administration
CAROL ROEDER VP – Marketing EDDIE SCANNELL VP – Mass Account & Digital Sales
COURTNEY SIMMONS Senior VP – Publicity & Communications
JIM (SKI) SOKOLOWSKI VP – Comic Book Specialty & Newsstand Sales SANDY YI Senior VP – Global Franchise Management

BATMAN/SUPERMAN VOLUME 3: SECOND CHANCE

Published by DC Comics. Compilation Copyright © 2015 DC Comics. All Rights Reserved.

Originally published in single magazine form as BATMAN/SUPERMAN 10-15 © 2014 DC Comics. All Rights Reserved. All characters, their
distinctive likenesses and related elements featured in this publication are trademarks of DC Comics. The stories, characters and incidents
featured in this publication are entirely fictional. DC Comics does not read or accept unsolicited ideas, stories or artwork.

DC Comics, 2900 West Alameda Avenue, Burbank, CA 91505
Printed by RR Donnelley, Salem, VA, USA. 11/13/15. First Printing.

ISBN: 978-1-4012-5754-5

PEFC Certified
Printed on paper from
sustainably managed
forests and controlled
sources
www.pefc.org
PEFC/29-31-75

Library of Congress Cataloging-in-Publication Data

Pak, Greg.
Batman/Superman. Volume 3, Second chance / Greg Pak ; illustrated by Jae Lee.
pages cm. — (The New 52!)
ISBN 978-1-4012-5754-5
1. Graphic novels. I. Lee, Jae, 1972- illustrator. II. Title. III. Title: Second chance.
PN6728.B36P344 2015
741.5'973·dc23
2015000605

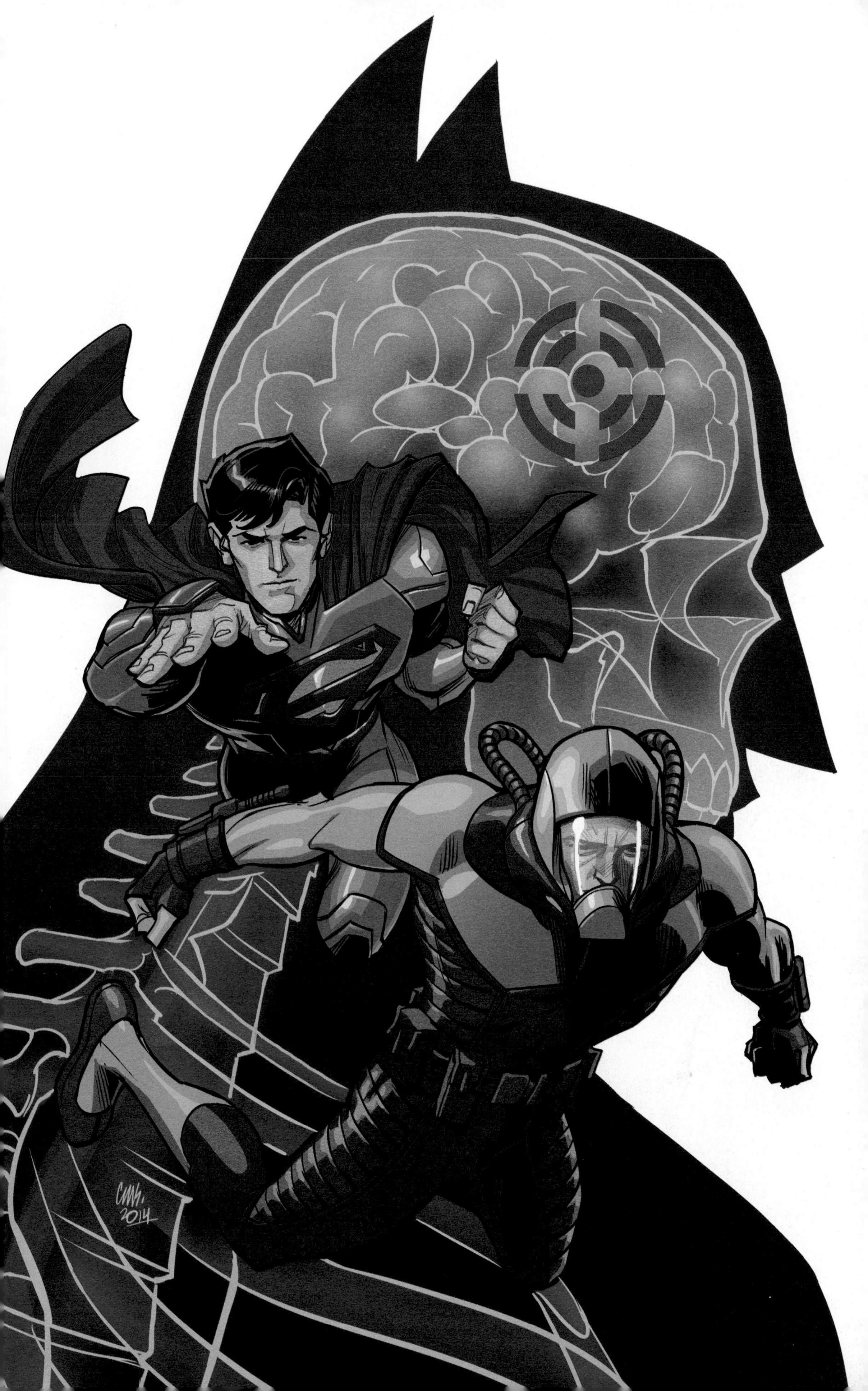

ENTER THE MICROVERSE

JEFF LEMIRE writer **KARL KERSCHL SCOTT HEPBURN** (pgs 12-15, 17-19, 22, 24) artists **GABE ELTAEB** colorist **ROB LEIGH** letterer
cover by **CAMERON STEWART**

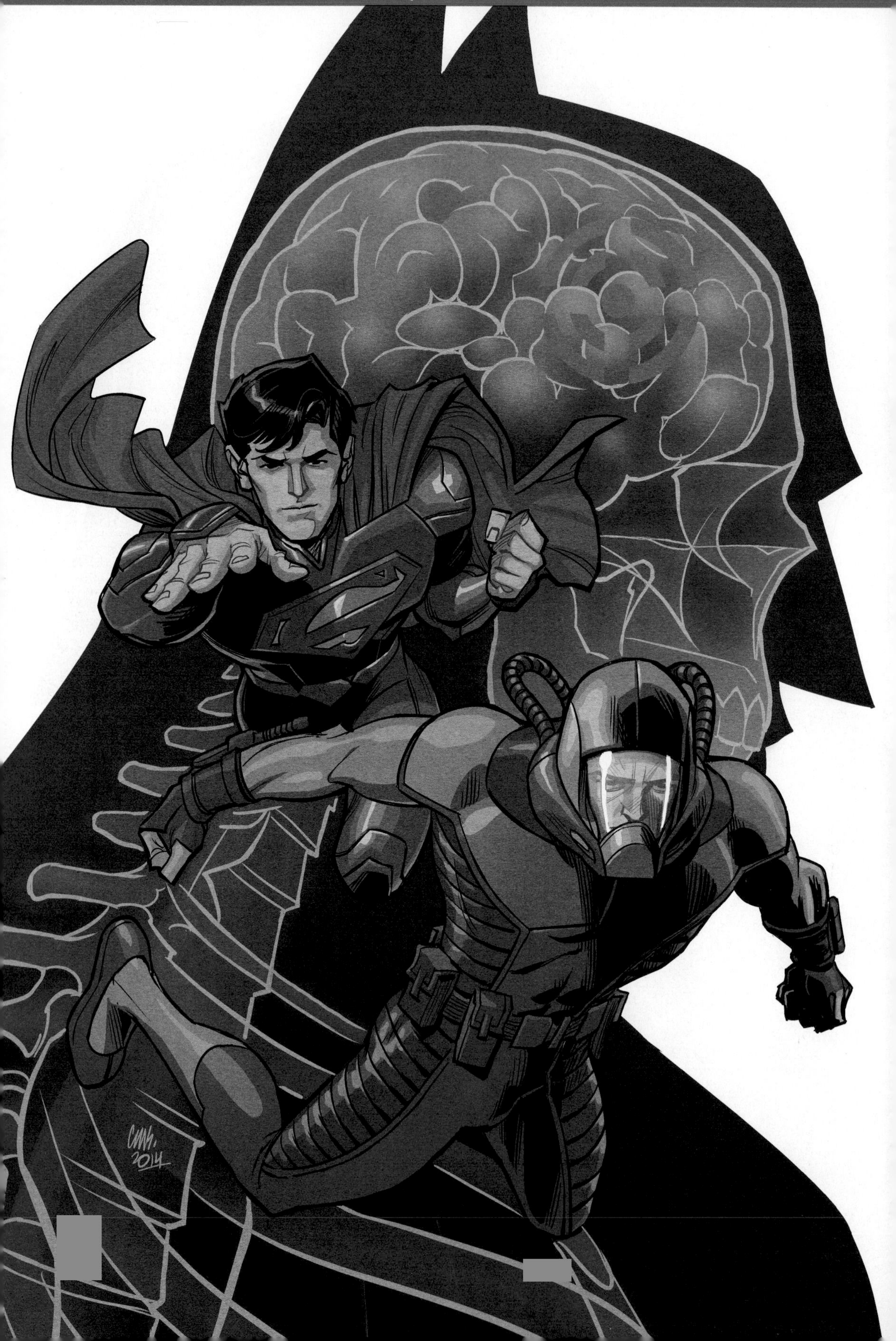

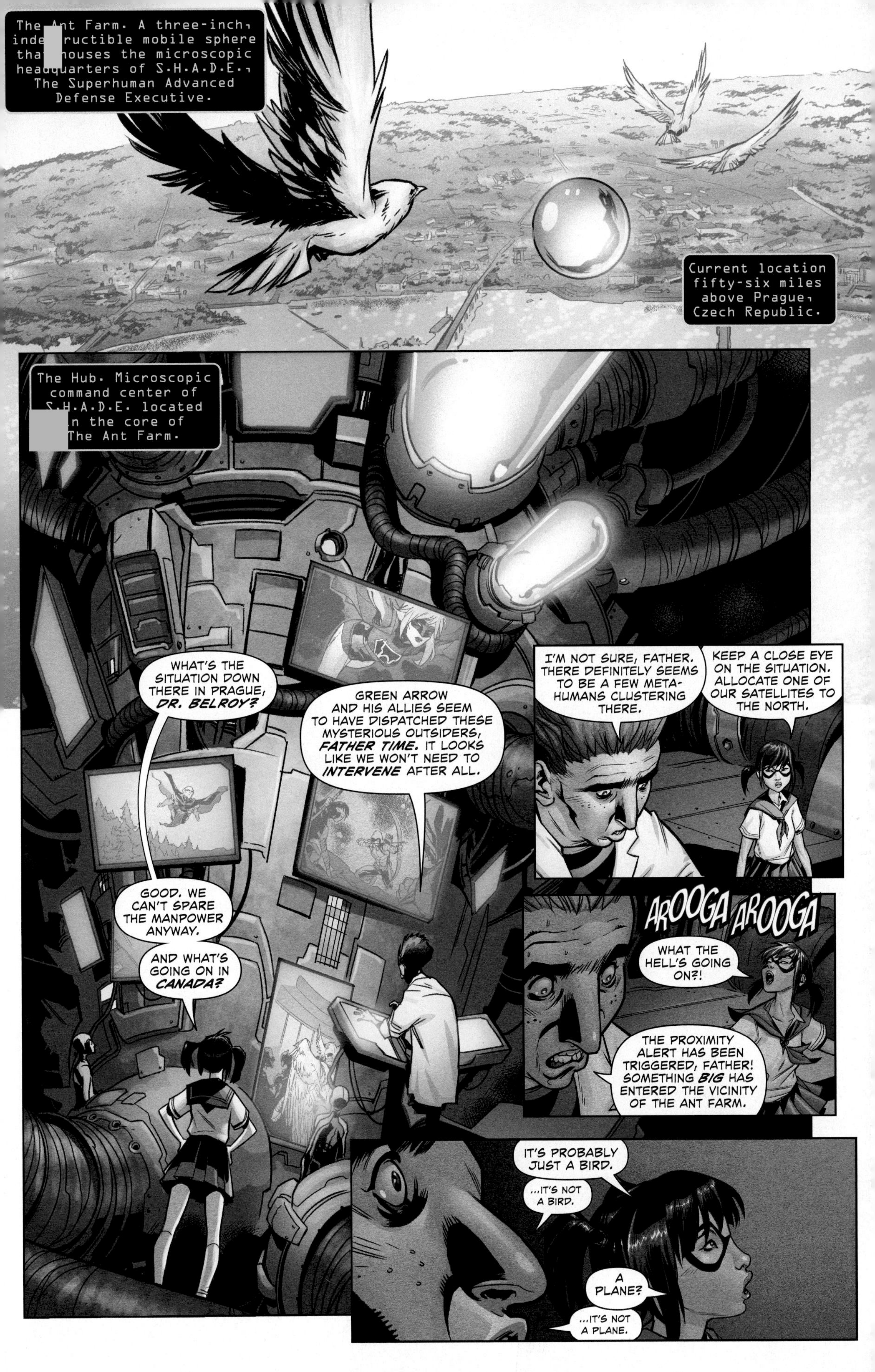

The Ant Farm. A three-inch, inde ructible mobile sphere tha houses the microscopic headquarters of S.H.A.D.E., The Superhuman Advanced Defense Executive.
Current location fifty-six miles above Prague, Czech Republic.
The Hub. Microscopic command center of S.H.A.D.E. located n the core of The Ant Farm.
WHAT'S THE SITUATION DOWN THERE IN PRAGUE, DR. BELROY?
GREEN ARROW AND HIS ALLIES SEEM TO HAVE DISPATCHED THESE MYSTERIOUS OUTSIDERS, FATHER TIME. IT LOOKS LIKE WE WON'T NEED TO INTERVENE AFTER ALL.
GOOD. WE CAN'T SPARE THE MANPOWER ANYWAY.
AND WHAT'S GOING ON IN CANADA?
I'M NOT SURE, FATHER. THERE DEFINITELY SEEMS TO BE A FEW META-HUMANS CLUSTERING THERE.
KEEP A CLOSE EYE ON THE SITUATION. ALLOCATE ONE OF OUR SATELLITES TO THE NORTH.
AROOGA AROOGA
WHAT THE HELL'S GOING ON?!
THE PROXIMITY ALERT HAS BEEN TRIGGERED, FATHER! SOMETHING BIG HAS ENTERED THE VICINITY OF THE ANT FARM.
IT'S PROBABLY JUST A BIRD.
...IT'S NOT A BIRD.
A PLANE?
...IT'S NOT A PLANE.

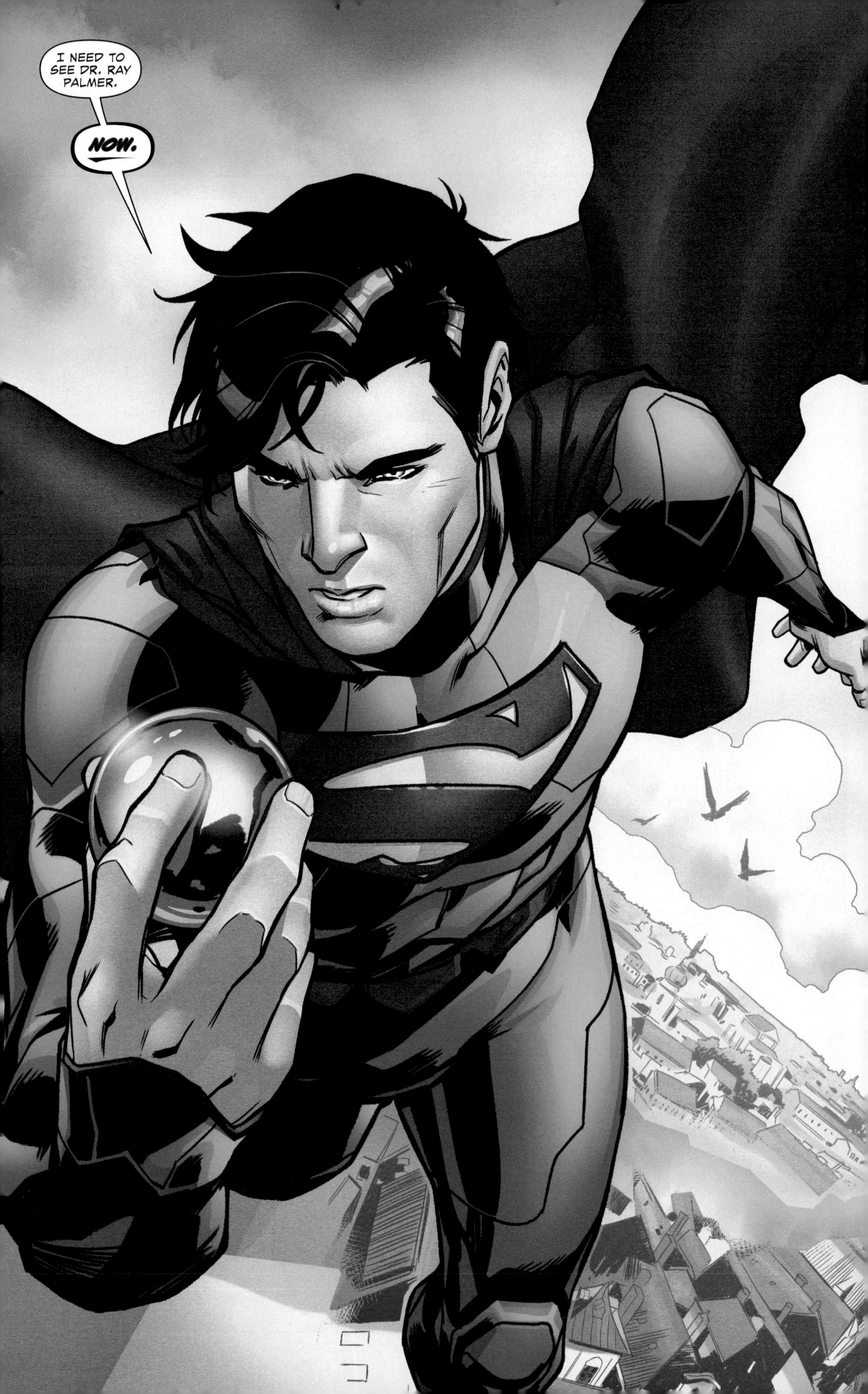
I NEED TO SEE DR. RAY PALMER.
NOW.

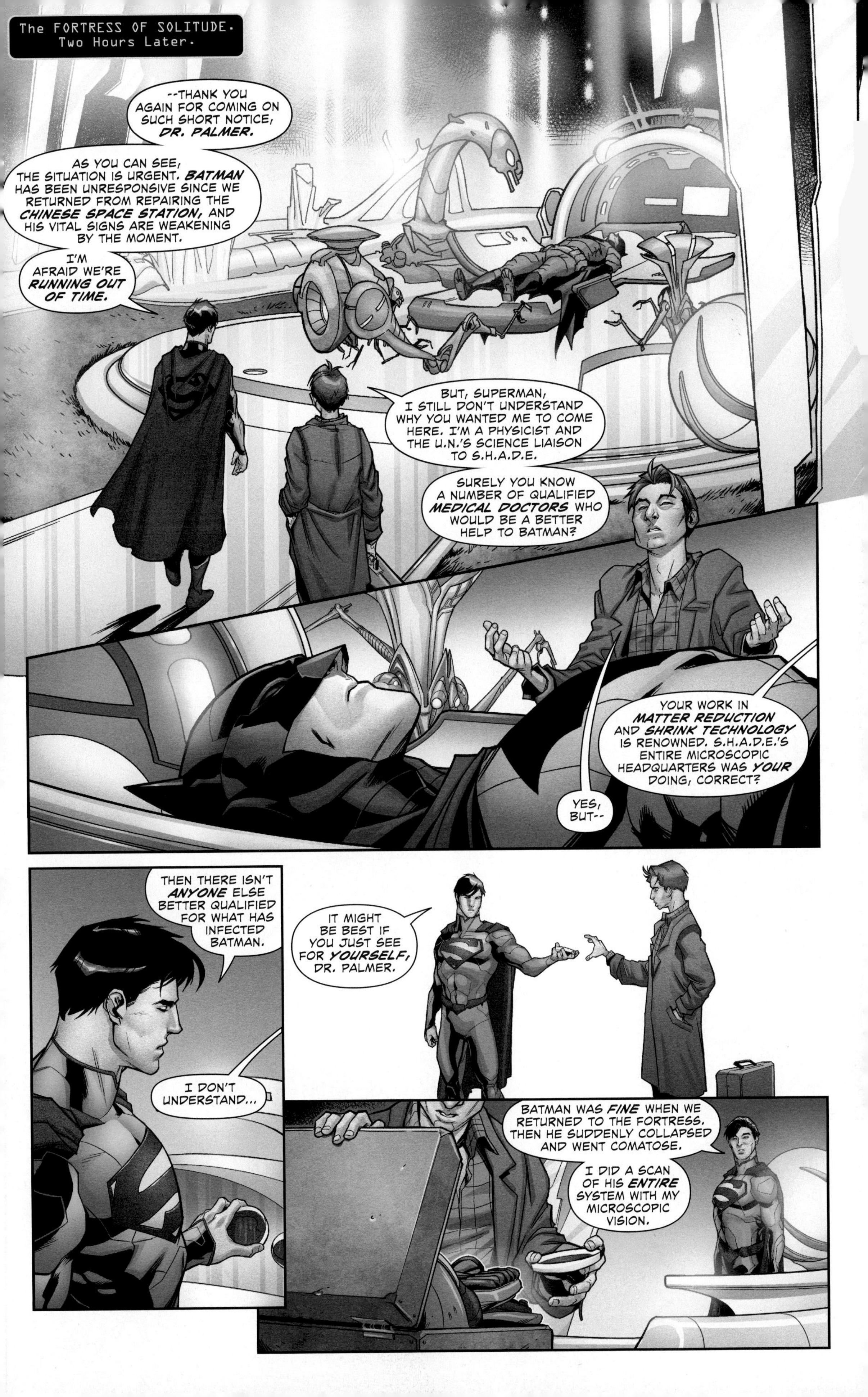
The FORTRESS OF SOLITUDE. Two Hours Later.
--THANK YOU AGAIN FOR COMING ON SUCH SHORT NOTICE, DR. PALMER.
AS YOU CAN SEE, THE SITUATION IS URGENT. BATMAN HAS BEEN UNRESPONSIVE SINCE WE RETURNED FROM REPAIRING THE CHINESE SPACE STATION, AND HIS VITAL SIGNS ARE WEAKENING BY THE MOMENT.
I'M AFRAID WE'RE RUNNING OUT OF TIME.
BUT, SUPERMAN, I STILL DON'T UNDERSTAND WHY YOU WANTED ME TO COME HERE. I'M A PHYSICIST AND THE U.N.'S SCIENCE LIAISON TO S.H.A.D.E.
SURELY YOU KNOW A NUMBER OF QUALIFIED MEDICAL DOCTORS WHO WOULD BE A BETTER HELP TO BATMAN?
YOUR WORK IN MATTER REDUCTION AND SHRINK TECHNOLOGY IS RENOWNED. S.H.A.D.E.'S ENTIRE MICROSCOPIC HEADQUARTERS WAS YOUR DOING, CORRECT?
YES, BUT--
THEN THERE ISN'T ANYONE ELSE BETTER QUALIFIED FOR WHAT HAS INFECTED BATMAN.
I DON'T UNDERSTAND...
IT MIGHT BE BEST IF YOU JUST SEE FOR YOURSELF, DR. PALMER.
BATMAN WAS FINE WHEN WE RETURNED TO THE FORTRESS. THEN HE SUDDENLY COLLAPSED AND WENT COMATOSE.
I DID A SCAN OF HIS ENTIRE SYSTEM WITH MY MICROSCOPIC VISION.

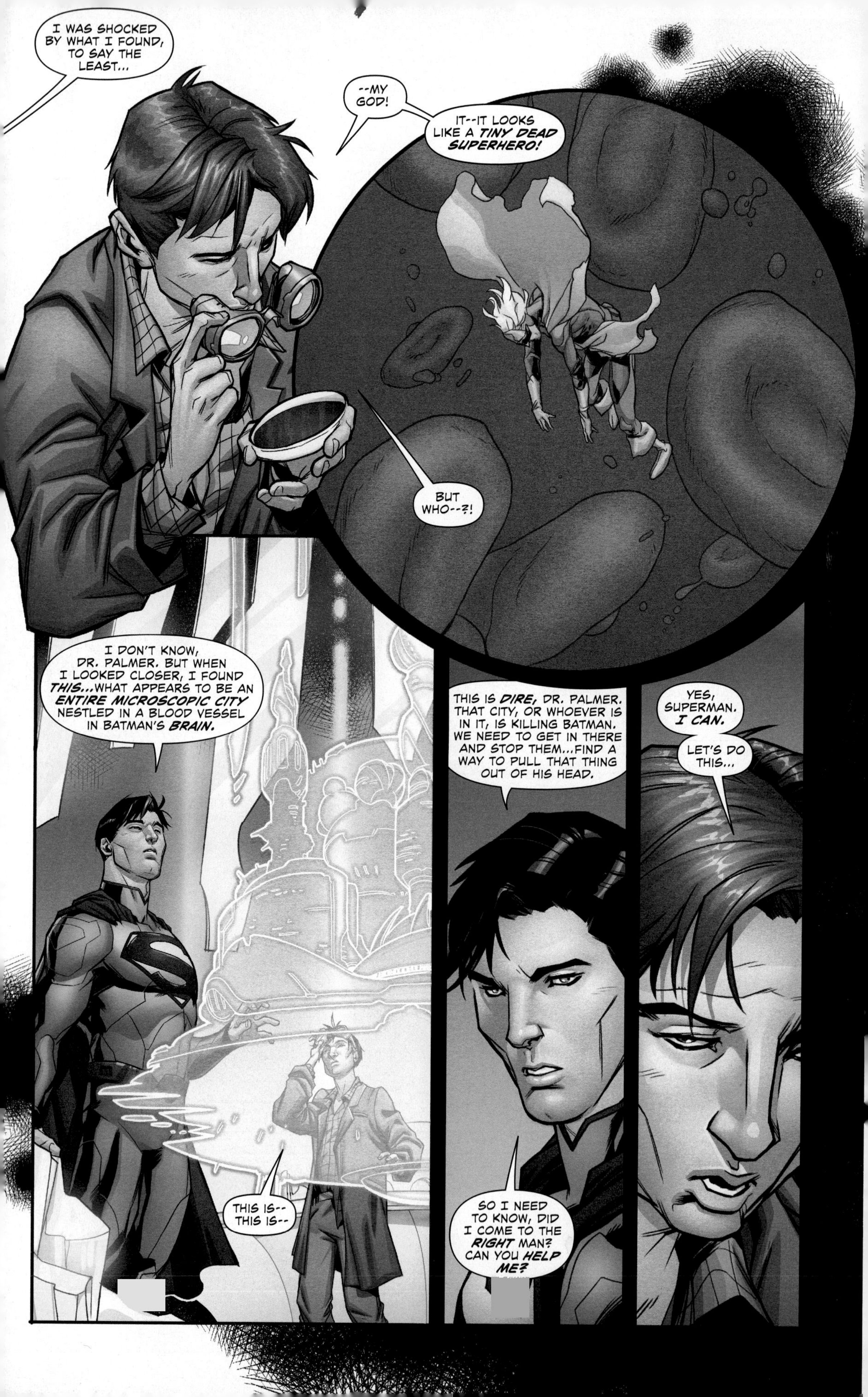
I WAS SHOCKED BY WHAT I FOUND, TO SAY THE LEAST...
--MY GOD!
IT--IT LOOKS LIKE A TINY DEAD SUPERHERO!
BUT WHO--?!
I DON'T KNOW, DR. PALMER. BUT WHEN I LOOKED CLOSER, I FOUND THIS...WHAT APPEARS TO BE AN ENTIRE MICROSCOPIC CITY NESTLED IN A BLOOD VESSEL IN BATMAN'S BRAIN.
THIS IS-- THIS IS--
THIS IS DIRE, DR. PALMER. THAT CITY, OR WHOEVER IS IN IT, IS KILLING BATMAN. WE NEED TO GET IN THERE AND STOP THEM...FIND A WAY TO PULL THAT THING OUT OF HIS HEAD.
SO I NEED TO KNOW, DID I COME TO THE RIGHT MAN? CAN YOU HELP ME?
YES, SUPERMAN. I CAN.
LET'S DO THIS...

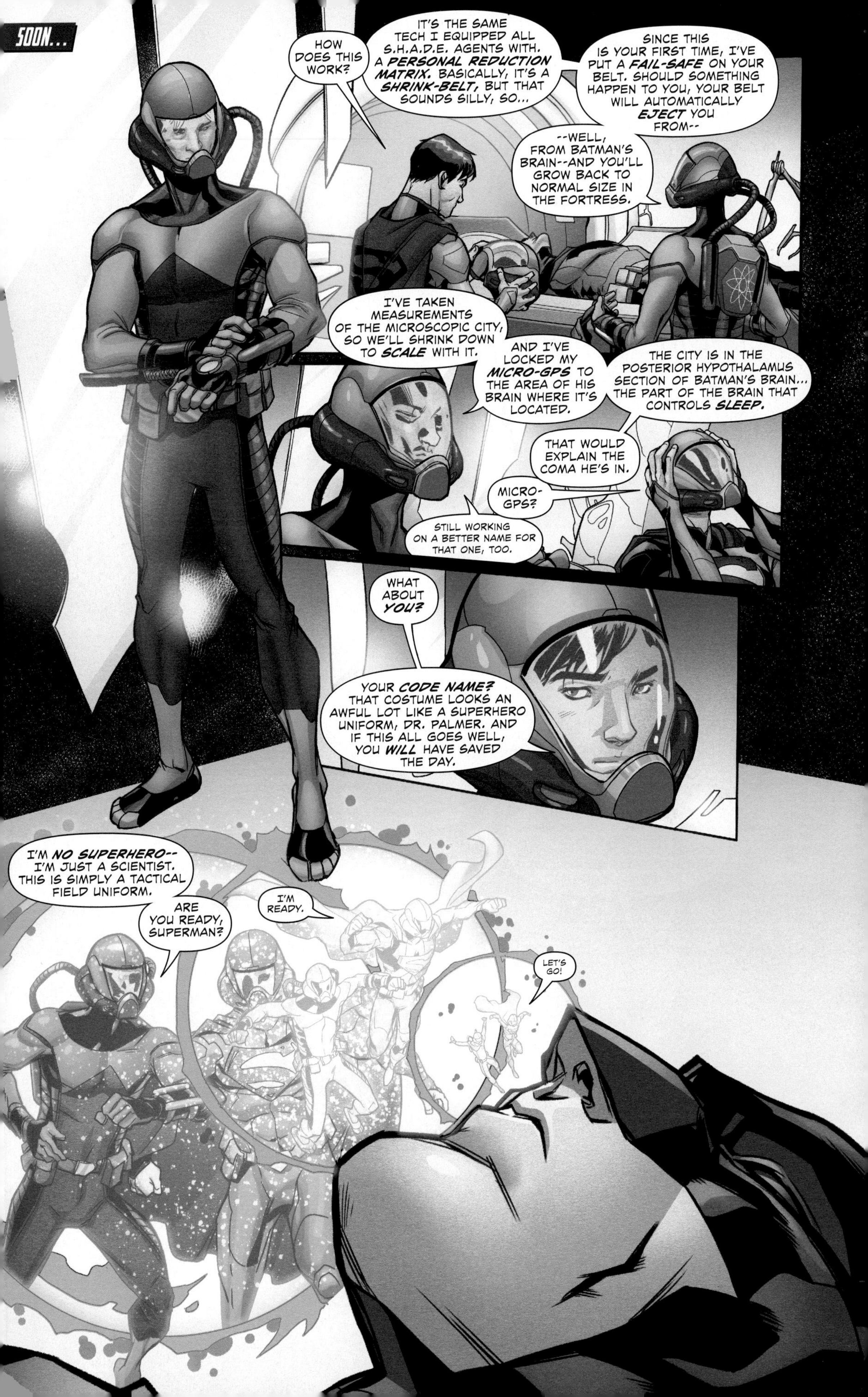
SOON...
HOW DOES THIS WORK?
IT'S THE SAME TECH I EQUIPPED ALL S.H.A.D.E. AGENTS WITH. A PERSONAL REDUCTION MATRIX. BASICALLY, IT'S A SHRINK-BELT, BUT THAT SOUNDS SILLY, SO...
SINCE THIS IS YOUR FIRST TIME, I'VE PUT A FAIL-SAFE ON YOUR BELT. SHOULD SOMETHING HAPPEN TO YOU, YOUR BELT WILL AUTOMATICALLY EJECT YOU FROM--
--WELL, FROM BATMAN'S BRAIN--AND YOU'LL GROW BACK TO NORMAL SIZE IN THE FORTRESS.
I'VE TAKEN MEASUREMENTS OF THE MICROSCOPIC CITY, SO WE'LL SHRINK DOWN TO SCALE WITH IT.
AND I'VE LOCKED MY MICRO-GPS TO THE AREA OF HIS BRAIN WHERE IT'S LOCATED.
THE CITY IS IN THE POSTERIOR HYPOTHALAMUS SECTION OF BATMAN'S BRAIN... THE PART OF THE BRAIN THAT CONTROLS SLEEP.
THAT WOULD EXPLAIN THE COMA HE'S IN.
MICRO-GPS?
STILL WORKING ON A BETTER NAME FOR THAT ONE, TOO.
WHAT ABOUT YOU?
YOUR CODE NAME? THAT COSTUME LOOKS AN AWFUL LOT LIKE A SUPERHERO UNIFORM, DR. PALMER. AND IF THIS ALL GOES WELL, YOU WILL HAVE SAVED THE DAY.
I'M NO SUPERHERO-- I'M JUST A SCIENTIST. THIS IS SIMPLY A TACTICAL FIELD UNIFORM.
ARE YOU READY, SUPERMAN?
I'M READY.
LET'S GO!

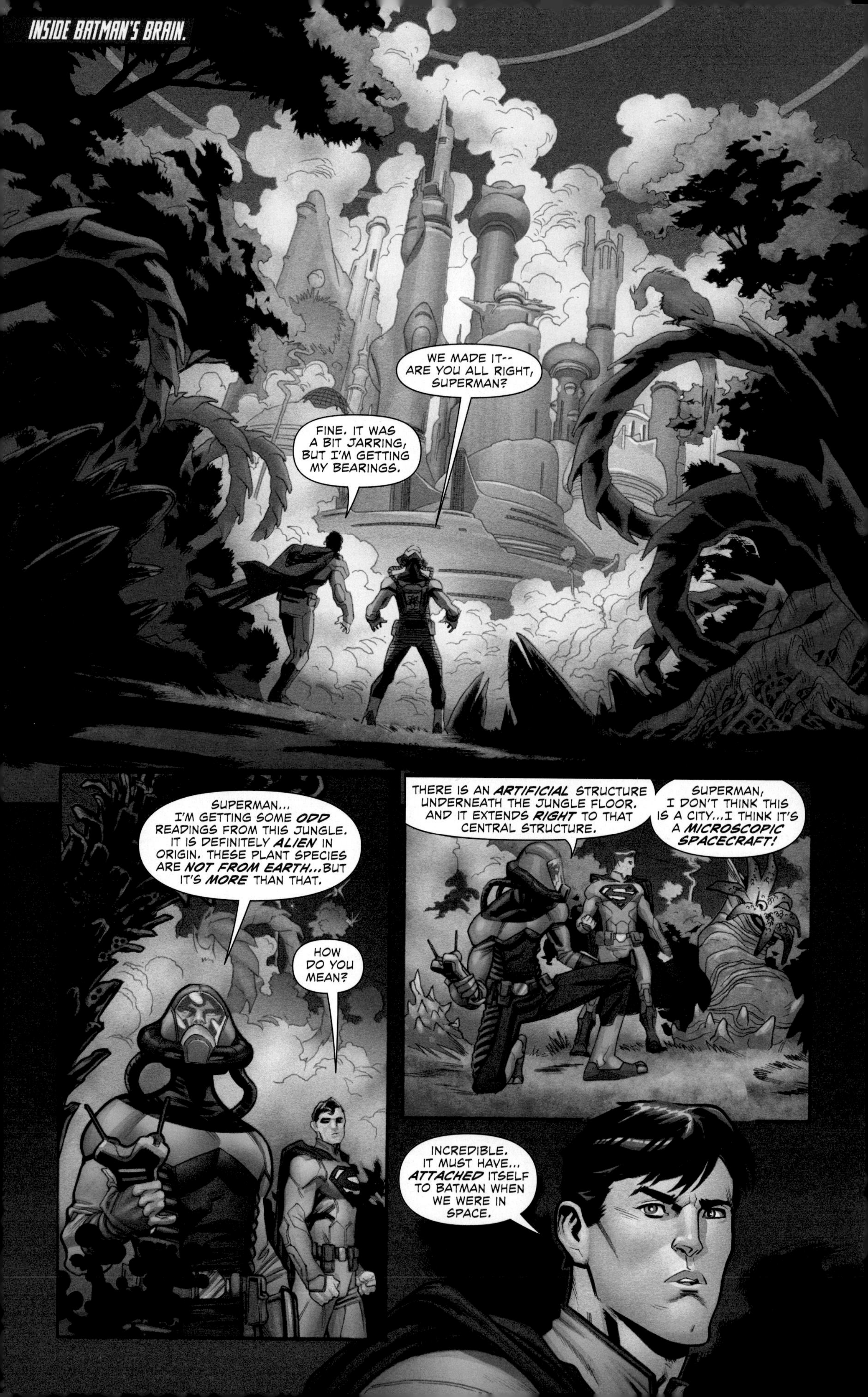
INSIDE BATMAN'S BRAIN.
WE MADE IT-- ARE YOU ALL RIGHT, SUPERMAN?
FINE. IT WAS A BIT JARRING, BUT I'M GETTING MY BEARINGS.
SUPERMAN... I'M GETTING SOME ODD READINGS FROM THIS JUNGLE. IT IS DEFINITELY ALIEN IN ORIGIN. THESE PLANT SPECIES ARE NOT FROM EARTH...BUT IT'S MORE THAN THAT.
HOW DO YOU MEAN?
THERE IS AN ARTIFICIAL STRUCTURE UNDERNEATH THE JUNGLE FLOOR. AND IT EXTENDS RIGHT TO THAT CENTRAL STRUCTURE.
SUPERMAN, I DON'T THINK THIS IS A CITY...I THINK IT'S A MICROSCOPIC SPACECRAFT!
INCREDIBLE. IT MUST HAVE... ATTACHED ITSELF TO BATMAN WHEN WE WERE IN SPACE.

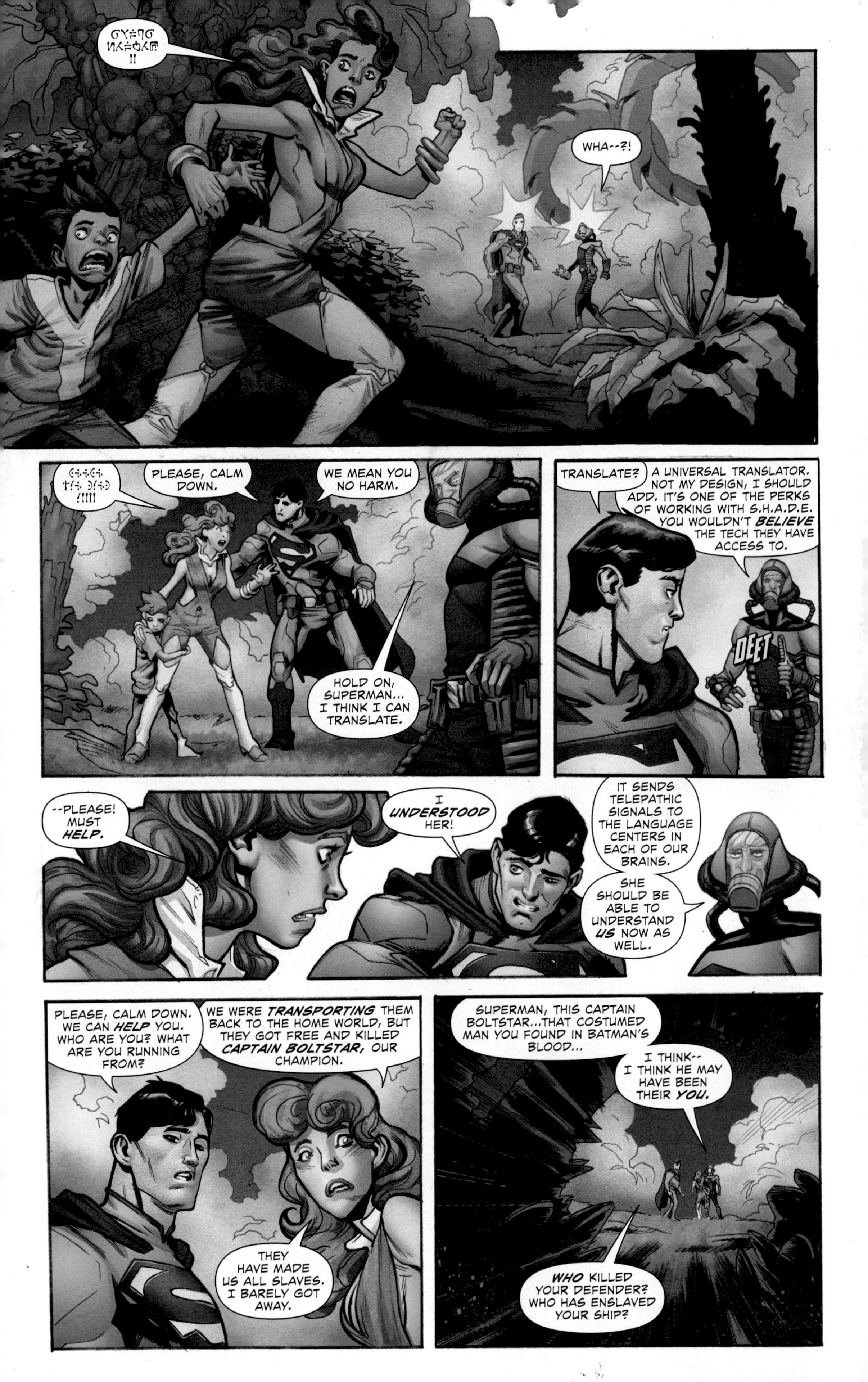
WHA--?!
PLEASE, CALM DOWN.
WE MEAN YOU NO HARM.
HOLD ON, SUPERMAN... I THINK I CAN TRANSLATE.
TRANSLATE?
A UNIVERSAL TRANSLATOR. NOT MY DESIGN, I SHOULD ADD. IT'S ONE OF THE PERKS OF WORKING WITH S.H.A.D.E. YOU WOULDN'T BELIEVE THE TECH THEY HAVE ACCESS TO.
DEET
--PLEASE! MUST HELP.
I UNDERSTOOD HER!
IT SENDS TELEPATHIC SIGNALS TO THE LANGUAGE CENTERS IN EACH OF OUR BRAINS.
SHE SHOULD BE ABLE TO UNDERSTAND US NOW AS WELL.
PLEASE, CALM DOWN. WE CAN HELP YOU. WHO ARE YOU? WHAT ARE YOU RUNNING FROM?
WE WERE TRANSPORTING THEM BACK TO THE HOME WORLD, BUT THEY GOT FREE AND KILLED CAPTAIN BOLTSTAR, OUR CHAMPION.
THEY HAVE MADE US ALL SLAVES. I BARELY GOT AWAY.
SUPERMAN, THIS CAPTAIN BOLTSTAR...THAT COSTUMED MAN YOU FOUND IN BATMAN'S BLOOD...
I THINK-- I THINK HE MAY HAVE BEEN THEIR YOU.
WHO KILLED YOUR DEFENDER? WHO HAS ENSLAVED YOUR SHIP?

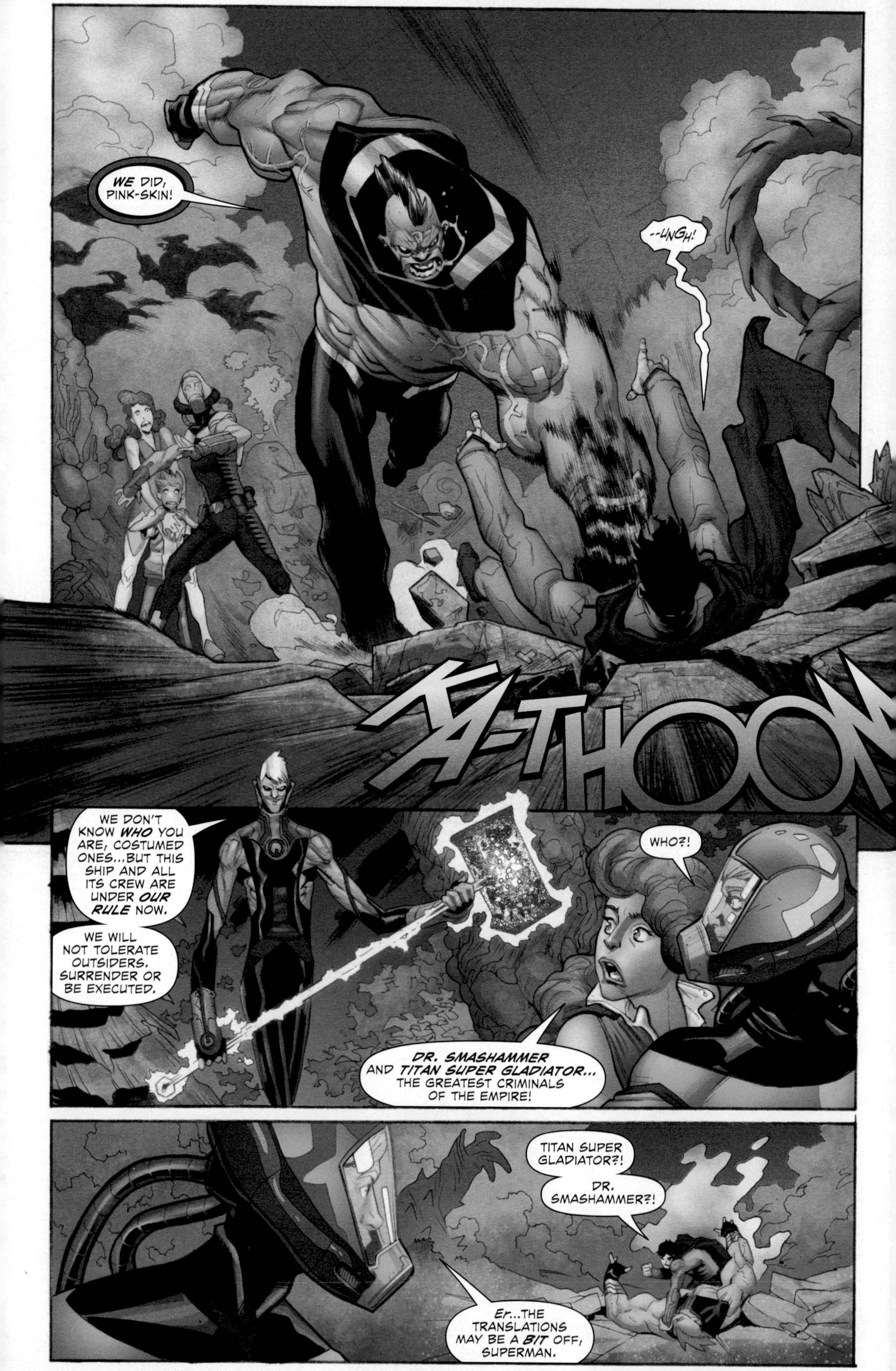
WE DID, PINK-SKIN!
--UNGH!
KA-THOOM
WE DON'T KNOW WHO YOU ARE, COSTUMED ONES...BUT THIS SHIP AND ALL ITS CREW ARE UNDER OUR RULE NOW.
WE WILL NOT TOLERATE OUTSIDERS. SURRENDER OR BE EXECUTED.
WHO?!
DR. SMASHAMMER AND TITAN SUPER GLADIATOR... THE GREATEST CRIMINALS OF THE EMPIRE!
TITAN SUPER GLADIATOR?!
DR. SMASHAMMER?!
Er...THE TRANSLATIONS MAY BE A BIT OFF, SUPERMAN.

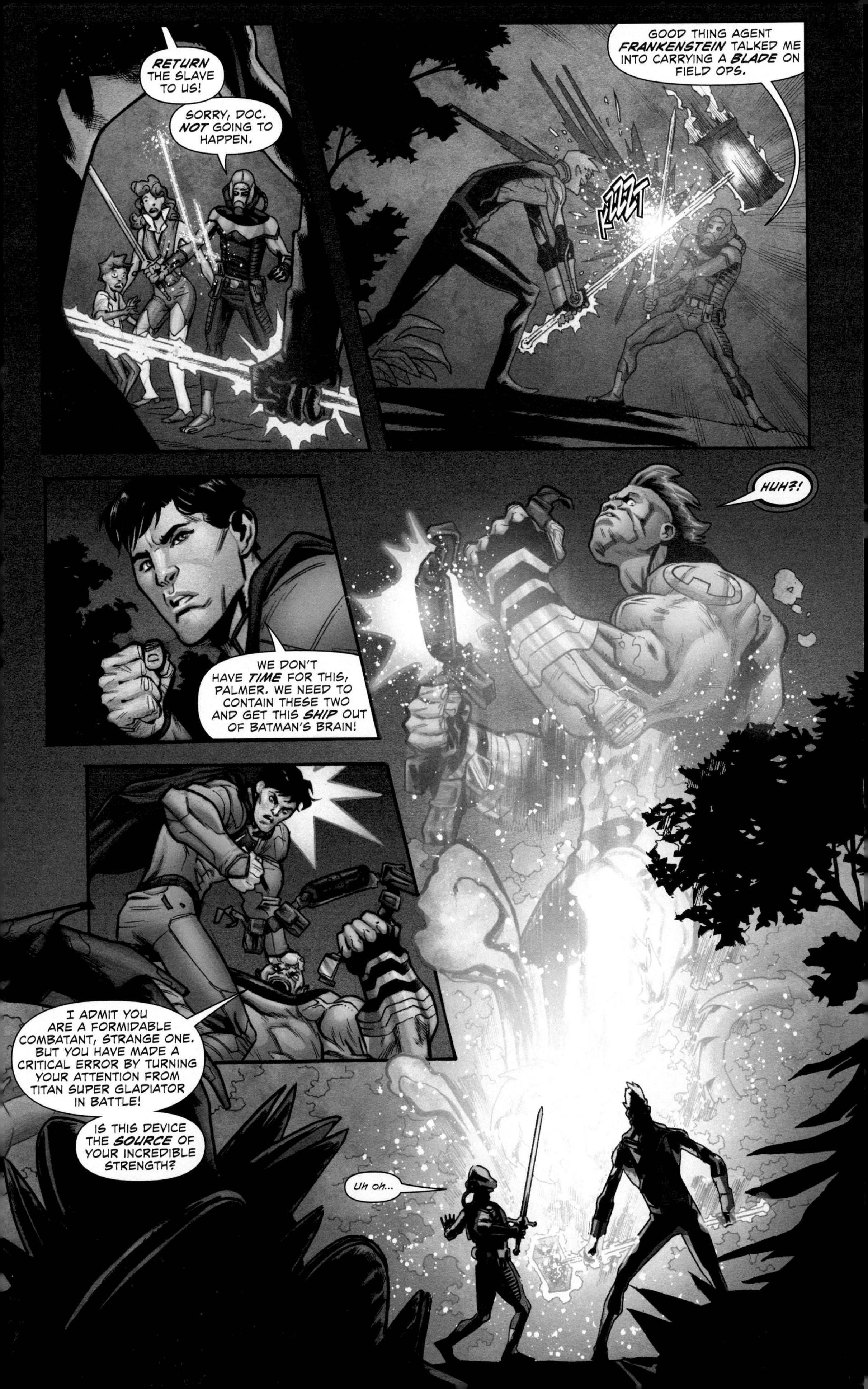
RETURN THE SLAVE TO US!
SORRY, DOC. NOT GOING TO HAPPEN.
GOOD THING AGENT FRANKENSTEIN TALKED ME INTO CARRYING A BLADE ON FIELD OPS.
KZZZT
WE DON'T HAVE TIME FOR THIS, PALMER. WE NEED TO CONTAIN THESE TWO AND GET THIS SHIP OUT OF BATMAN'S BRAIN!
HUH?!
I ADMIT YOU ARE A FORMIDABLE COMBATANT, STRANGE ONE. BUT YOU HAVE MADE A CRITICAL ERROR BY TURNING YOUR ATTENTION FROM TITAN SUPER GLADIATOR IN BATTLE!
IS THIS DEVICE THE SOURCE OF YOUR INCREDIBLE STRENGTH?
Uh oh...

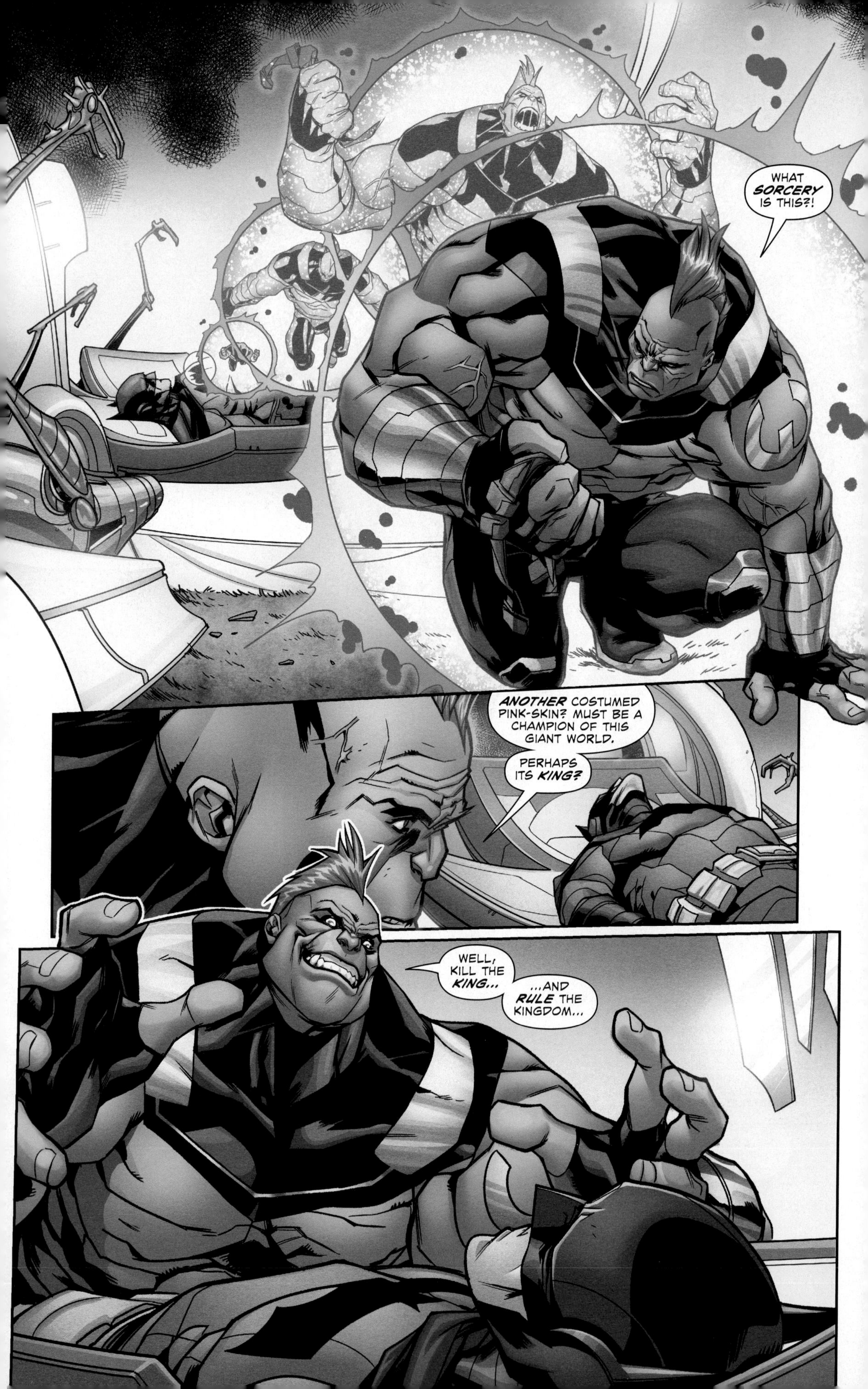
WHAT SORCERY IS THIS?!
ANOTHER COSTUMED PINK-SKIN? MUST BE A CHAMPION OF THIS GIANT WORLD.
PERHAPS ITS KING?
WELL, KILL THE KING...
...AND RULE THE KINGDOM...

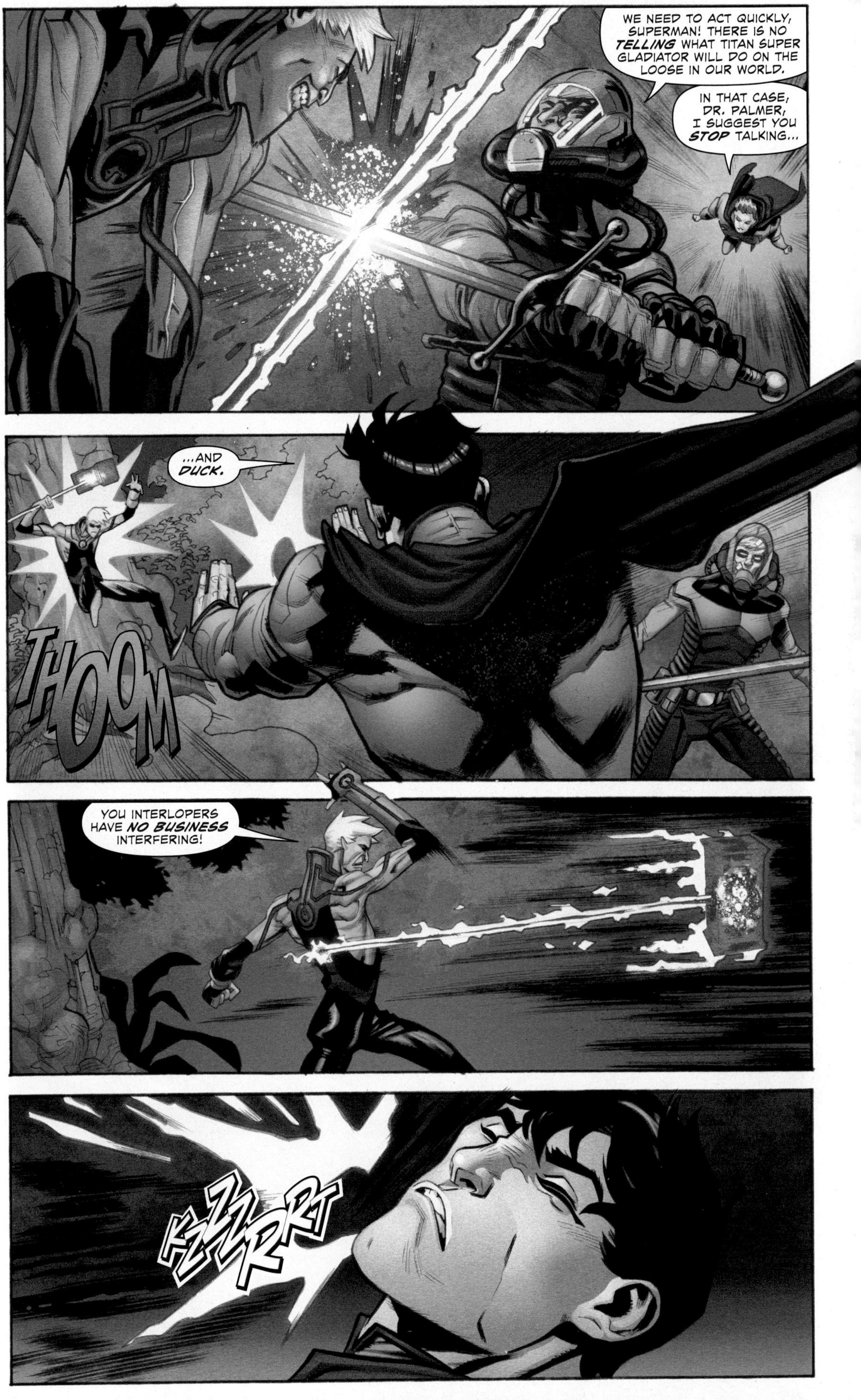
WE NEED TO ACT QUICKLY, SUPERMAN! THERE IS NO TELLING WHAT TITAN SUPER GLADIATOR WILL DO ON THE LOOSE IN OUR WORLD.
IN THAT CASE, DR. PALMER, I SUGGEST YOU STOP TALKING...
...AND DUCK.
THOOM
YOU INTERLOPERS HAVE NO BUSINESS INTERFERING!
KZZZRRT

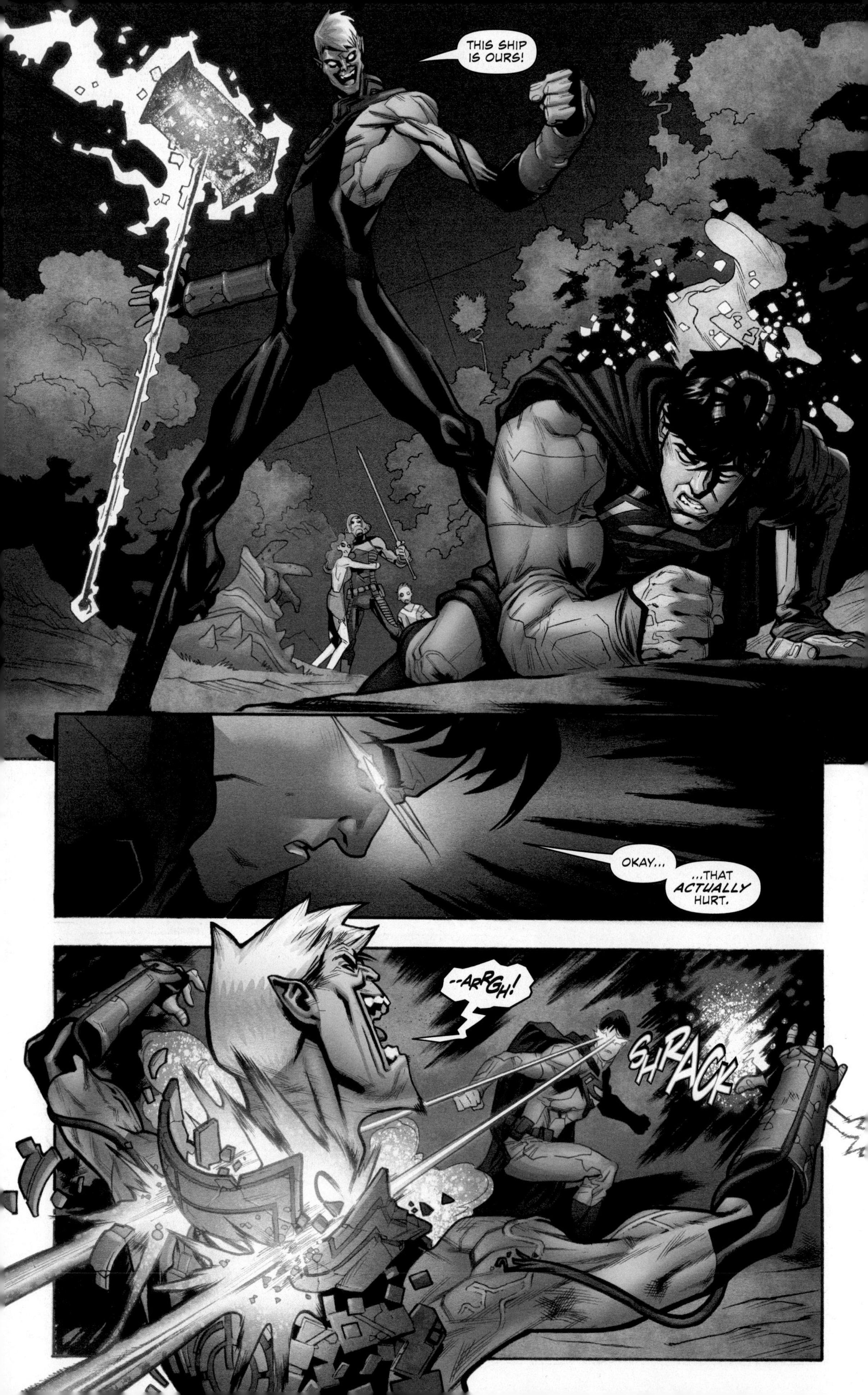
THIS SHIP IS OURS!
OKAY...
...THAT *ACTUALLY* HURT.
--ARRGH!
SHRACK

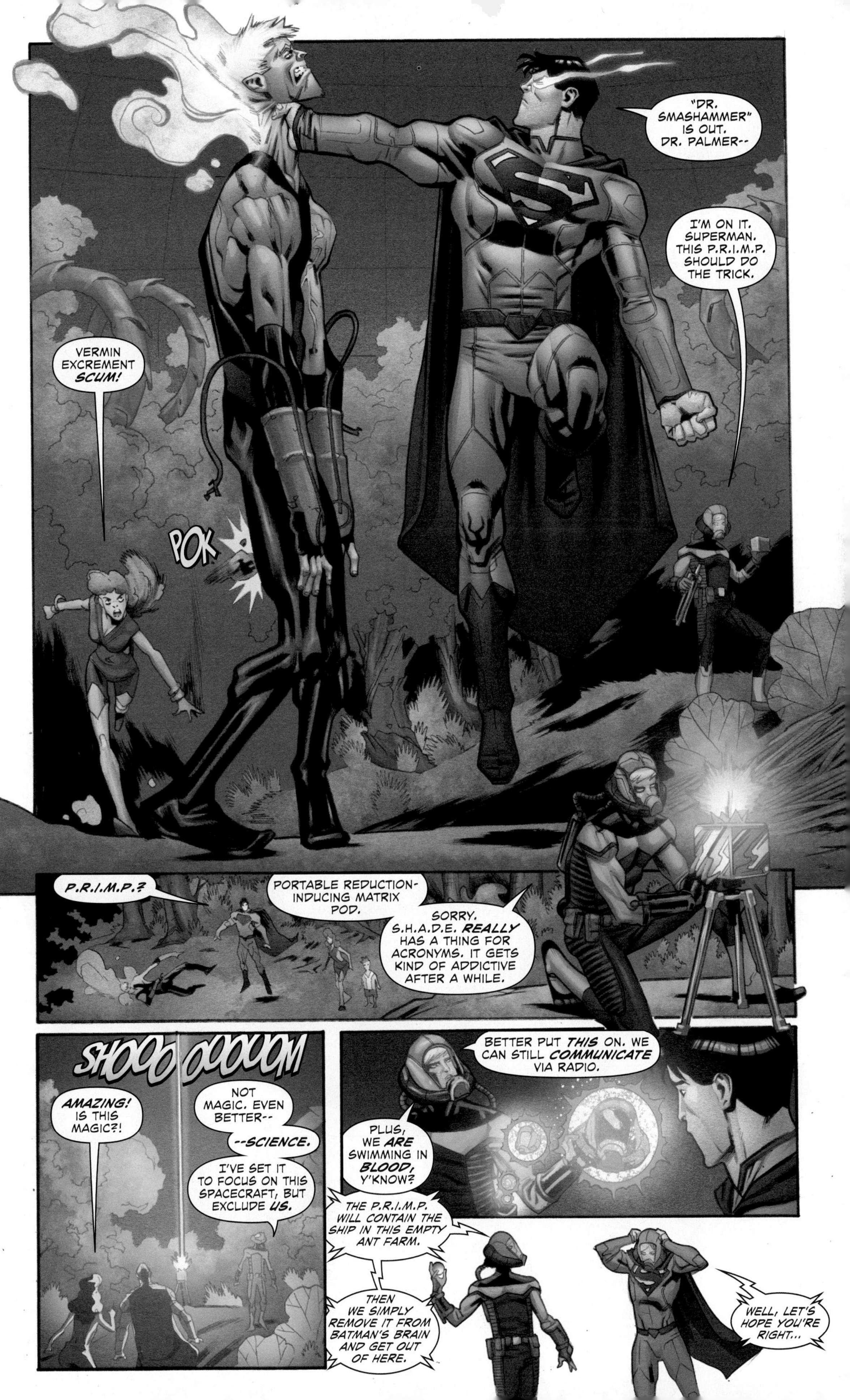

"DR. SMASHAMMER" IS OUT. DR. PALMER--
I'M ON IT. SUPERMAN. THIS P.R.I.M.P. SHOULD DO THE TRICK.
VERMIN EXCREMENT SCUM!
POK
P.R.I.M.P.?
PORTABLE REDUCTION-INDUCING MATRIX POD.
SORRY. S.H.A.D.E. REALLY HAS A THING FOR ACRONYMS. IT GETS KIND OF ADDICTIVE AFTER A WHILE.
SHOOOOOOOOM
AMAZING! IS THIS MAGIC?!
NOT MAGIC. EVEN BETTER--
--SCIENCE.
I'VE SET IT TO FOCUS ON THIS SPACECRAFT, BUT EXCLUDE US.
BETTER PUT THIS ON. WE CAN STILL COMMUNICATE VIA RADIO.
PLUS, WE ARE SWIMMING IN BLOOD, Y'KNOW?
THE P.R.I.M.P. WILL CONTAIN THE SHIP IN THIS EMPTY ANT FARM.
THEN WE SIMPLY REMOVE IT FROM BATMAN'S BRAIN AND GET OUT OF HERE.
WELL, LET'S HOPE YOU'RE RIGHT...

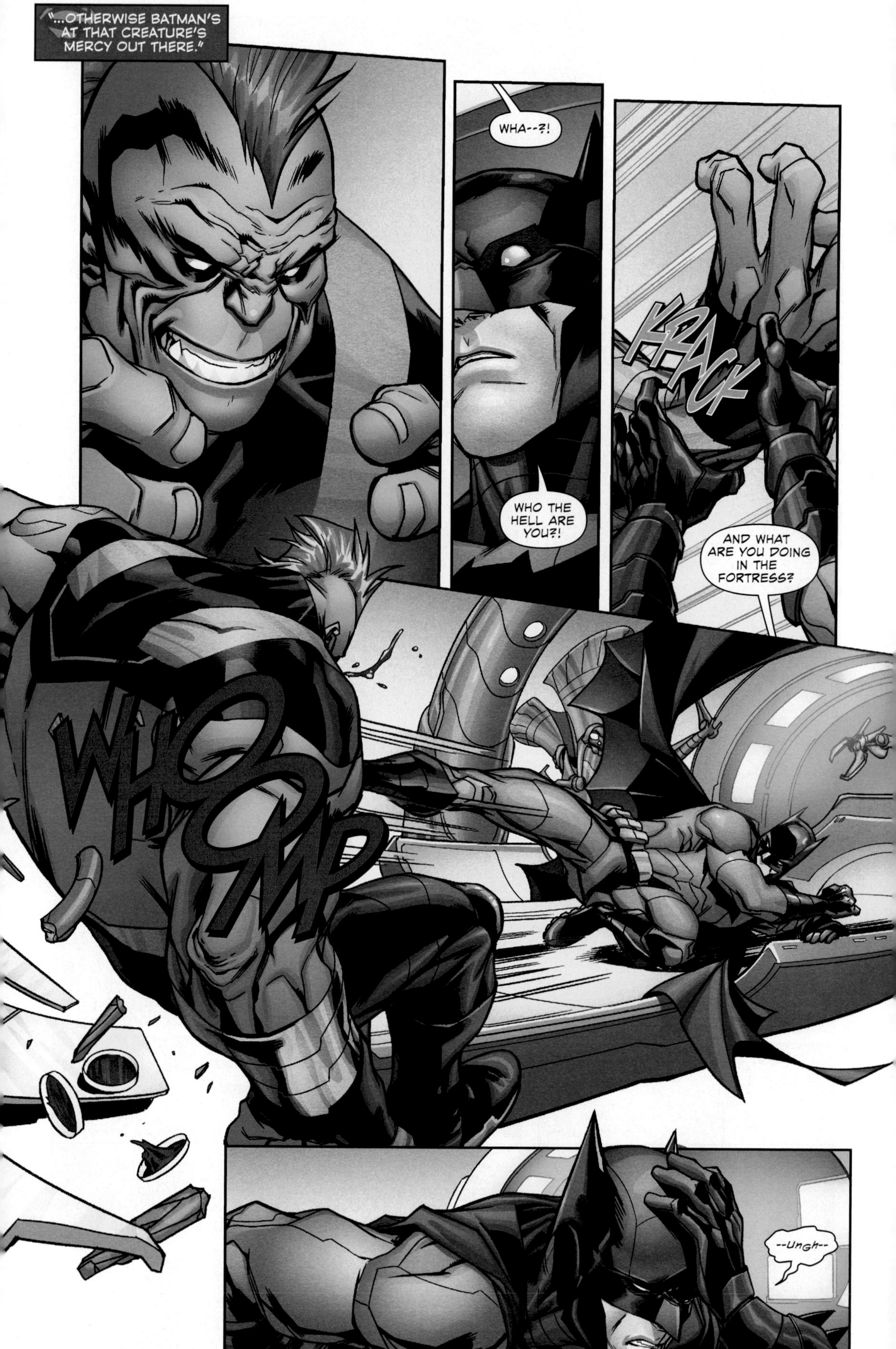
"...OTHERWISE BATMAN'S AT THAT CREATURE'S MERCY OUT THERE."
WHA--?!
WHO THE HELL ARE YOU?!
KRACK
AND WHAT ARE YOU DOING IN THE FORTRESS?
WHOOMP
--Ungh--

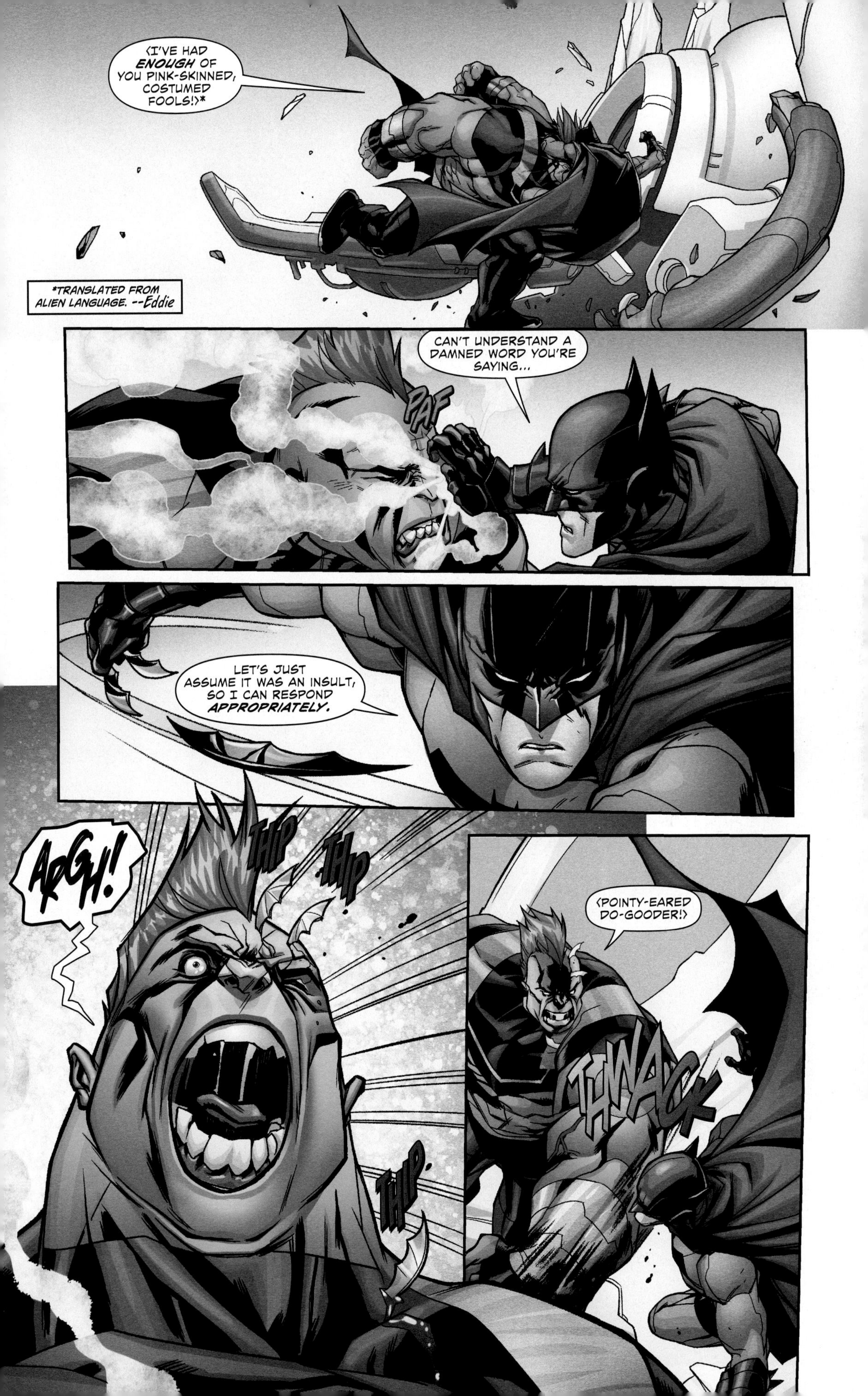
〈I'VE HAD ENOUGH OF YOU PINK-SKINNED, COSTUMED FOOLS!〉*
*TRANSLATED FROM ALIEN LANGUAGE. --Eddie
CAN'T UNDERSTAND A DAMNED WORD YOU'RE SAYING...
PAF
LET'S JUST ASSUME IT WAS AN INSULT, SO I CAN RESPOND APPROPRIATELY.
ARGH!
THIP
THIP
THIP
〈POINTY-EARED DO-GOODER!〉
THWACK

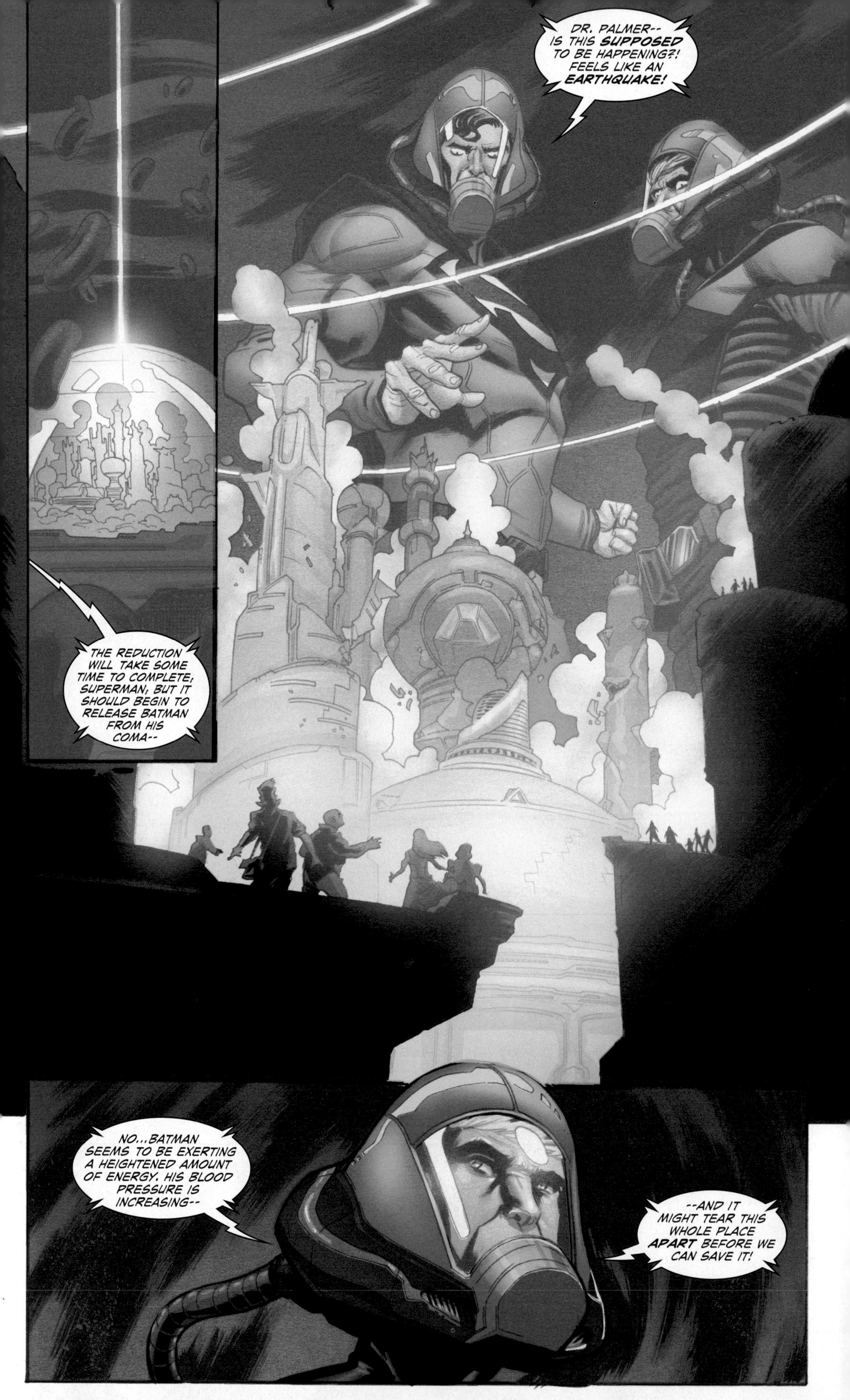

DR. PALMER-- IS THIS SUPPOSED TO BE HAPPENING?! FEELS LIKE AN EARTHQUAKE!
THE REDUCTION WILL TAKE SOME TIME TO COMPLETE, SUPERMAN, BUT IT SHOULD BEGIN TO RELEASE BATMAN FROM HIS COMA--
NO...BATMAN SEEMS TO BE EXERTING A HEIGHTENED AMOUNT OF ENERGY. HIS BLOOD PRESSURE IS INCREASING--
--AND IT MIGHT TEAR THIS WHOLE PLACE APART BEFORE WE CAN SAVE IT!

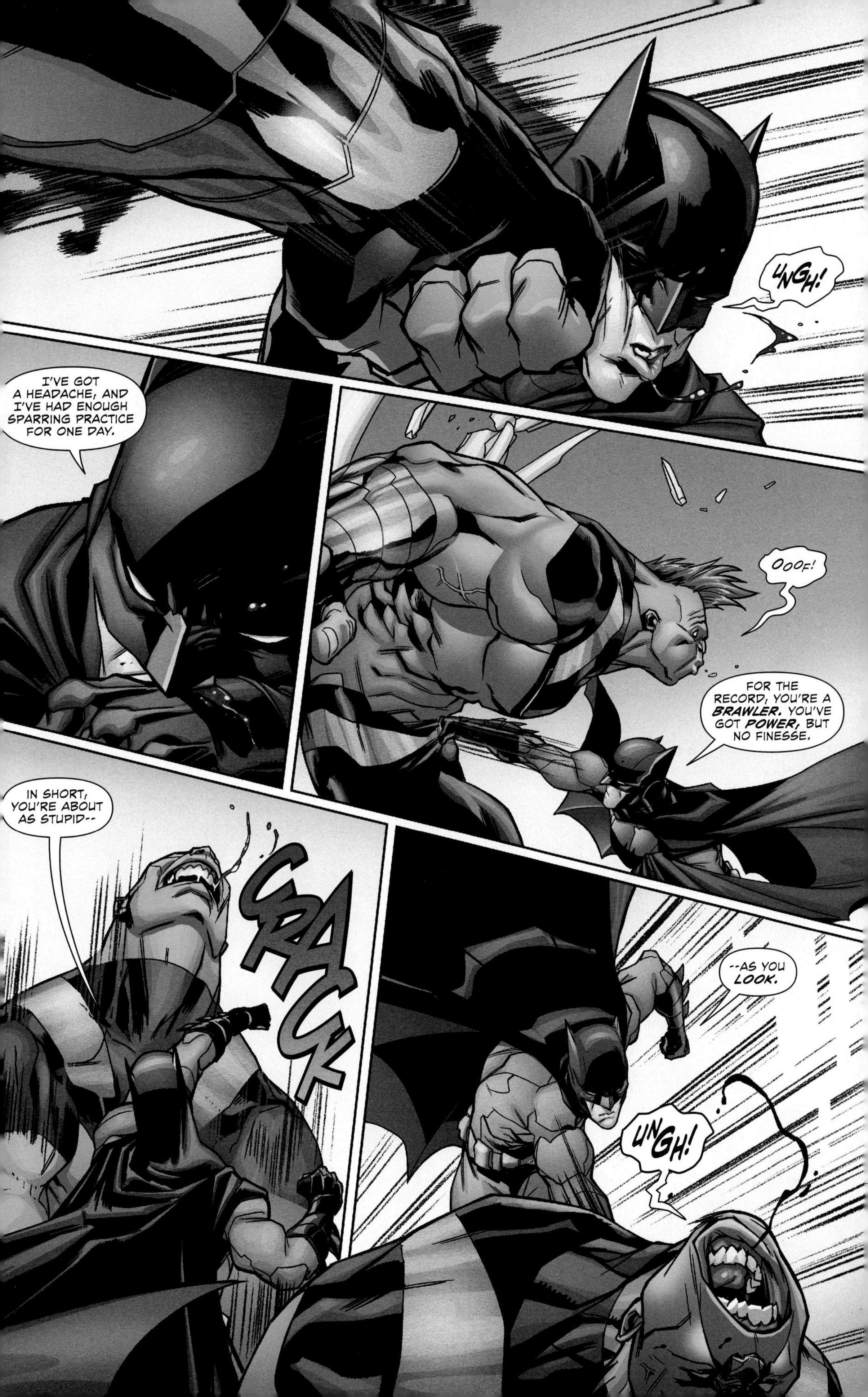
UNGH!
I'VE GOT A HEADACHE, AND I'VE HAD ENOUGH SPARRING PRACTICE FOR ONE DAY.
OOOF!
FOR THE RECORD, YOU'RE A BRAWLER. YOU'VE GOT POWER, BUT NO FINESSE.
IN SHORT, YOU'RE ABOUT AS STUPID--
CRACK
--AS YOU LOOK.
UNGH!

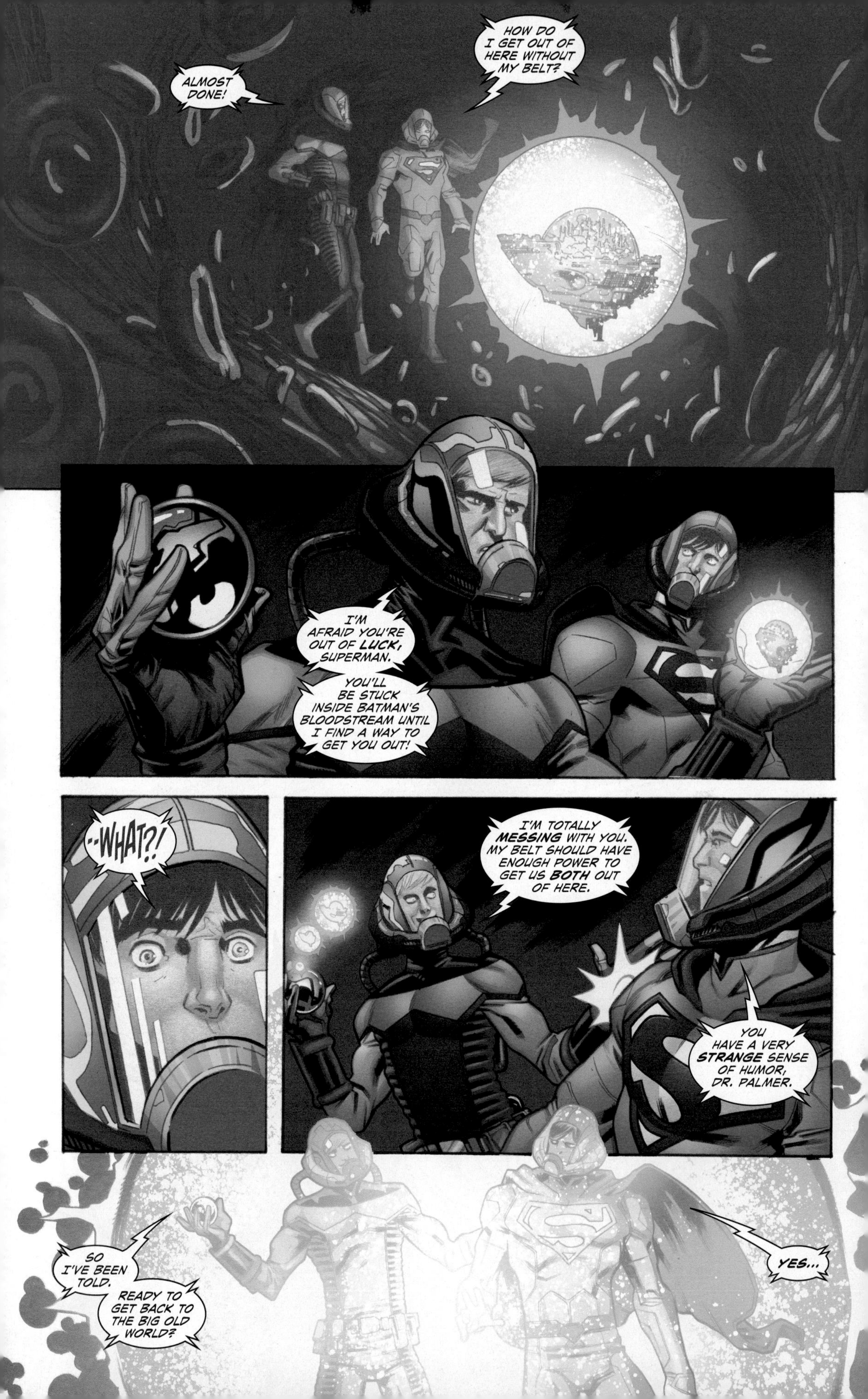
ALMOST DONE!
HOW DO I GET OUT OF HERE WITHOUT MY BELT?
I'M AFRAID YOU'RE OUT OF LUCK, SUPERMAN.
YOU'LL BE STUCK INSIDE BATMAN'S BLOODSTREAM UNTIL I FIND A WAY TO GET YOU OUT!
--WHAT?!
I'M TOTALLY MESSING WITH YOU. MY BELT SHOULD HAVE ENOUGH POWER TO GET US BOTH OUT OF HERE.
YOU HAVE A VERY STRANGE SENSE OF HUMOR, DR. PALMER.
SO I'VE BEEN TOLD.
READY TO GET BACK TO THE BIG OLD WORLD?
YES...

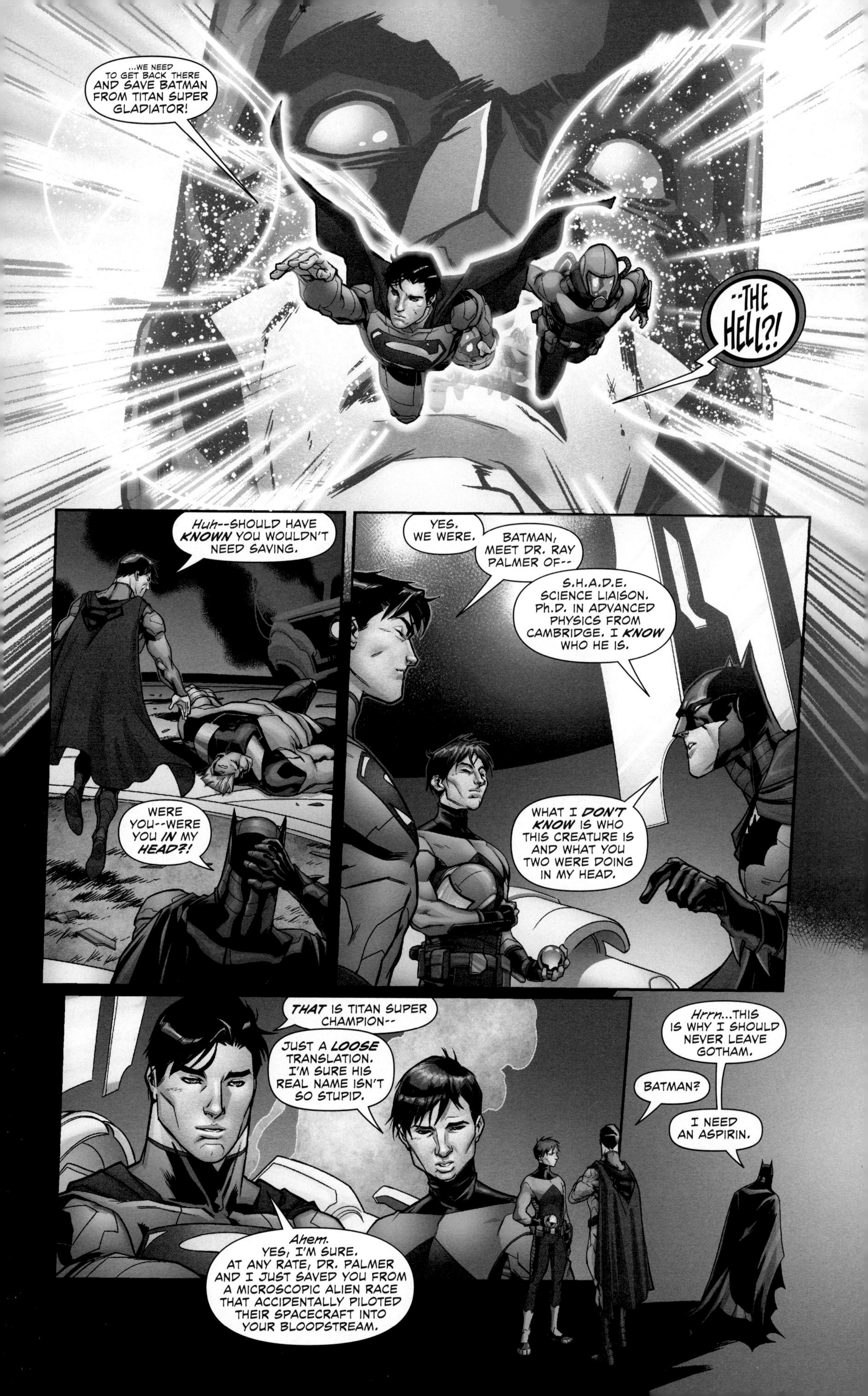
...WE NEED TO GET BACK THERE AND SAVE BATMAN FROM TITAN SUPER GLADIATOR!
--THE HELL?!
Huh--SHOULD HAVE **KNOWN** YOU WOULDN'T NEED SAVING.
WERE YOU--WERE YOU ***IN*** MY ***HEAD?!***
YES. WE WERE.
BATMAN, MEET DR. RAY PALMER OF--
S.H.A.D.E. SCIENCE LIAISON. Ph.D. IN ADVANCED PHYSICS FROM CAMBRIDGE. I ***KNOW*** WHO HE IS.
WHAT I ***DON'T KNOW*** IS WHO THIS CREATURE IS AND WHAT YOU TWO WERE DOING IN MY HEAD.
THAT IS TITAN SUPER CHAMPION--
JUST A ***LOOSE*** TRANSLATION. I'M SURE HIS REAL NAME ISN'T SO STUPID.
Ahem. YES, I'M SURE. AT ANY RATE, DR. PALMER AND I JUST SAVED YOU FROM A MICROSCOPIC ALIEN RACE THAT ACCIDENTALLY PILOTED THEIR SPACECRAFT INTO YOUR BLOODSTREAM.
Hrrn...THIS IS WHY I SHOULD NEVER LEAVE GOTHAM.
BATMAN?
I NEED AN ASPIRIN.

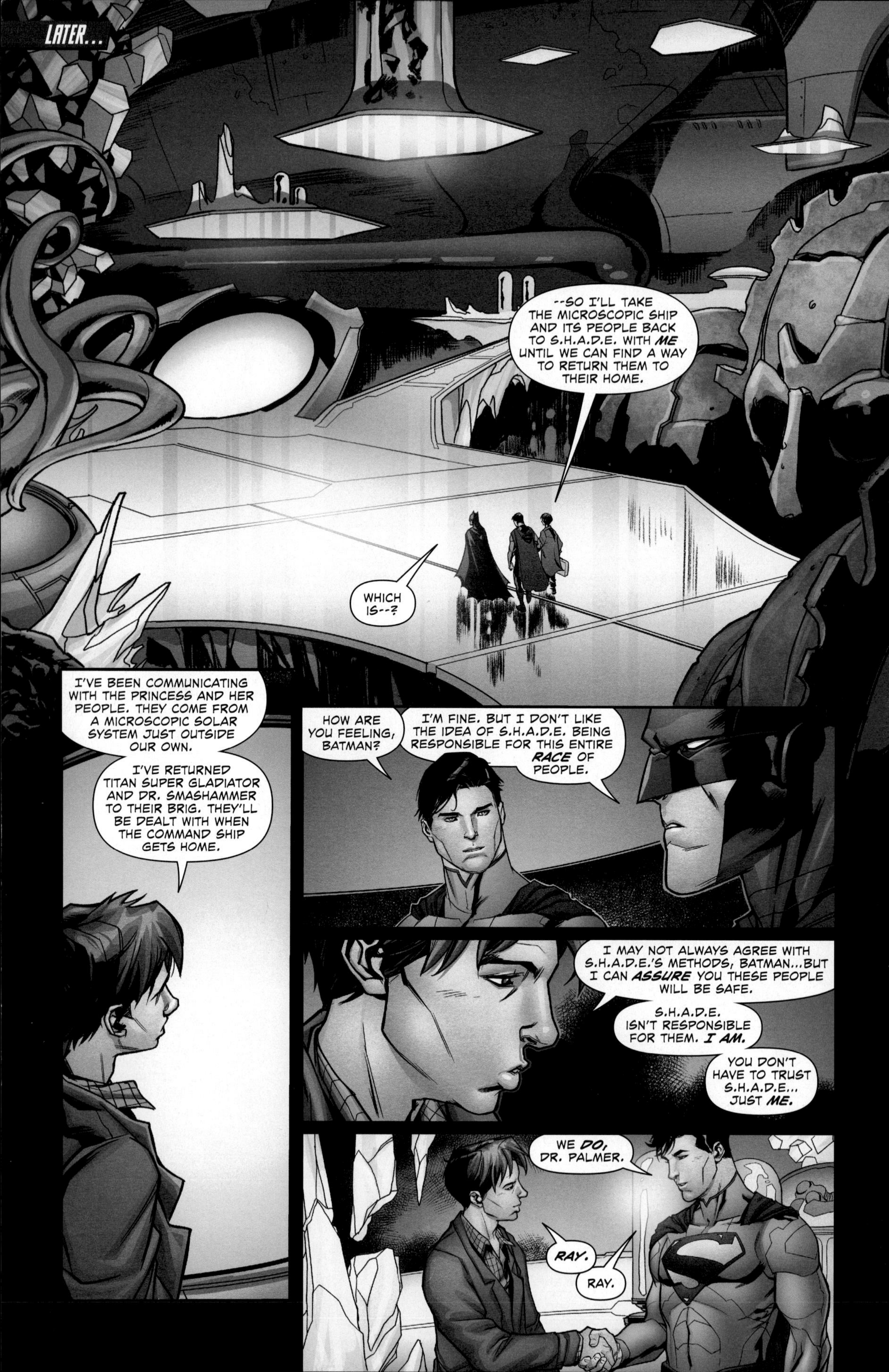
LATER...
--SO I'LL TAKE THE MICROSCOPIC SHIP AND ITS PEOPLE BACK TO S.H.A.D.E. WITH ME UNTIL WE CAN FIND A WAY TO RETURN THEM TO THEIR HOME.
WHICH IS--?
I'VE BEEN COMMUNICATING WITH THE PRINCESS AND HER PEOPLE. THEY COME FROM A MICROSCOPIC SOLAR SYSTEM JUST OUTSIDE OUR OWN.
I'VE RETURNED TITAN SUPER GLADIATOR AND DR. SMASHAMMER TO THEIR BRIG. THEY'LL BE DEALT WITH WHEN THE COMMAND SHIP GETS HOME.
HOW ARE YOU FEELING, BATMAN?
I'M FINE. BUT I DON'T LIKE THE IDEA OF S.H.A.D.E. BEING RESPONSIBLE FOR THIS ENTIRE RACE OF PEOPLE.
I MAY NOT ALWAYS AGREE WITH S.H.A.D.E.'S METHODS, BATMAN...BUT I CAN ASSURE YOU THESE PEOPLE WILL BE SAFE.
S.H.A.D.E. ISN'T RESPONSIBLE FOR THEM. I AM.
YOU DON'T HAVE TO TRUST S.H.A.D.E... JUST ME.
WE DO, DR. PALMER.
RAY.
RAY.

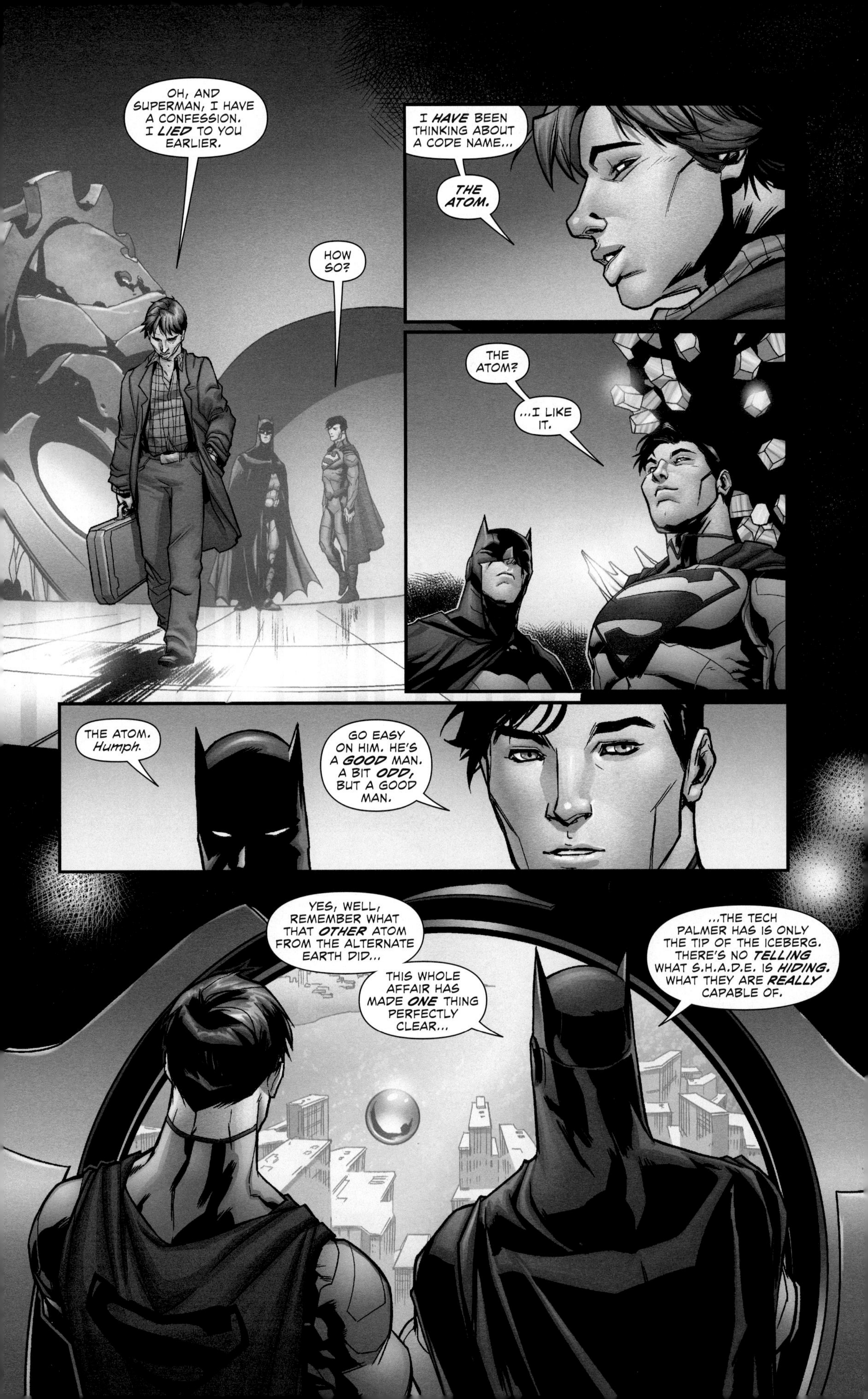
OH, AND SUPERMAN, I HAVE A CONFESSION. I LIED TO YOU EARLIER.
HOW SO?
I HAVE BEEN THINKING ABOUT A CODE NAME...
THE ATOM.
THE ATOM?
...I LIKE IT.
THE ATOM. Humph.
GO EASY ON HIM. HE'S A GOOD MAN. A BIT ODD, BUT A GOOD MAN.
YES, WELL, REMEMBER WHAT THAT OTHER ATOM FROM THE ALTERNATE EARTH DID...
THIS WHOLE AFFAIR HAS MADE ONE THING PERFECTLY CLEAR...
...THE TECH PALMER HAS IS ONLY THE TIP OF THE ICEBERG. THERE'S NO TELLING WHAT S.H.A.D.E. IS HIDING. WHAT THEY ARE REALLY CAPABLE OF.

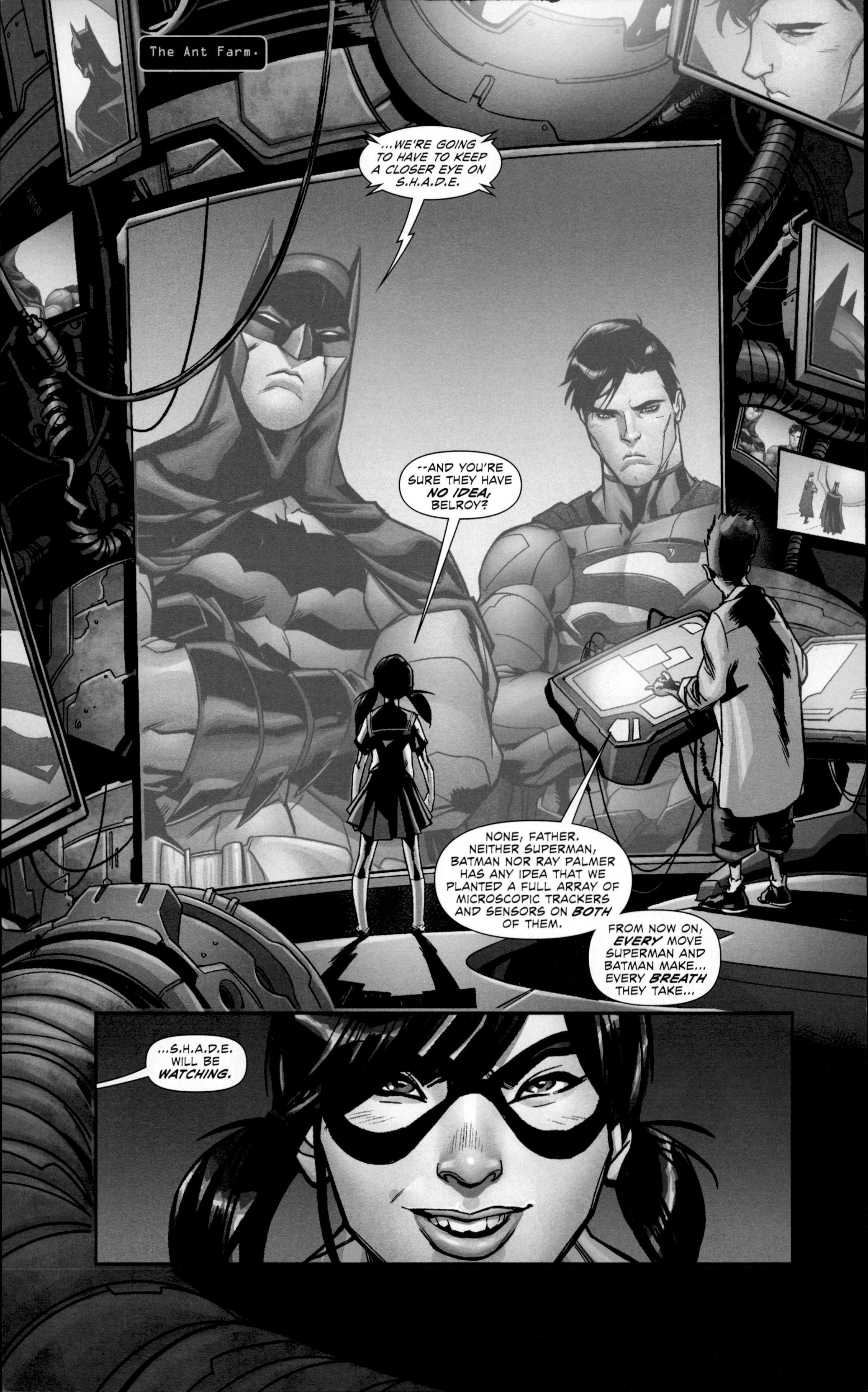
The Ant Farm.
...WE'RE GOING TO HAVE TO KEEP A CLOSER EYE ON S.H.A.D.E.
--AND YOU'RE SURE THEY HAVE NO IDEA, BELROY?
NONE, FATHER. NEITHER SUPERMAN, BATMAN NOR RAY PALMER HAS ANY IDEA THAT WE PLANTED A FULL ARRAY OF MICROSCOPIC TRACKERS AND SENSORS ON BOTH OF THEM.
FROM NOW ON, EVERY MOVE SUPERMAN AND BATMAN MAKE... EVERY BREATH THEY TAKE...
...S.H.A.D.E. WILL BE WATCHING.

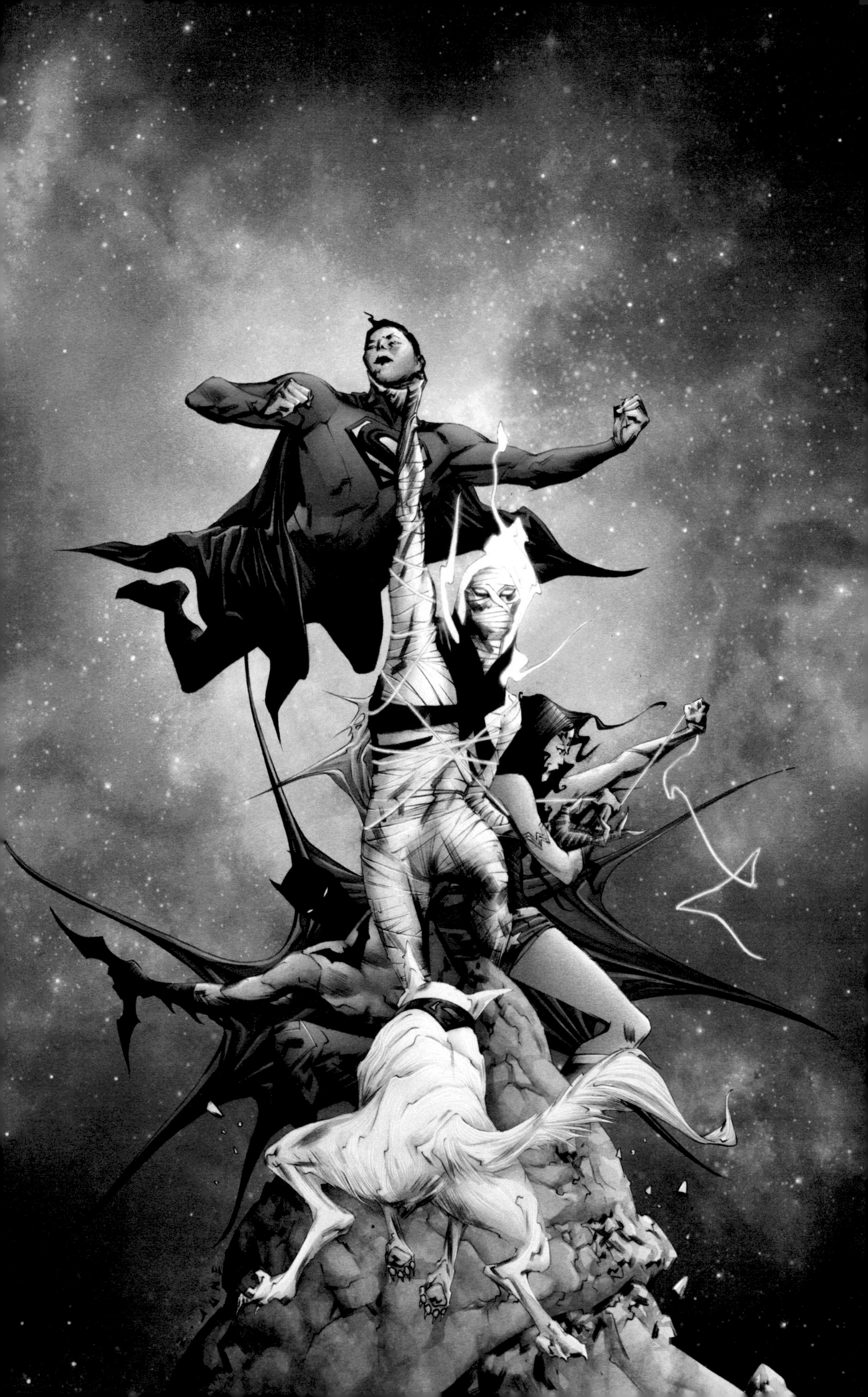

DANGER ZONE

GREG PAK writer **KARL KERSCHL TOM DERENICK DANIEL SAMPERE** pencillers **KARL KERSCHL VICENTE CIFUENTES MARC DEERING WAYNE FAUCHER DANIEL SAMPERE** inkers **HI-FI** colorist **ROB LEIGH** letterer cover by **JAE LEE** with **JUNE CHUNG**

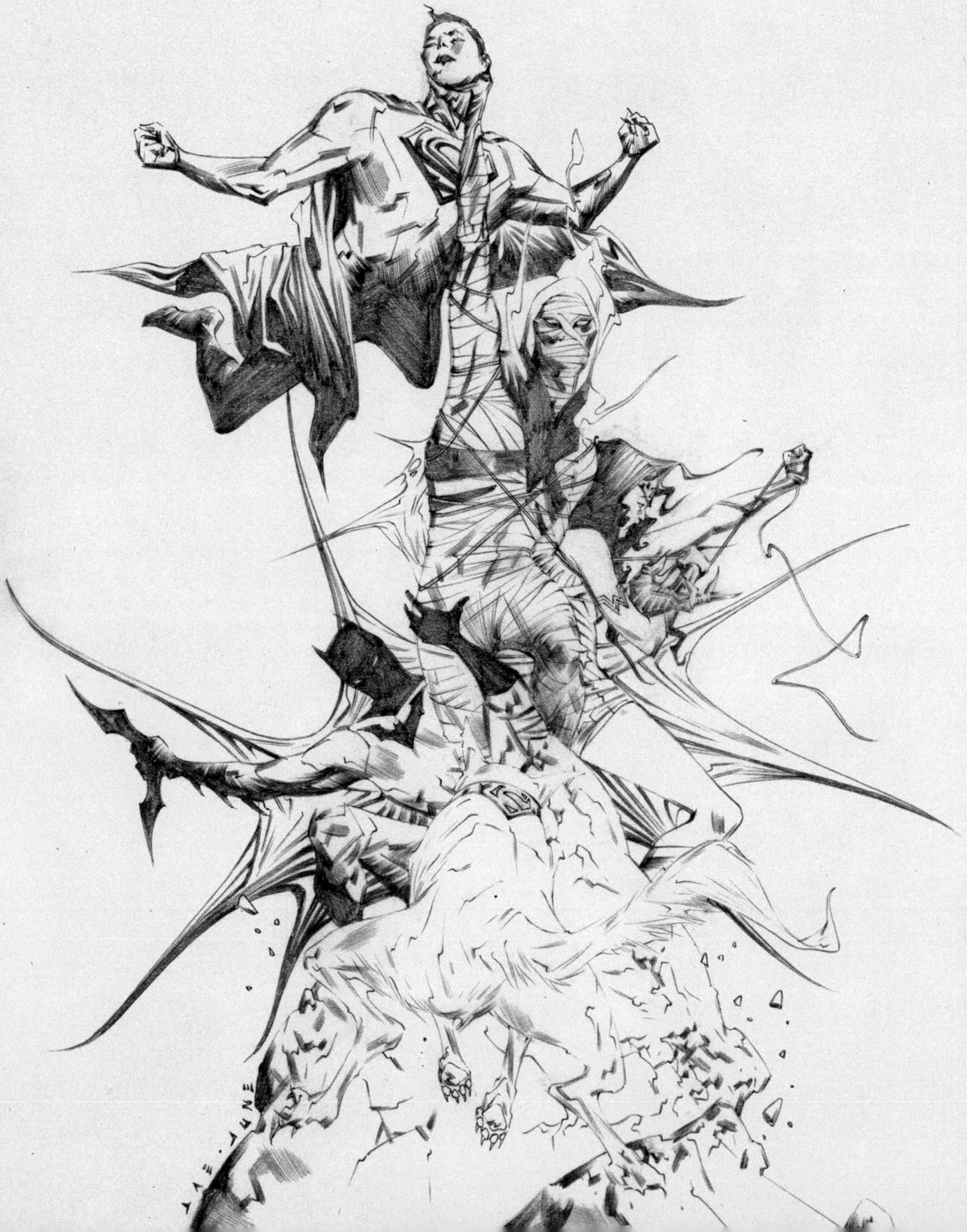

WORLD   U.S.   METROPOLIS   BUSINESS   OPINION   SPORTS   ARTS   STYLE   VIDEO

May 21, 2014

Daily Planet

DAILY PLANET

SUPER-MENACE!

Photo by James Olsen

By Lois Lane

It was the Boom heard around the world. Everyone's worst fears have come true as Superman seems to be infected with what S.T.A.R. Labs officials can only speculate is a virus from the creature the world has come to know as Doomsday.

The Kryptonian's affliction became public knowledge after fellow Justice Leaguers Wonder Woman and Batman tried to contain him in a battle that shook the entirety of New Troy island in Metropolis.

Miraculously, no one was hurt, but many residents on Clinton Street report severe property damage from the fight.

At present, it seems that Superman has turned himself in to authorities, and at the behest of Senator Samuel Lane many prominent scientists have been brought in to study the case, among them Dr. Ray Palmer, Dr. Shay Veritas and Lex Luthor, who just had this to say: "We do not know what is happening to Superman. We hope for the best, but none of us have ever faced anything like this," adding, "Unfortunately, we do know what this could evolve into, and we have to be prepared to contain it, or exterminate it in any way possible."

Watch exclusive video footage of the destruction in the Bahamas.

Metropolis Mayhem, locals report their Super-encounters

"Doomsday" origins recovery in the northwestern Indies

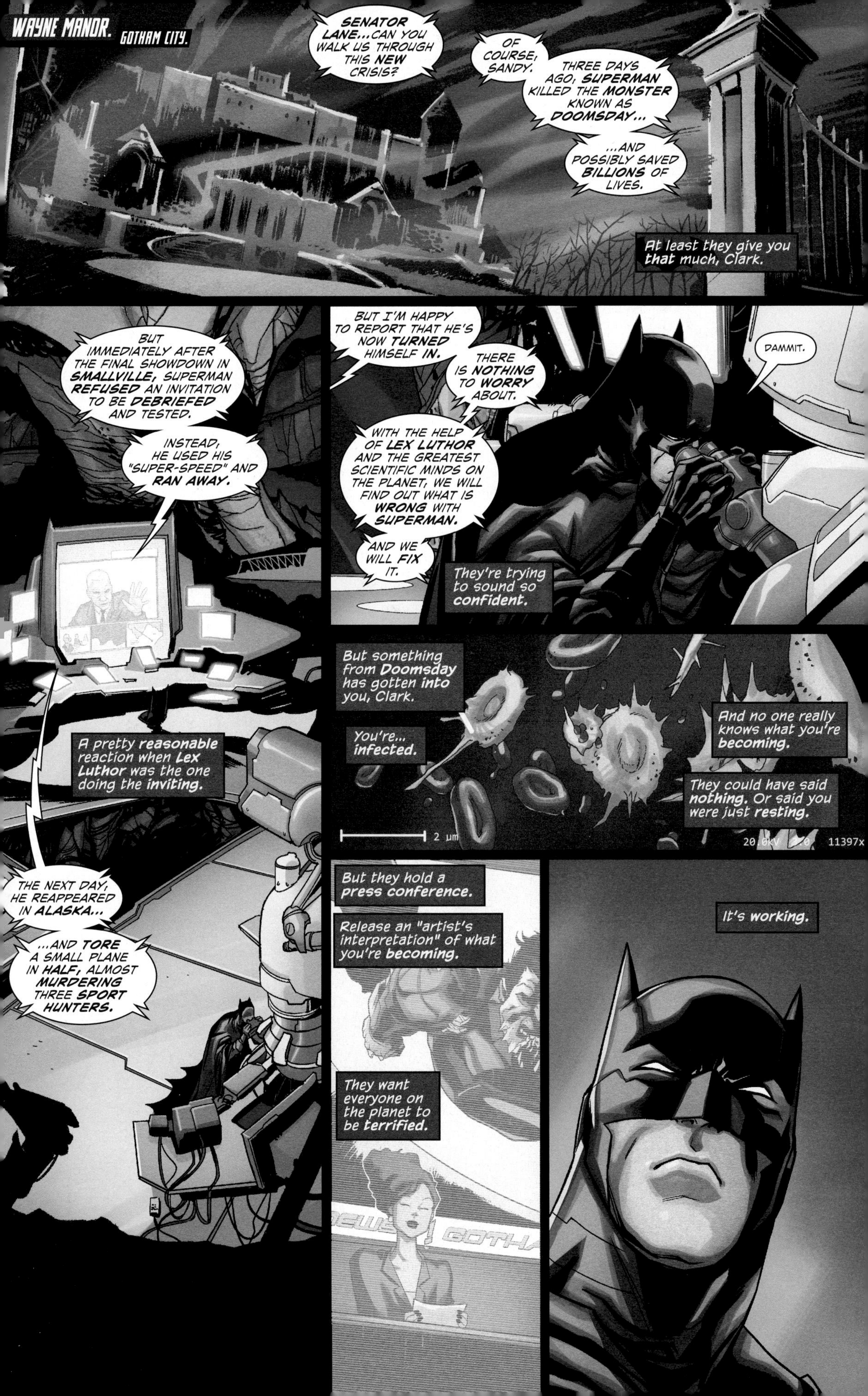

WAYNE MANOR. GOTHAM CITY.
SENATOR LANE...CAN YOU WALK US THROUGH THIS NEW CRISIS?
OF COURSE, SANDY.
THREE DAYS AGO, SUPERMAN KILLED THE MONSTER KNOWN AS DOOMSDAY...
...AND POSSIBLY SAVED BILLIONS OF LIVES.
At least they give you that much, Clark.
BUT IMMEDIATELY AFTER THE FINAL SHOWDOWN IN SMALLVILLE, SUPERMAN REFUSED AN INVITATION TO BE DEBRIEFED AND TESTED.
INSTEAD, HE USED HIS "SUPER-SPEED" AND RAN AWAY.
A pretty reasonable reaction when Lex Luthor was the one doing the inviting.
THE NEXT DAY, HE REAPPEARED IN ALASKA...
...AND TORE A SMALL PLANE IN HALF, ALMOST MURDERING THREE SPORT HUNTERS.
BUT I'M HAPPY TO REPORT THAT HE'S NOW TURNED HIMSELF IN.
THERE IS NOTHING TO WORRY ABOUT.
WITH THE HELP OF LEX LUTHOR AND THE GREATEST SCIENTIFIC MINDS ON THE PLANET, WE WILL FIND OUT WHAT IS WRONG WITH SUPERMAN.
AND WE WILL FIX IT.
They're trying to sound so confident.
DAMMIT.
But something from Doomsday has gotten into you, Clark.
You're... infected.
And no one really knows what you're becoming.
They could have said nothing. Or said you were just resting.
2 µm
11397x
But they hold a press conference.
Release an "artist's interpretation" of what you're becoming.
They want everyone on the planet to be terrified.
It's working.

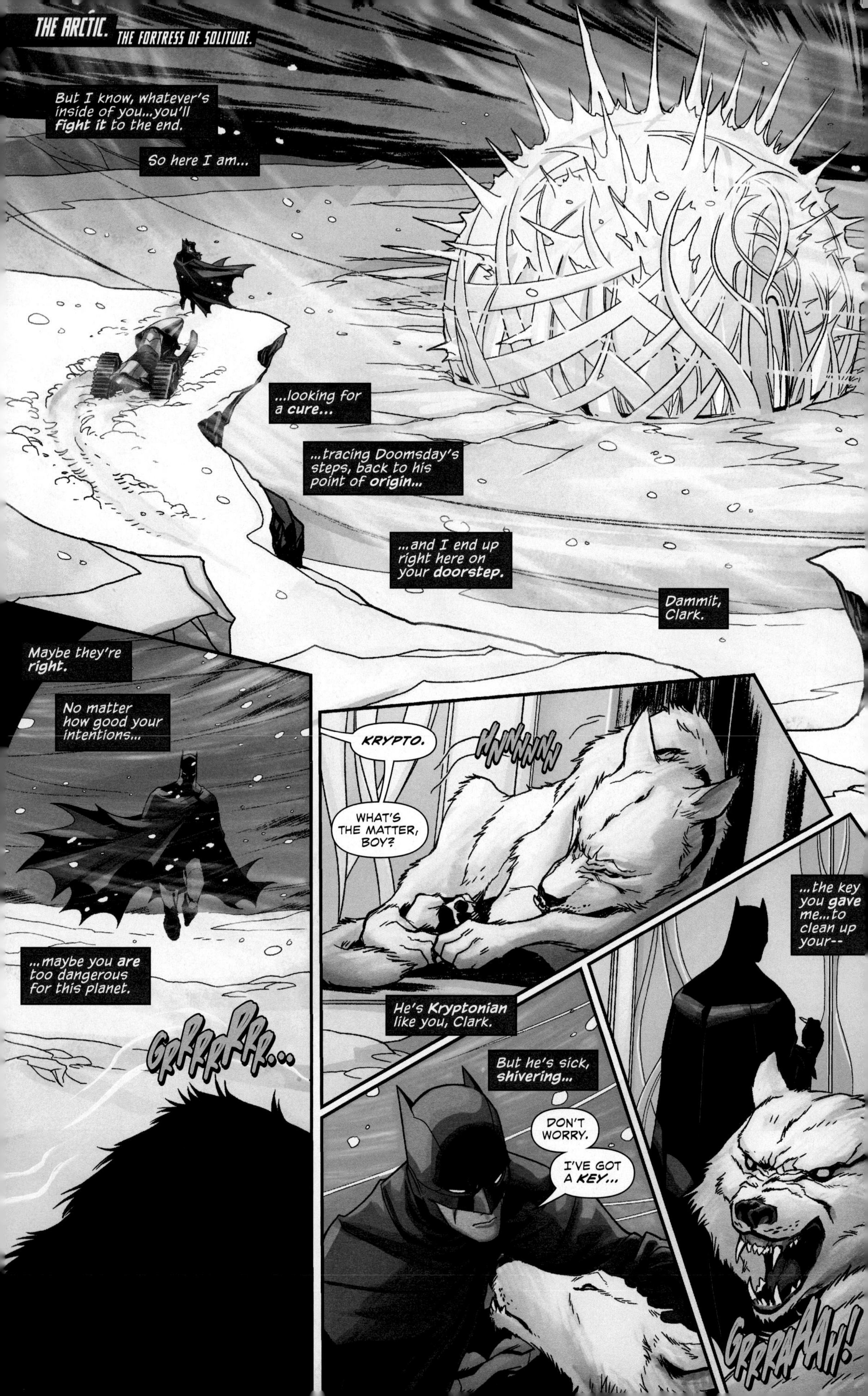
THE ARCTIC. THE FORTRESS OF SOLITUDE.
But I know, whatever's inside of you...you'll fight it to the end.
So here I am...
...looking for a cure...
...tracing Doomsday's steps, back to his point of origin...
...and I end up right here on your doorstep.
Dammit, Clark.
Maybe they're right.
No matter how good your intentions...
...maybe you are too dangerous for this planet.
GRRRRRRR...
KRYPTO.
WHAT'S THE MATTER, BOY?
HNNNNN
He's Kryptonian like you, Clark.
But he's sick, shivering...
DON'T WORRY.
I'VE GOT A KEY...
...the key you gave me...to clean up your--
GRRRAAAH!

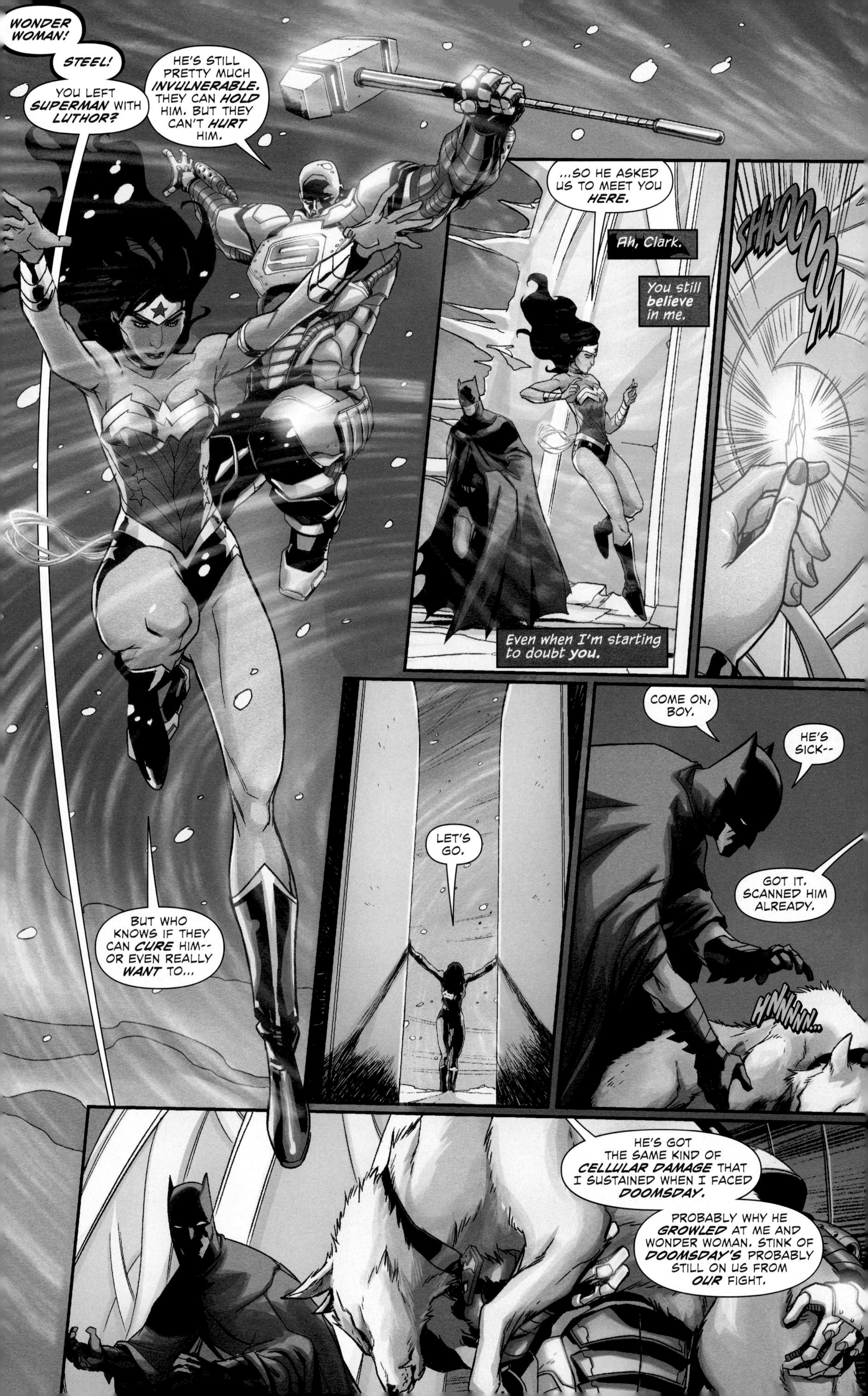
WONDER WOMAN!
STEEL!
YOU LEFT SUPERMAN WITH LUTHOR?
HE'S STILL PRETTY MUCH INVULNERABLE. THEY CAN HOLD HIM. BUT THEY CAN'T HURT HIM.
BUT WHO KNOWS IF THEY CAN CURE HIM-- OR EVEN REALLY WANT TO...
...SO HE ASKED US TO MEET YOU HERE.
Ah, Clark.
You still believe in me.
Even when I'm starting to doubt you.
SHHOOOOM
LET'S GO.
COME ON, BOY.
HE'S SICK--
GOT IT. SCANNED HIM ALREADY.
HNNNNN...
HE'S GOT THE SAME KIND OF CELLULAR DAMAGE THAT I SUSTAINED WHEN I FACED DOOMSDAY.
PROBABLY WHY HE GROWLED AT ME AND WONDER WOMAN. STINK OF DOOMSDAY'S PROBABLY STILL ON US FROM OUR FIGHT.

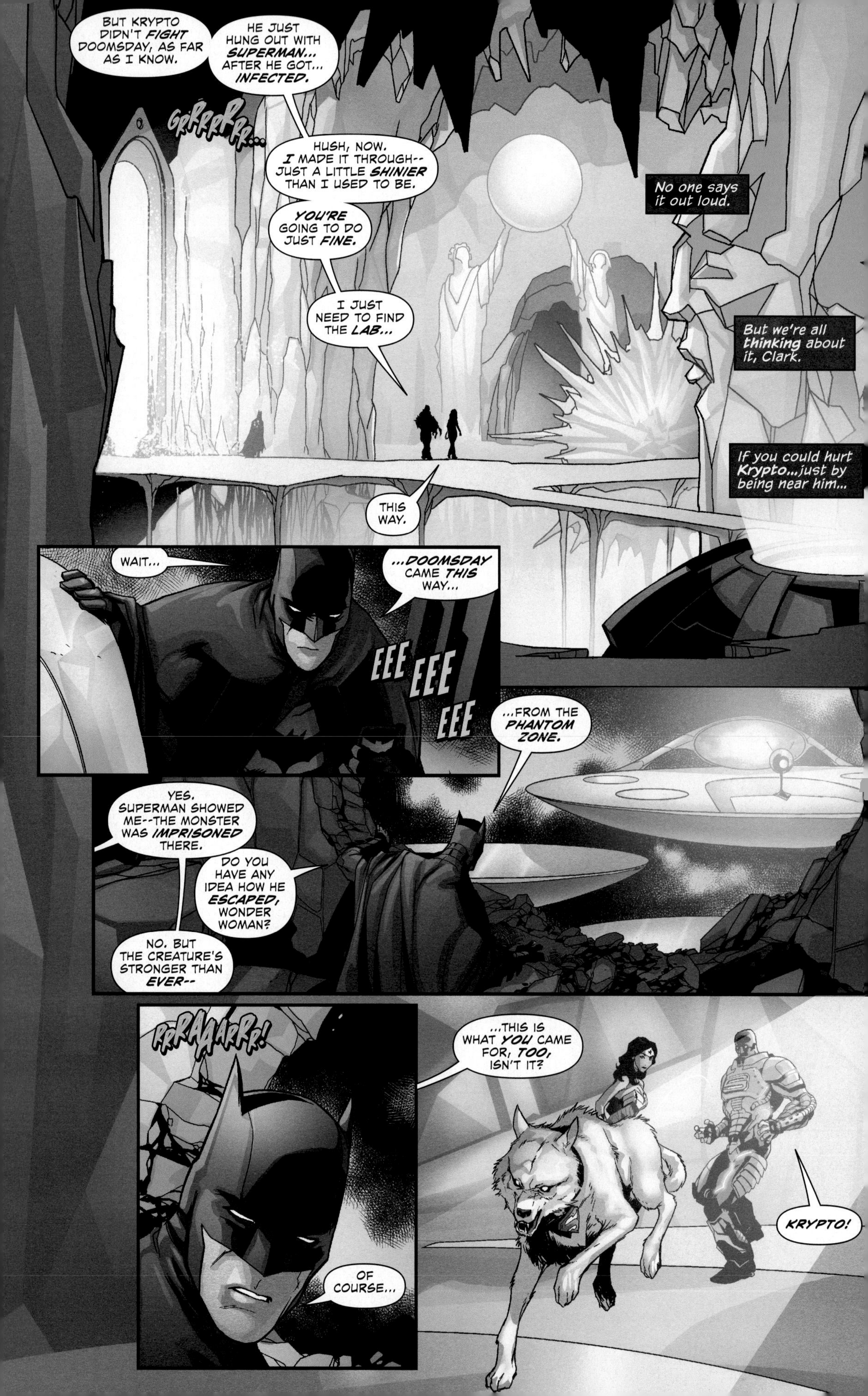
BUT KRYPTO DIDN'T FIGHT DOOMSDAY, AS FAR AS I KNOW.
HE JUST HUNG OUT WITH SUPERMAN... AFTER HE GOT... INFECTED.
GRRRRRRR...
HUSH, NOW. I MADE IT THROUGH-- JUST A LITTLE SHINIER THAN I USED TO BE.
YOU'RE GOING TO DO JUST FINE.
I JUST NEED TO FIND THE LAB...
No one says it out loud.
But we're all thinking about it, Clark.
If you could hurt Krypto...just by being near him...
THIS WAY.
WAIT...
...DOOMSDAY CAME THIS WAY...
EEE EEE EEE
...FROM THE PHANTOM ZONE.
YES. SUPERMAN SHOWED ME--THE MONSTER WAS IMPRISONED THERE.
DO YOU HAVE ANY IDEA HOW HE ESCAPED, WONDER WOMAN?
NO. BUT THE CREATURE'S STRONGER THAN EVER--
RRRAAARRR!
...THIS IS WHAT YOU CAME FOR, TOO, ISN'T IT?
OF COURSE...
KRYPTO!

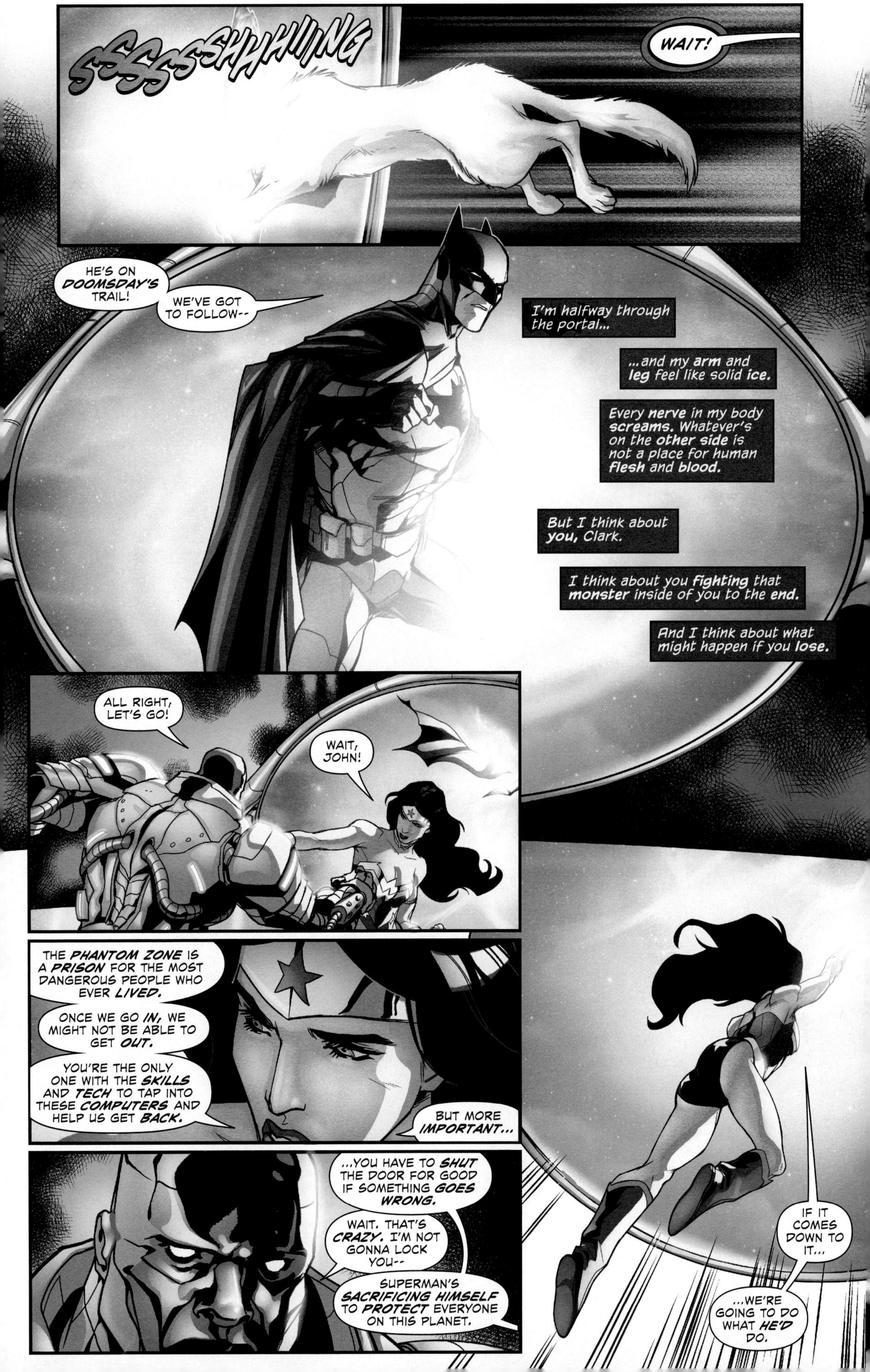
SSSSSSHHHIIIING
WAIT!
HE'S ON DOOMSDAY'S TRAIL!
WE'VE GOT TO FOLLOW--
I'm halfway through the portal...
...and my arm and leg feel like solid ice.
Every nerve in my body screams. Whatever's on the other side is not a place for human flesh and blood.
But I think about you, Clark.
I think about you fighting that monster inside of you to the end.
And I think about what might happen if you lose.
ALL RIGHT, LET'S GO!
WAIT, JOHN!
THE PHANTOM ZONE IS A PRISON FOR THE MOST DANGEROUS PEOPLE WHO EVER LIVED.
ONCE WE GO IN, WE MIGHT NOT BE ABLE TO GET OUT.
YOU'RE THE ONLY ONE WITH THE SKILLS AND TECH TO TAP INTO THESE COMPUTERS AND HELP US GET BACK.
BUT MORE IMPORTANT...
...YOU HAVE TO SHUT THE DOOR FOR GOOD IF SOMETHING GOES WRONG.
WAIT. THAT'S CRAZY. I'M NOT GONNA LOCK YOU--
SUPERMAN'S SACRIFICING HIMSELF TO PROTECT EVERYONE ON THIS PLANET.
IF IT COMES DOWN TO IT...
...WE'RE GOING TO DO WHAT HE'D DO.

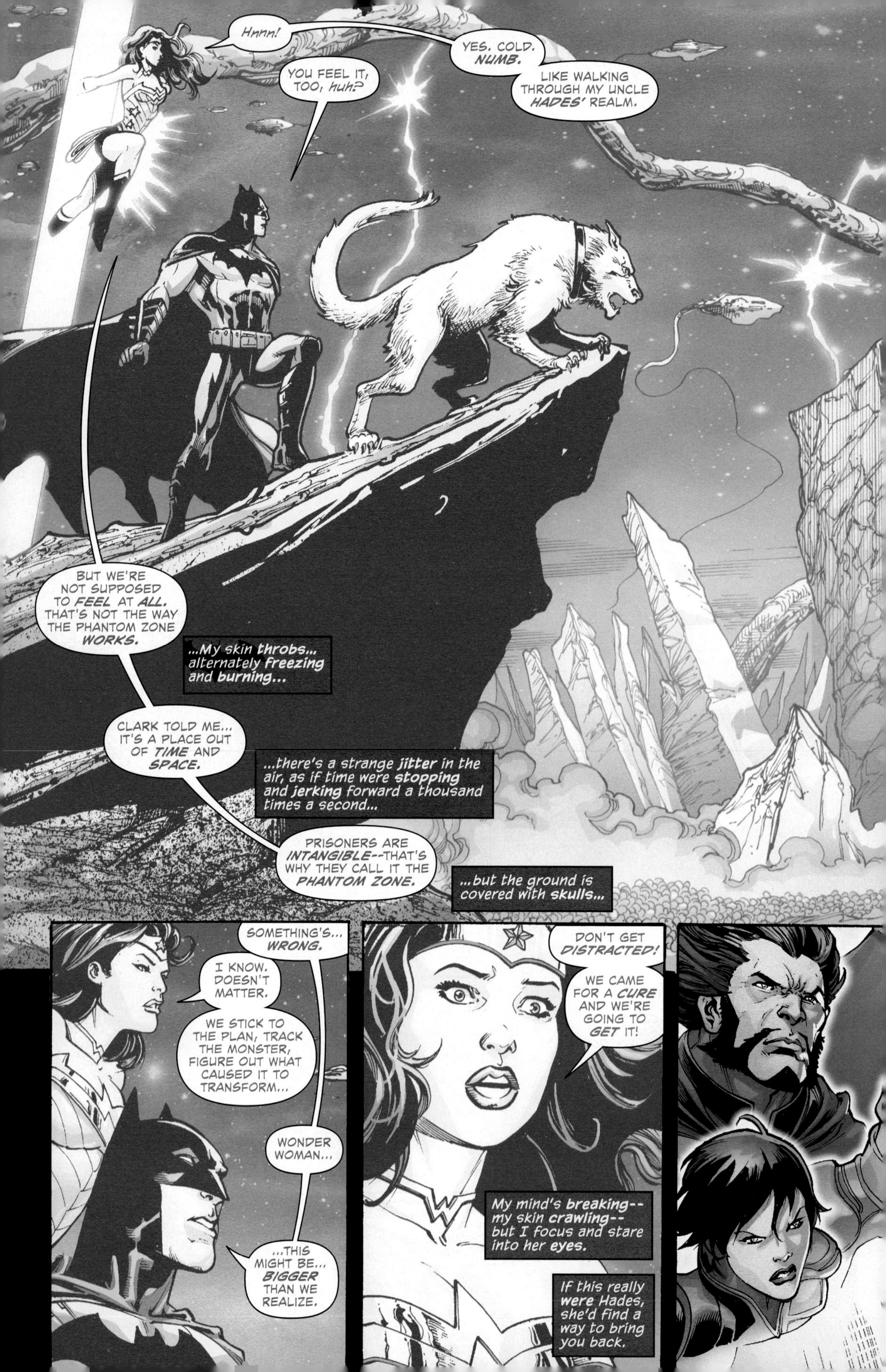
Hnnn!
YOU FEEL IT, TOO, huh?
YES. COLD. NUMB.
LIKE WALKING THROUGH MY UNCLE HADES' REALM.
BUT WE'RE NOT SUPPOSED TO FEEL AT ALL. THAT'S NOT THE WAY THE PHANTOM ZONE WORKS.
...My skin throbs... alternately freezing and burning...
CLARK TOLD ME... IT'S A PLACE OUT OF TIME AND SPACE.
...there's a strange jitter in the air, as if time were stopping and jerking forward a thousand times a second...
PRISONERS ARE INTANGIBLE--THAT'S WHY THEY CALL IT THE PHANTOM ZONE.
...but the ground is covered with skulls...
SOMETHING'S... WRONG.
I KNOW. DOESN'T MATTER.
WE STICK TO THE PLAN, TRACK THE MONSTER, FIGURE OUT WHAT CAUSED IT TO TRANSFORM...
WONDER WOMAN...
...THIS MIGHT BE... BIGGER THAN WE REALIZE.
DON'T GET DISTRACTED!
WE CAME FOR A CURE AND WE'RE GOING TO GET IT!
My mind's breaking-- my skin crawling-- but I focus and stare into her eyes.
If this really were Hades, she'd find a way to bring you back.

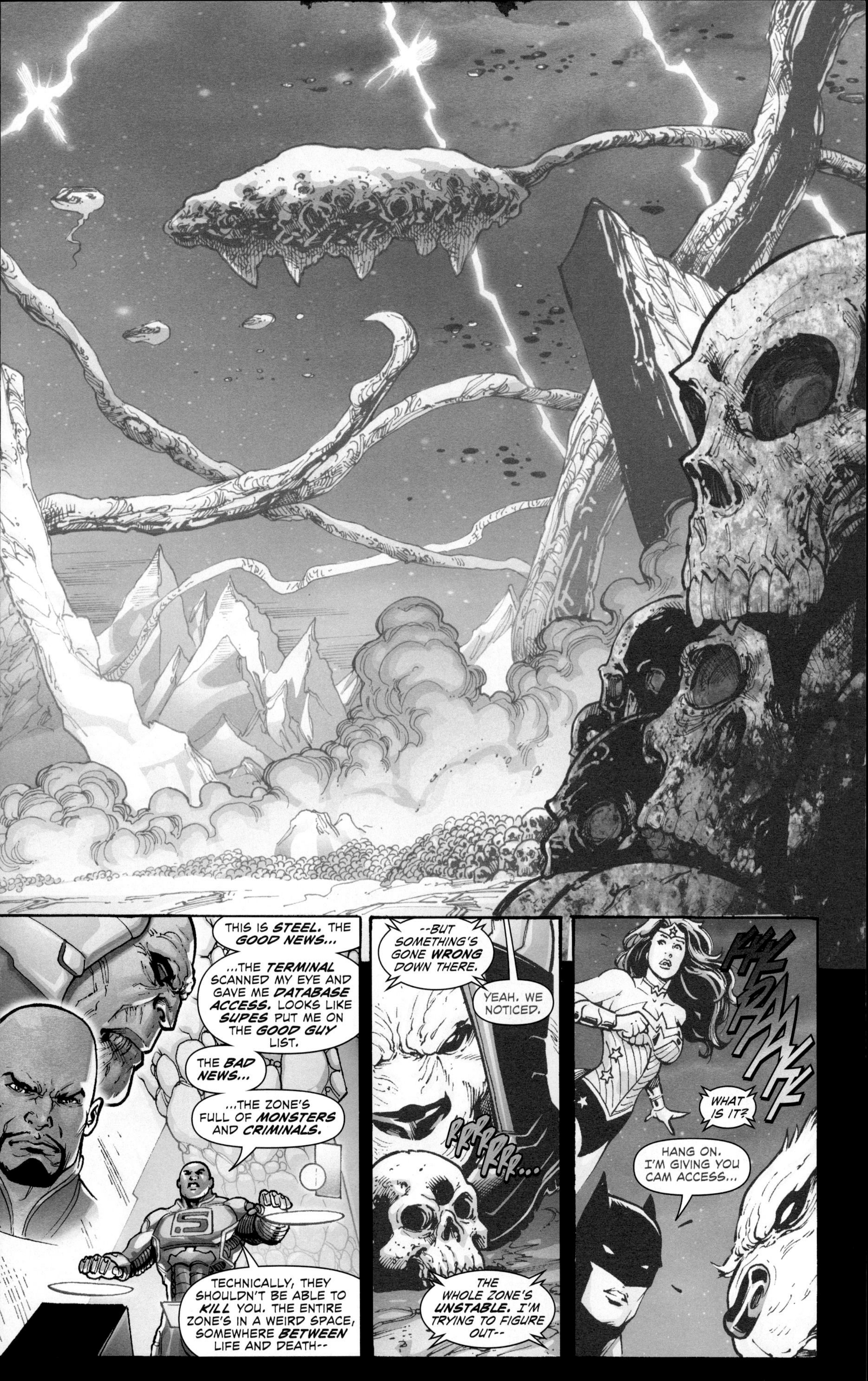
THIS IS STEEL. THE GOOD NEWS...
...THE TERMINAL SCANNED MY EYE AND GAVE ME DATABASE ACCESS. LOOKS LIKE SUPES PUT ME ON THE GOOD GUY LIST.
THE BAD NEWS...
...THE ZONE'S FULL OF MONSTERS AND CRIMINALS.
TECHNICALLY, THEY SHOULDN'T BE ABLE TO KILL YOU. THE ENTIRE ZONE'S IN A WEIRD SPACE, SOMEWHERE BETWEEN LIFE AND DEATH--
--BUT SOMETHING'S GONE WRONG DOWN THERE.
YEAH. WE NOTICED.
RRRRRRRR...
THE WHOLE ZONE'S UNSTABLE. I'M TRYING TO FIGURE OUT--
KRAKK
WHAT IS IT?
HANG ON. I'M GIVING YOU CAM ACCESS...

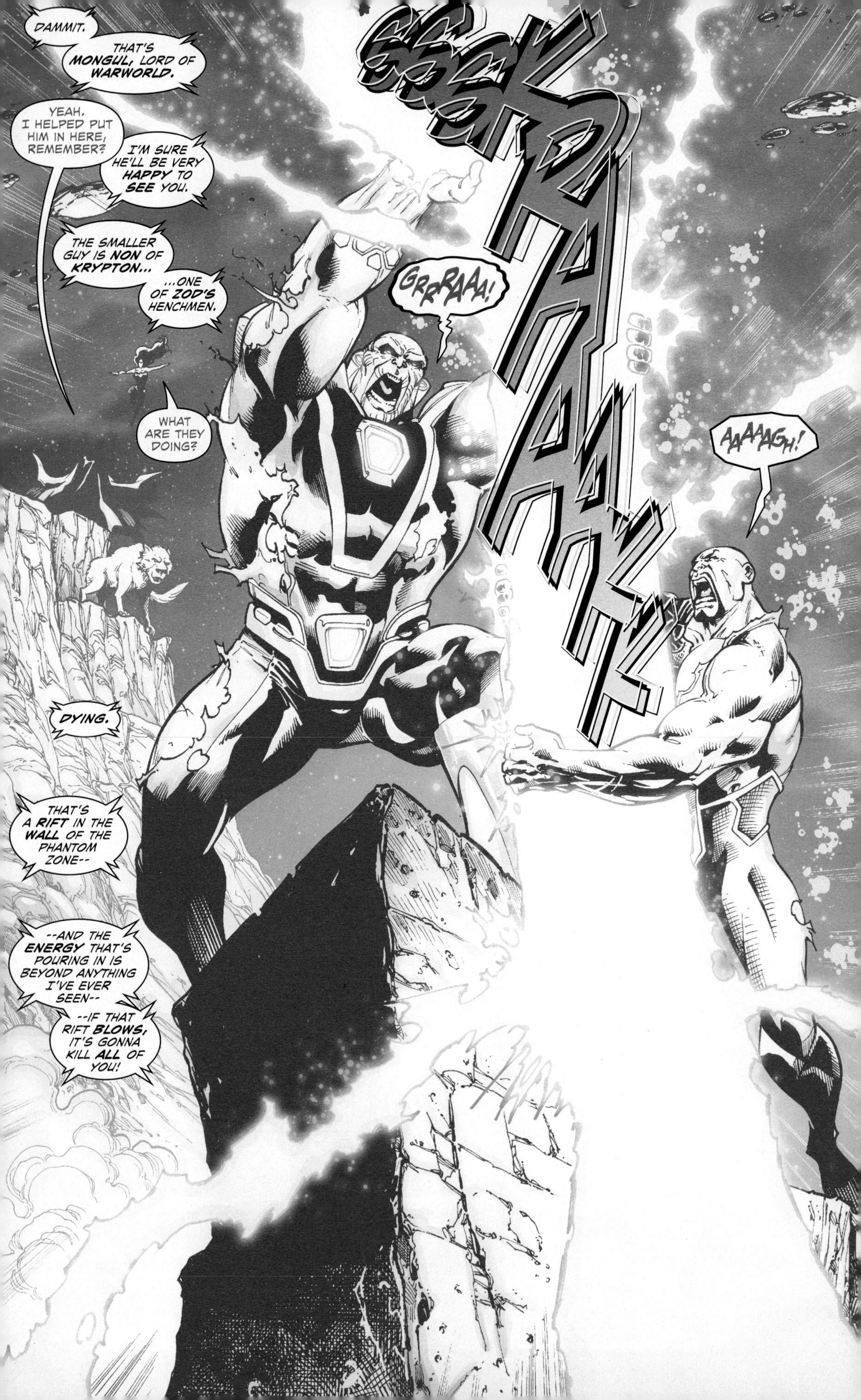
DAMMIT.
THAT'S MONGUL, LORD OF WARWORLD.
YEAH. I HELPED PUT HIM IN HERE, REMEMBER?
I'M SURE HE'LL BE VERY HAPPY TO SEE YOU.
THE SMALLER GUY IS NON OF KRYPTON...
...ONE OF ZOD'S HENCHMEN.
WHAT ARE THEY DOING?
GRRRAAA!
AAAAAGH!
DYING.
THAT'S A RIFT IN THE WALL OF THE PHANTOM ZONE--
--AND THE ENERGY THAT'S POURING IN IS BEYOND ANYTHING I'VE EVER SEEN--
--IF THAT RIFT BLOWS, IT'S GONNA KILL ALL OF YOU!

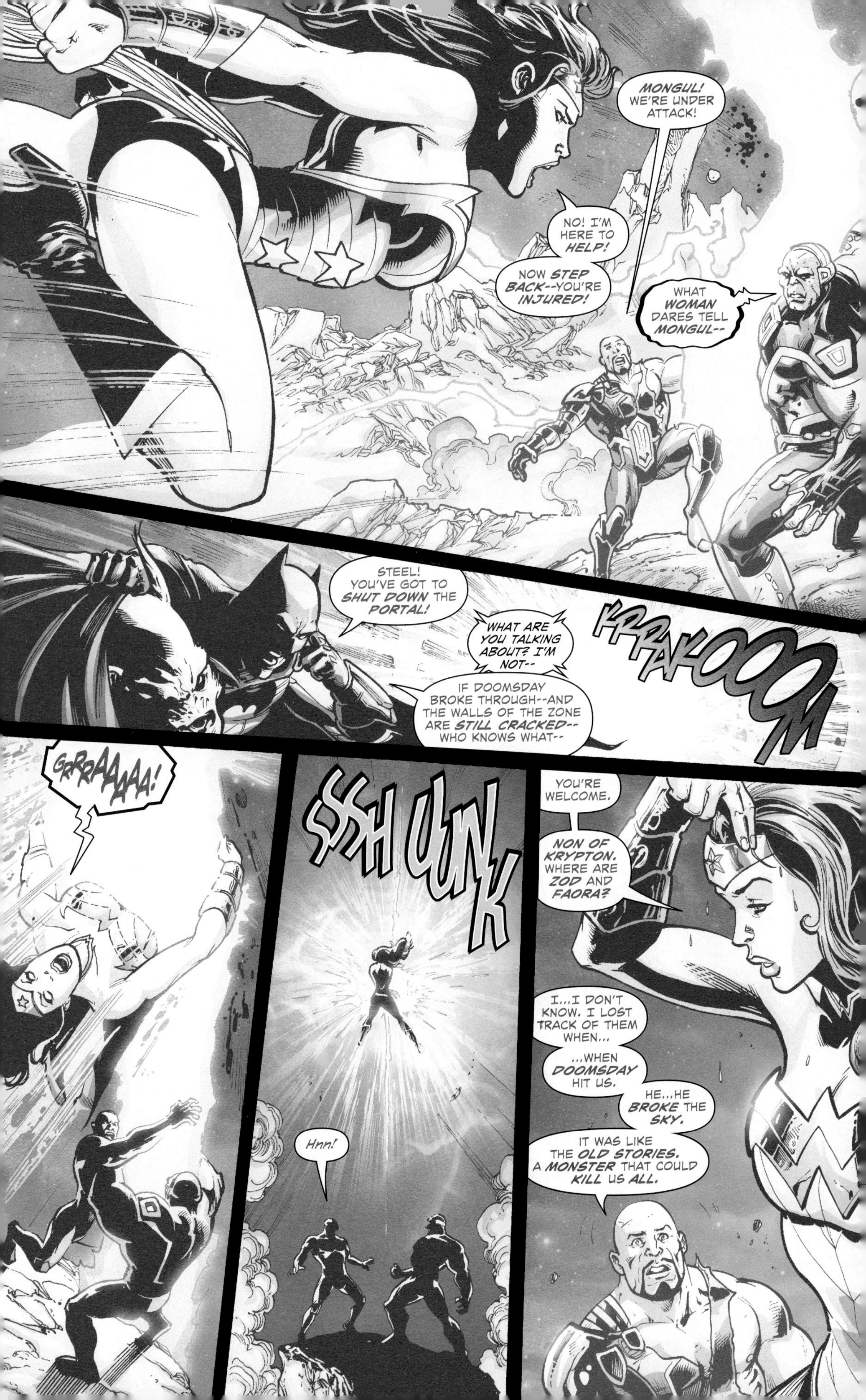
MONGUL! WE'RE UNDER ATTACK!
NO! I'M HERE TO HELP!
NOW STEP BACK--YOU'RE INJURED!
WHAT WOMAN DARES TELL MONGUL--
STEEL! YOU'VE GOT TO SHUT DOWN THE PORTAL!
WHAT ARE YOU TALKING ABOUT? I'M NOT--
IF DOOMSDAY BROKE THROUGH--AND THE WALLS OF THE ZONE ARE STILL CRACKED-- WHO KNOWS WHAT--
KRRAKOOOM
GRRRAAAAAA!
SSHUUNK
Hnn!
YOU'RE WELCOME.
NON OF KRYPTON. WHERE ARE ZOD AND FAORA?
I...I DON'T KNOW. I LOST TRACK OF THEM WHEN...
...WHEN DOOMSDAY HIT US.
HE...HE BROKE THE SKY.
IT WAS LIKE THE OLD STORIES. A MONSTER THAT COULD KILL US ALL.

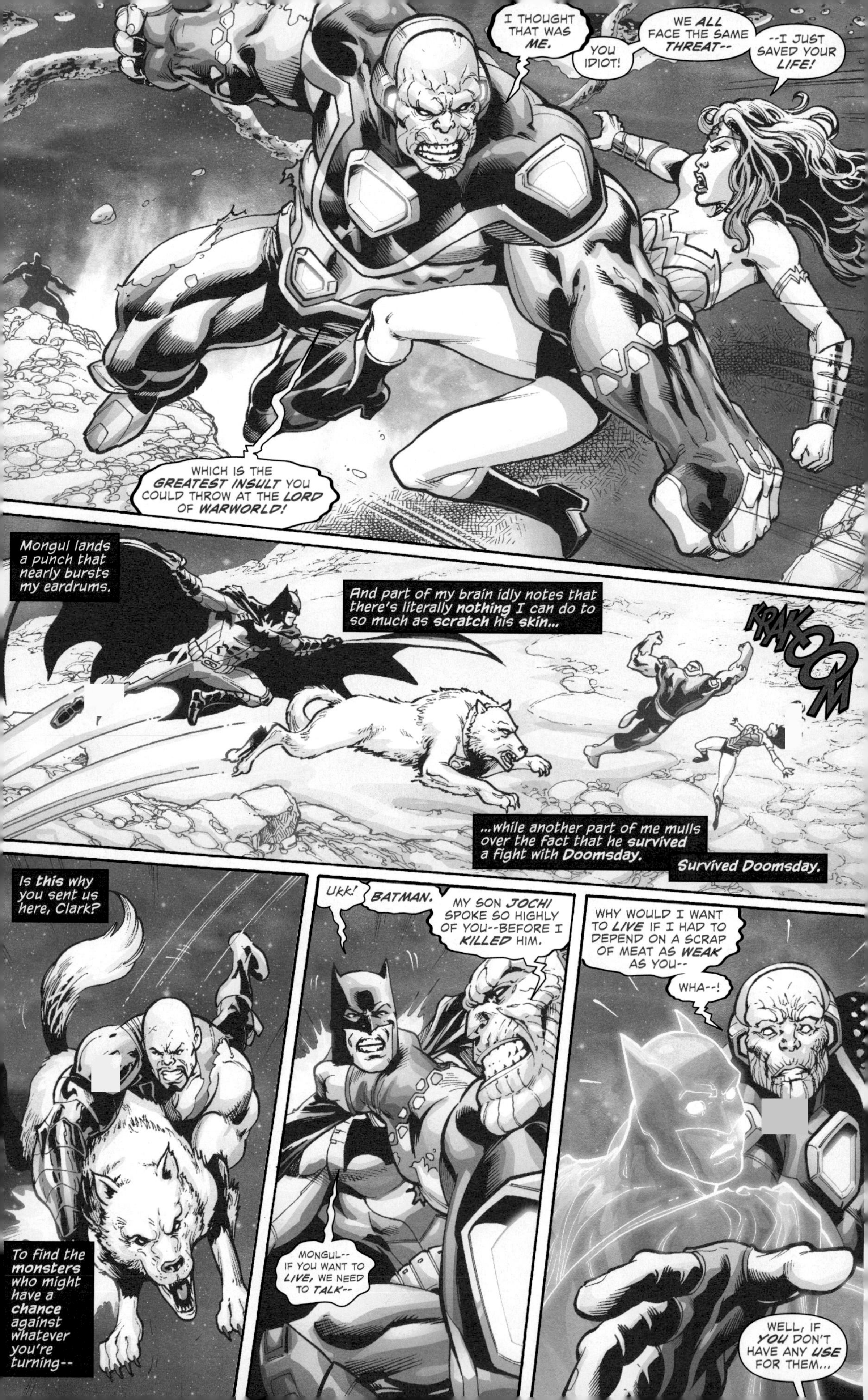
I THOUGHT THAT WAS ME.
YOU IDIOT!
WE ALL FACE THE SAME THREAT--
--I JUST SAVED YOUR LIFE!
WHICH IS THE GREATEST INSULT YOU COULD THROW AT THE LORD OF WARWORLD!
Mongul lands a punch that nearly bursts my eardrums.
And part of my brain idly notes that there's literally nothing I can do to so much as scratch his skin...
KRAKOOM
...while another part of me mulls over the fact that he survived a fight with Doomsday.
Survived Doomsday.
Is this why you sent us here, Clark?
To find the monsters who might have a chance against whatever you're turning--
Ukk!
BATMAN.
MY SON JOCHI SPOKE SO HIGHLY OF YOU--BEFORE I KILLED HIM.
MONGUL-- IF YOU WANT TO LIVE, WE NEED TO TALK--
WHY WOULD I WANT TO LIVE IF I HAD TO DEPEND ON A SCRAP OF MEAT AS WEAK AS YOU--
WHA--!
WELL, IF YOU DON'T HAVE ANY USE FOR THEM...

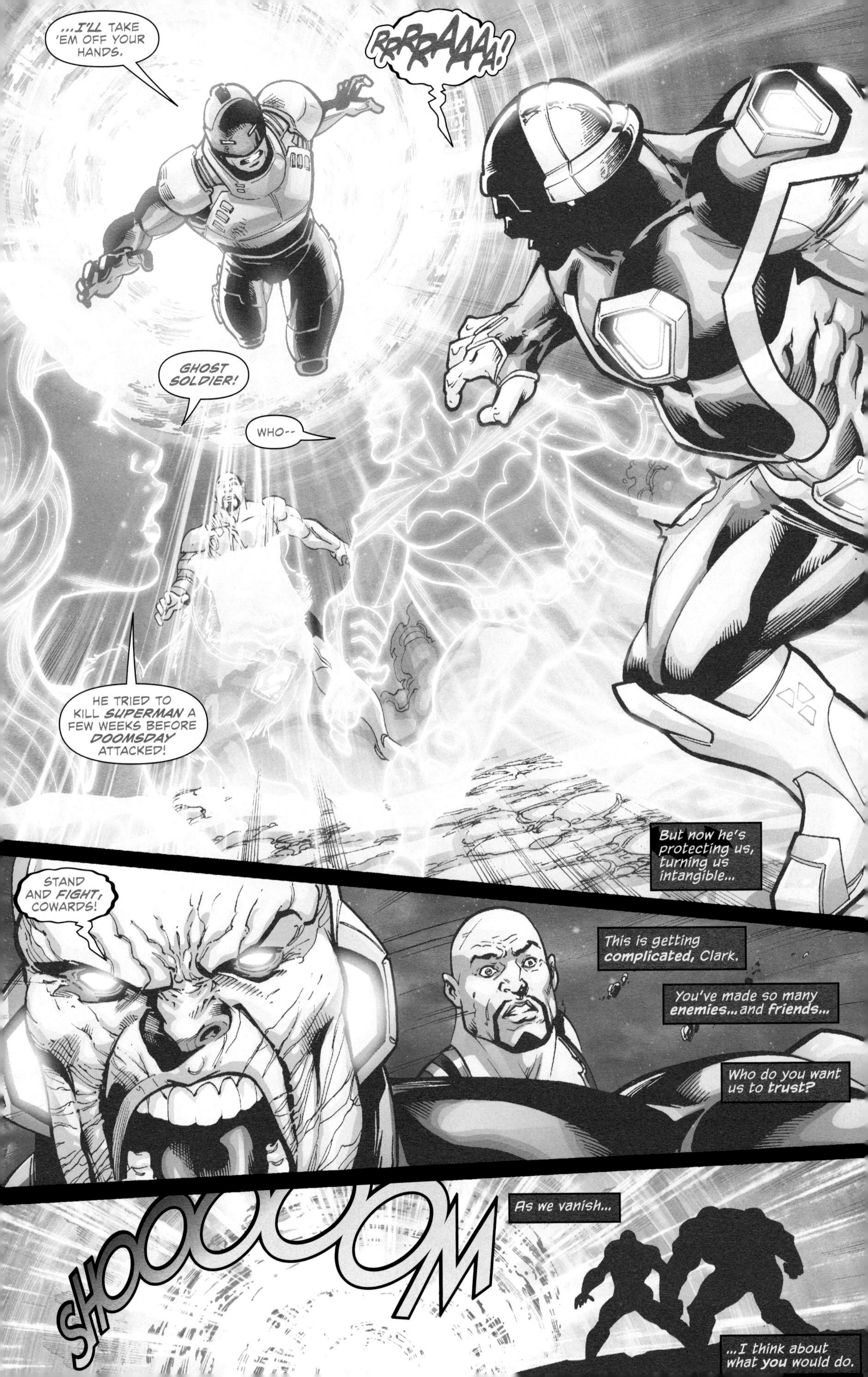
...I'LL TAKE 'EM OFF YOUR HANDS.
RRRRAAAAA!
GHOST SOLDIER!
WHO--
HE TRIED TO KILL SUPERMAN A FEW WEEKS BEFORE DOOMSDAY ATTACKED!
But now he's protecting us, turning us intangible...
STAND AND FIGHT, COWARDS!
This is getting complicated, Clark.
You've made so many enemies...and friends...
Who do you want us to trust?
SHOOOOOOM
As we vanish...
...I think about what you would do.

And as we reappear in another part of the Zone...

...I imagine you *holding* out your hand, with that small little half smile...

...and getting *stabbed* in the *chest.*

APOLOGIES FOR THE *UNANNOUNCED* TELEPORTATION.

YOU MAY FEEL A LITTLE QUEASY FOR--

GAH!

FTOOOM

I'm not you, Clark.

With so much at stake, I can't afford to be.

The liquid nitrogen barely slows him down...

...but it's enough to let *Diana* get to work.

YOU'RE BOUND BY THE *LASSO* OF *TRUTH.*

TELL ME-- WHAT DO YOU WANT?

SAME THING AS YOU.

I WORKED FOR THE *TOWER.* THEY'RE THE ONES WHO SET *DOOMSDAY* LOOSE. THEY THOUGHT SUPERMAN WAS... *DANGEROUS...*

YOU SURE THAT LASSO WORKS ON *GHOSTS?*

NO.

BUT IF HE MEANT US *HARM,* HE COULD HAVE TURNED US SOLID *INSIDE* THE ROCKS INSTEAD OF ON *TOP* OF THEM.

RRROOOOWL!

AND *KRYPTO* DOESN'T SEEM TOO WORRIED ABOUT HIM.

NO...

...BUT I DIDN'T KNOW THEY'D RISK KILLING *MILLIONS* TO TAKE HIM OUT. SO I'M HERE TO HELP.

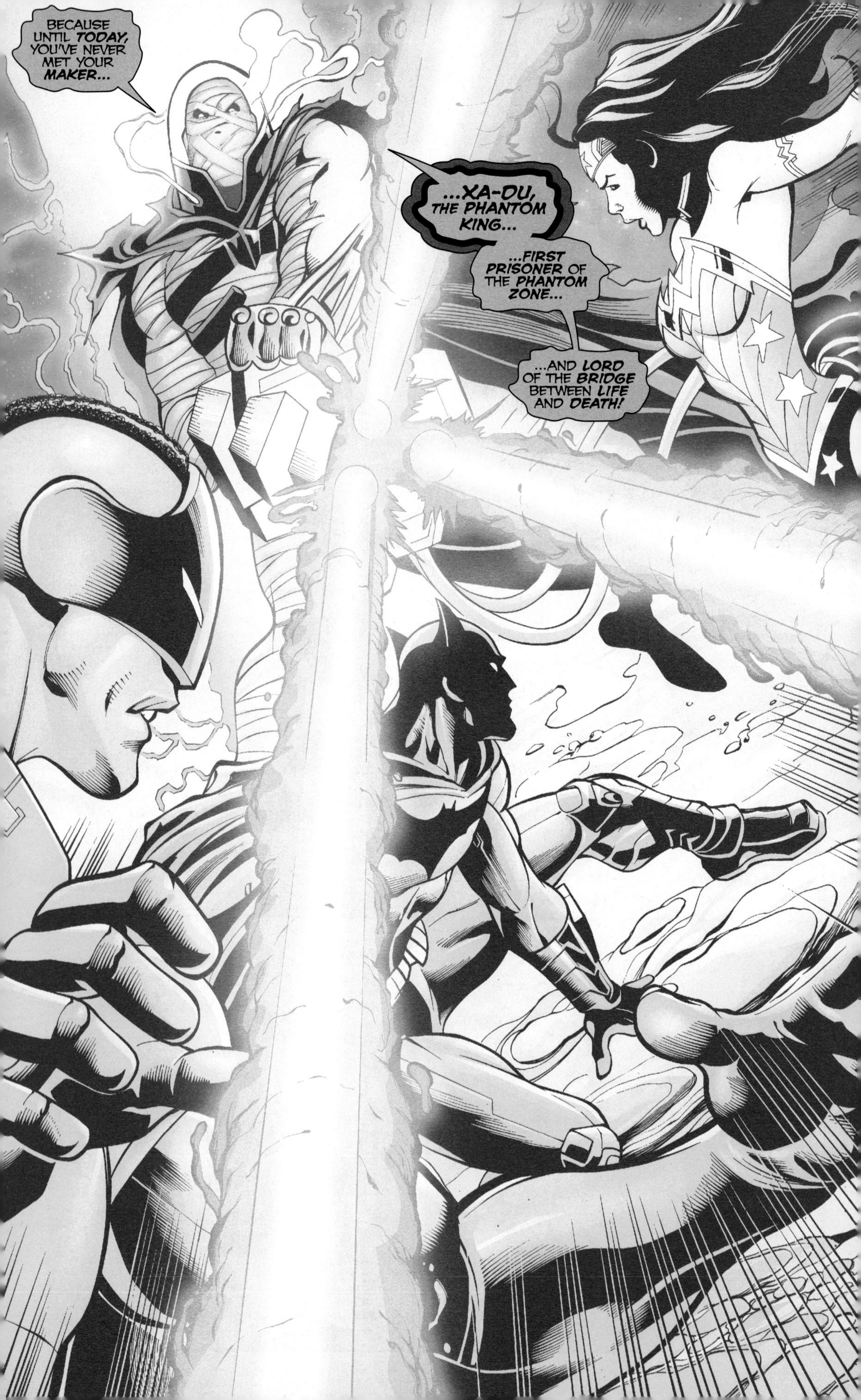
BECAUSE UNTIL TODAY, YOU'VE NEVER MET YOUR MAKER...
...XA-DU, THE PHANTOM KING...
...FIRST PRISONER OF THE PHANTOM ZONE...
...AND LORD OF THE BRIDGE BETWEEN LIFE AND DEATH!

BATCAVE.

BOOOOOM

WHERE--

SMALLVILLE.

AND YOU CAN GET UP AND CLEAN OUT THOSE GUTTERS WHEN YOU'RE DONE THERE.

MOM!

YES, DEAR.

DAD?

THEY CAN'T HEAR YOU.

WE'RE INTANGIBLE, HERE.

AND THEY'RE NOT YOUR PARENTS. THIS IS THE OTHER WORLD.

I... I KNOW.

BUT YOU HAVE NO IDEA WHAT IT FEELS LIKE.

IF MY FOLKS HAD LIVED...

HE JOKES ABOUT HIS CREAKY BACK...

...SHE SAYS IF HE'D STOP EATING SO MUCH PIE HIS BELLY WOULDN'T PUT SO MUCH STRAIN ON IT.

HE WINKS AND SAYS SOMETHING ABOUT HER PIE.

SHE BLUSHES AND MY HEART BREAKS AND--

BOOOOOM

OH, LORD.

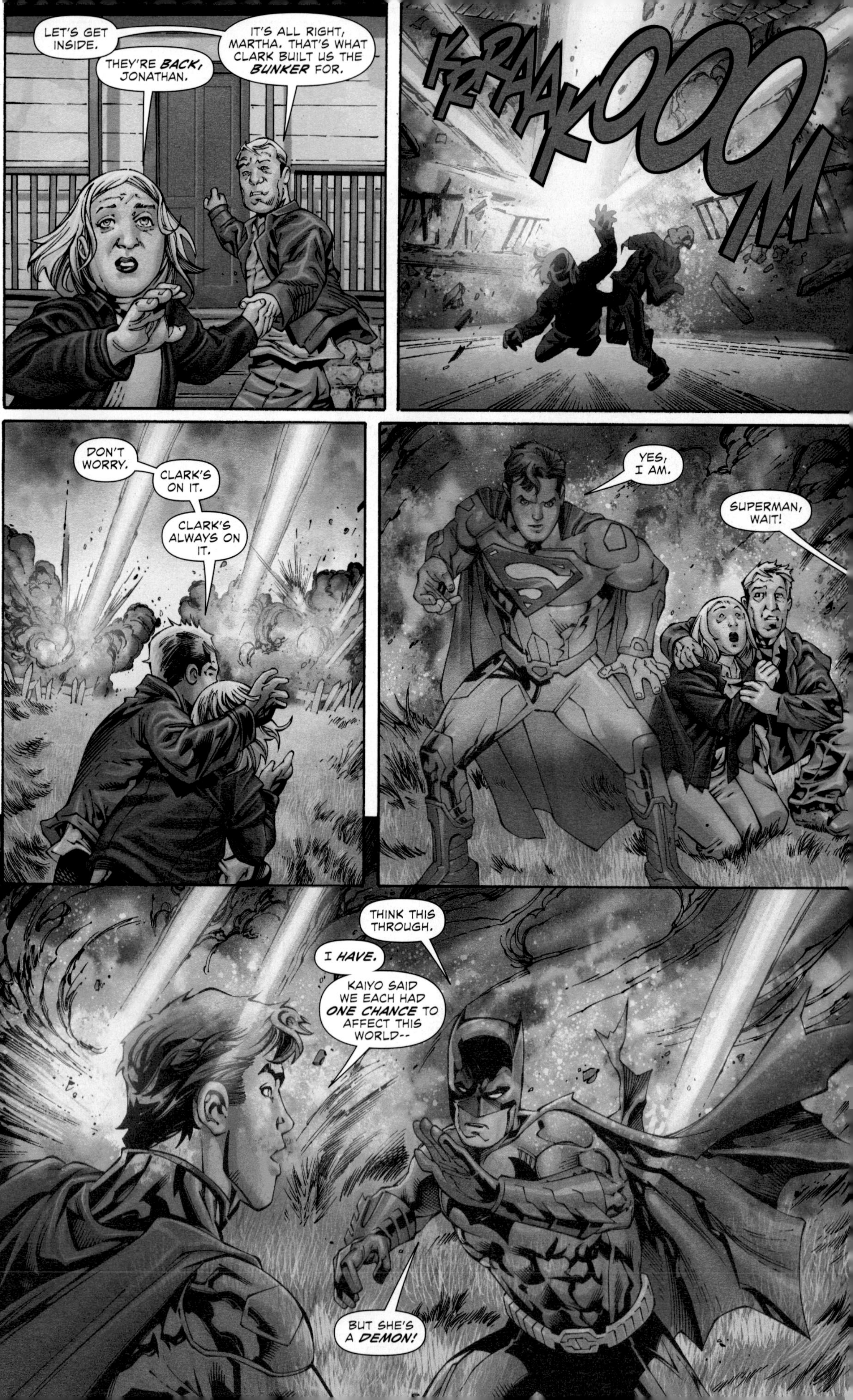
LET'S GET INSIDE.
THEY'RE BACK, JONATHAN.
IT'S ALL RIGHT, MARTHA. THAT'S WHAT CLARK BUILT US THE BUNKER FOR.
KRAAKOOOM
DON'T WORRY.
CLARK'S ON IT.
CLARK'S ALWAYS ON IT.
YES, I AM.
SUPERMAN, WAIT!
THINK THIS THROUGH.
I HAVE.
KAIYO SAID WE EACH HAD ONE CHANCE TO AFFECT THIS WORLD--
BUT SHE'S A DEMON!

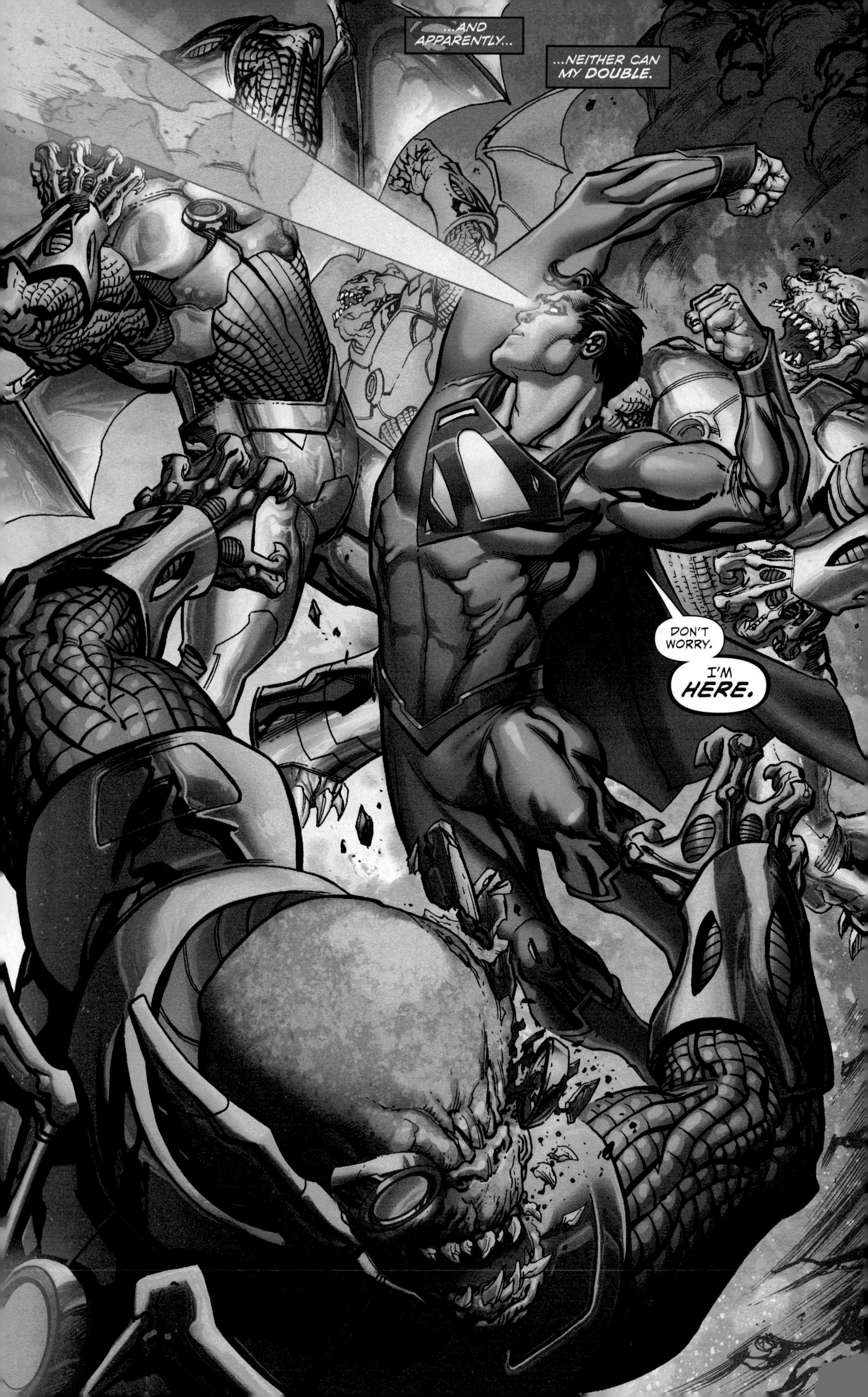
...AND APPARENTLY...
...NEITHER CAN MY DOUBLE.
DON'T WORRY.
I'M HERE.

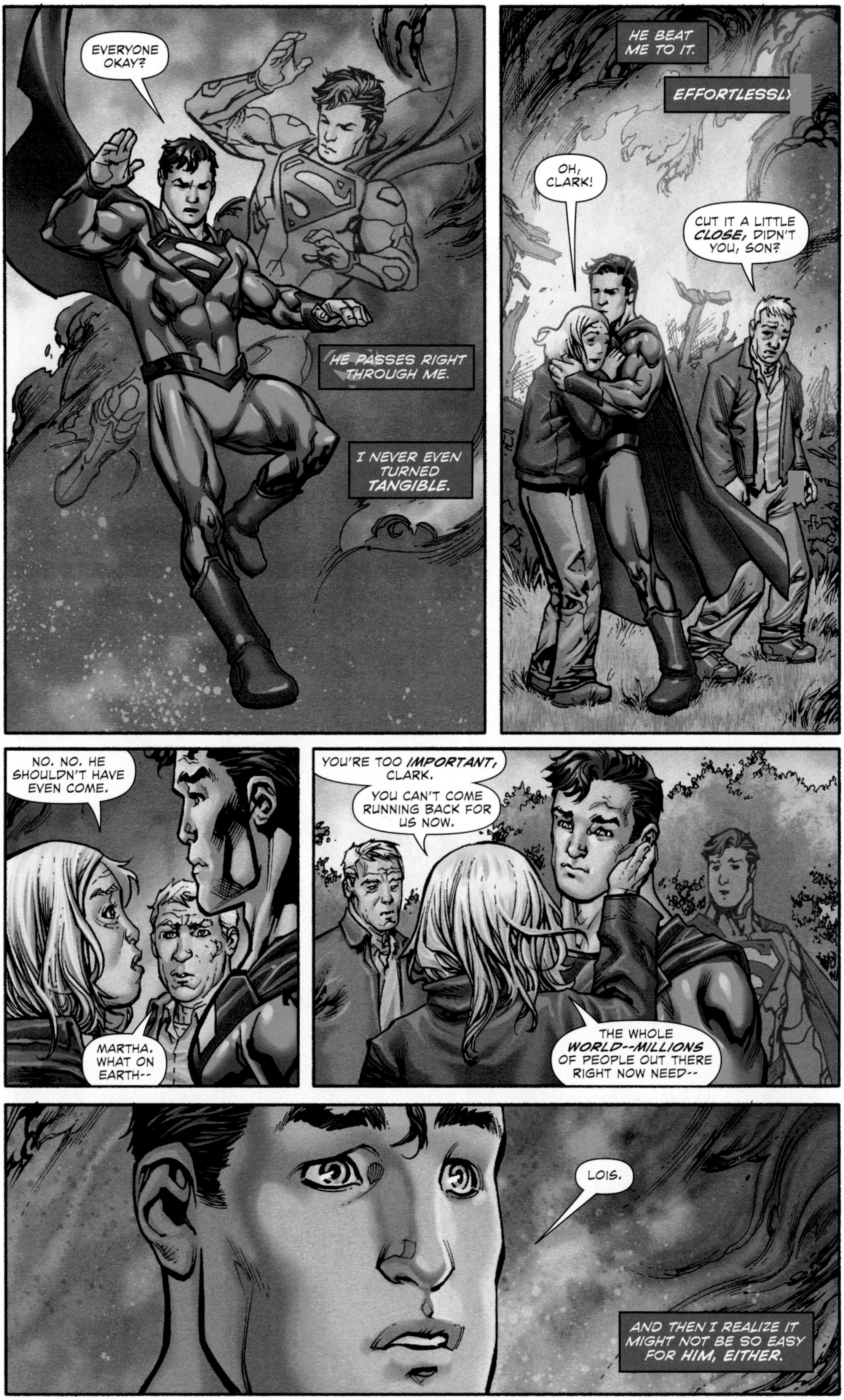
EVERYONE OKAY?
HE PASSES RIGHT THROUGH ME.
I NEVER EVEN TURNED TANGIBLE.
HE BEAT ME TO IT.
EFFORTLESSLY
OH, CLARK!
CUT IT A LITTLE CLOSE, DIDN'T YOU, SON?
NO. NO. HE SHOULDN'T HAVE EVEN COME.
MARTHA. WHAT ON EARTH--
YOU'RE TOO IMPORTANT, CLARK.
YOU CAN'T COME RUNNING BACK FOR US NOW.
THE WHOLE WORLD--MILLIONS OF PEOPLE OUT THERE RIGHT NOW NEED--
LOIS.
AND THEN I REALIZE IT MIGHT NOT BE SO EASY FOR HIM, EITHER.

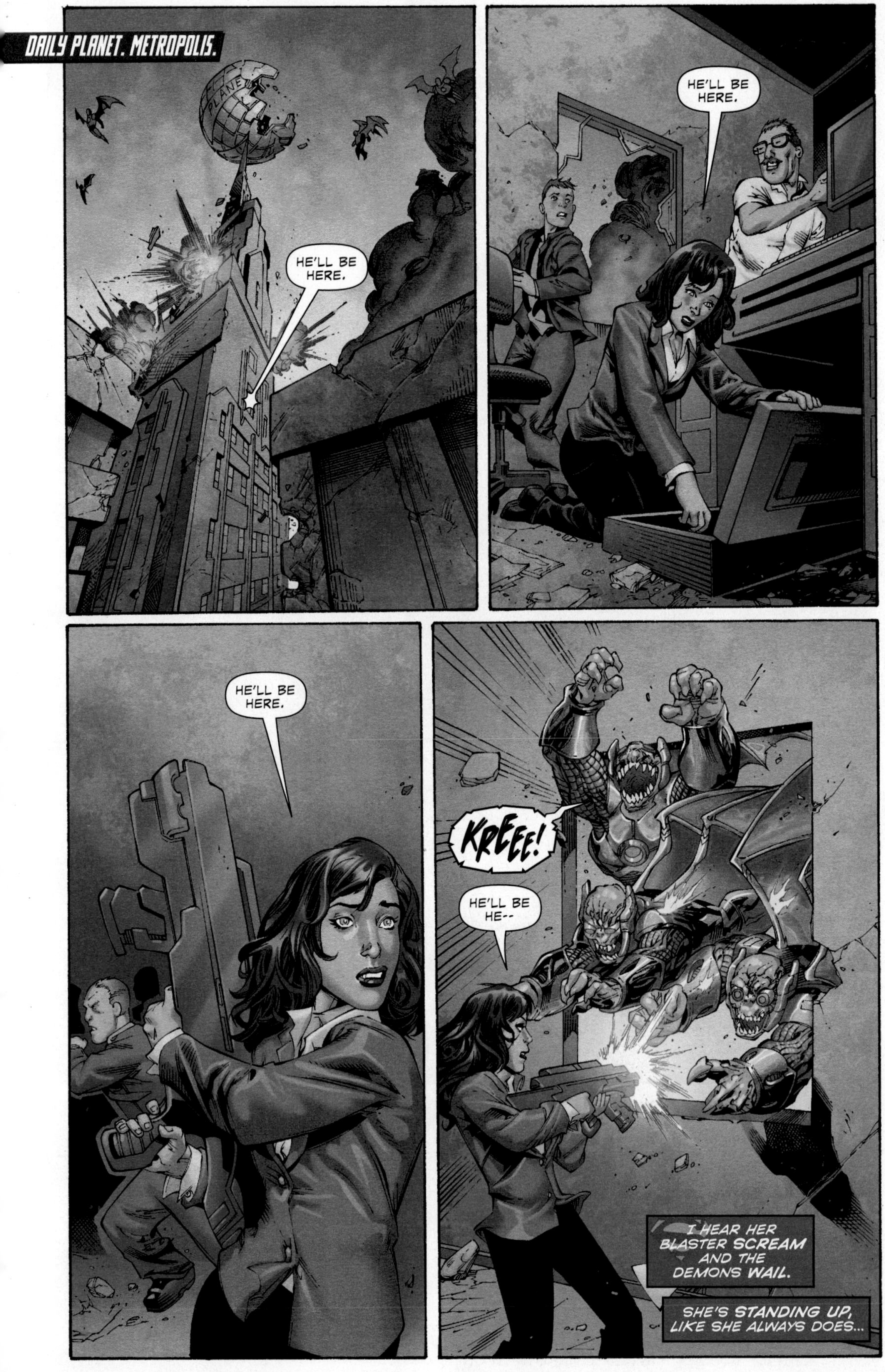
DAILY PLANET. METROPOLIS.
PLANET
HE'LL BE HERE.
HE'LL BE HERE.
HE'LL BE HERE.
KREEE!
HE'LL BE HE--
I HEAR HER BLASTER SCREAM AND THE DEMONS WAIL.
SHE'S STANDING UP, LIKE SHE ALWAYS DOES...

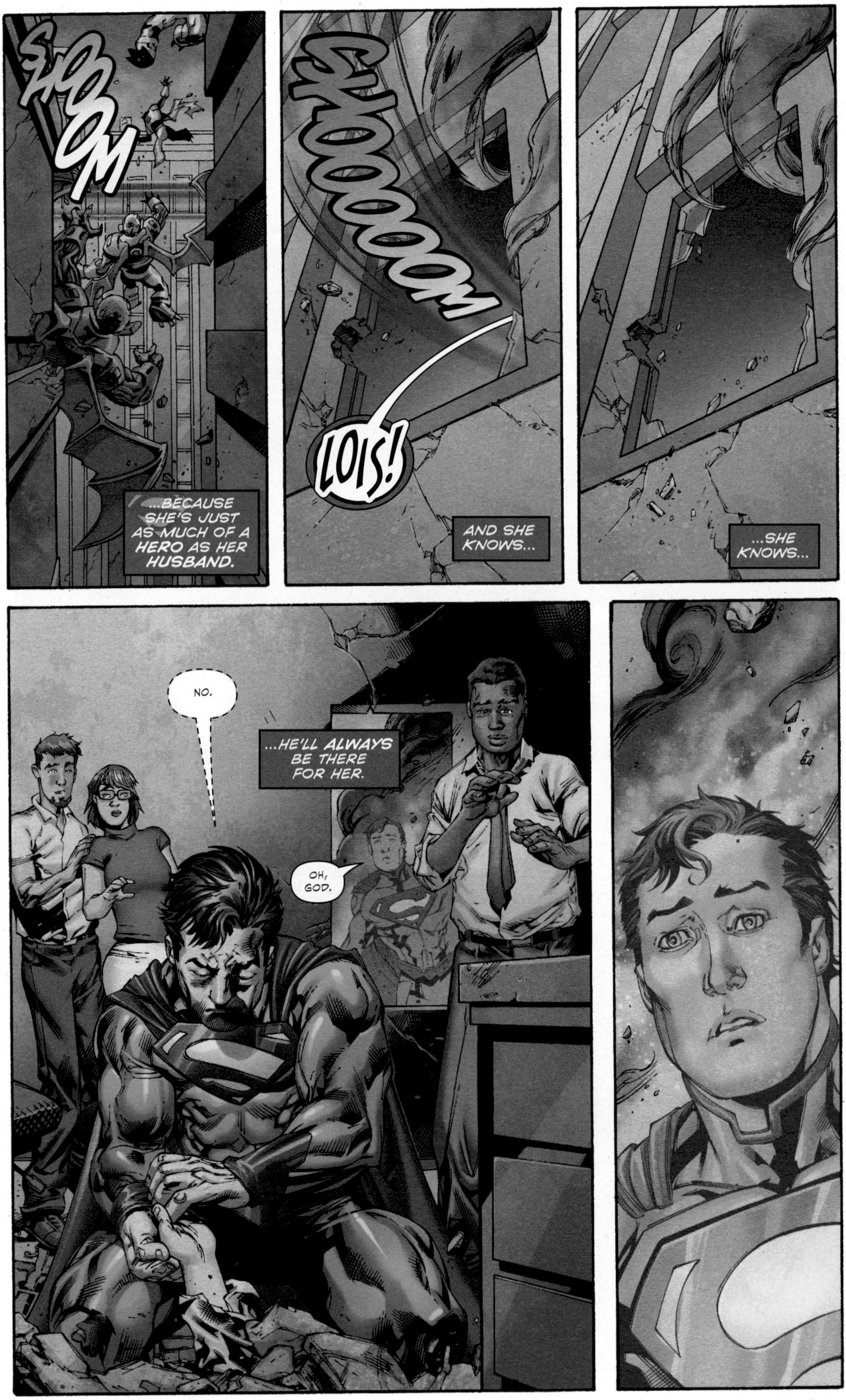
SHOOM
...BECAUSE SHE'S JUST AS MUCH OF A HERO AS HER HUSBAND.
SHOOOOOM
LOIS!
AND SHE KNOWS...
...SHE KNOWS...
NO.
...HE'LL ALWAYS BE THERE FOR HER.
OH, GOD.

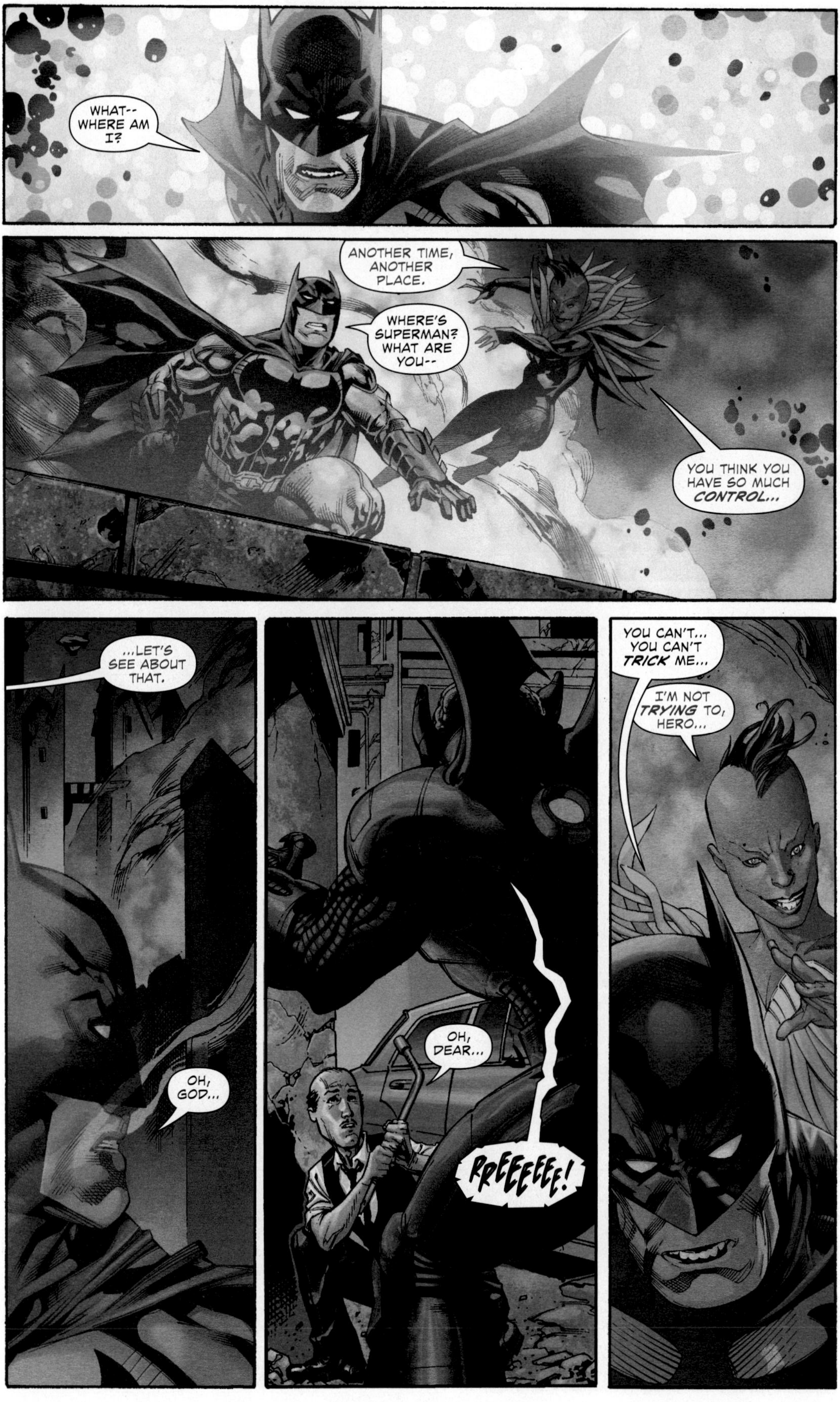
WHAT-- WHERE AM I?
ANOTHER TIME, ANOTHER PLACE.
WHERE'S SUPERMAN? WHAT ARE YOU--
YOU THINK YOU HAVE SO MUCH *CONTROL*...
...LET'S SEE ABOUT THAT.
OH, GOD...
OH, DEAR...
RREEEEEE!
YOU CAN'T... YOU CAN'T *TRICK* ME...
I'M NOT *TRYING* TO, HERO...

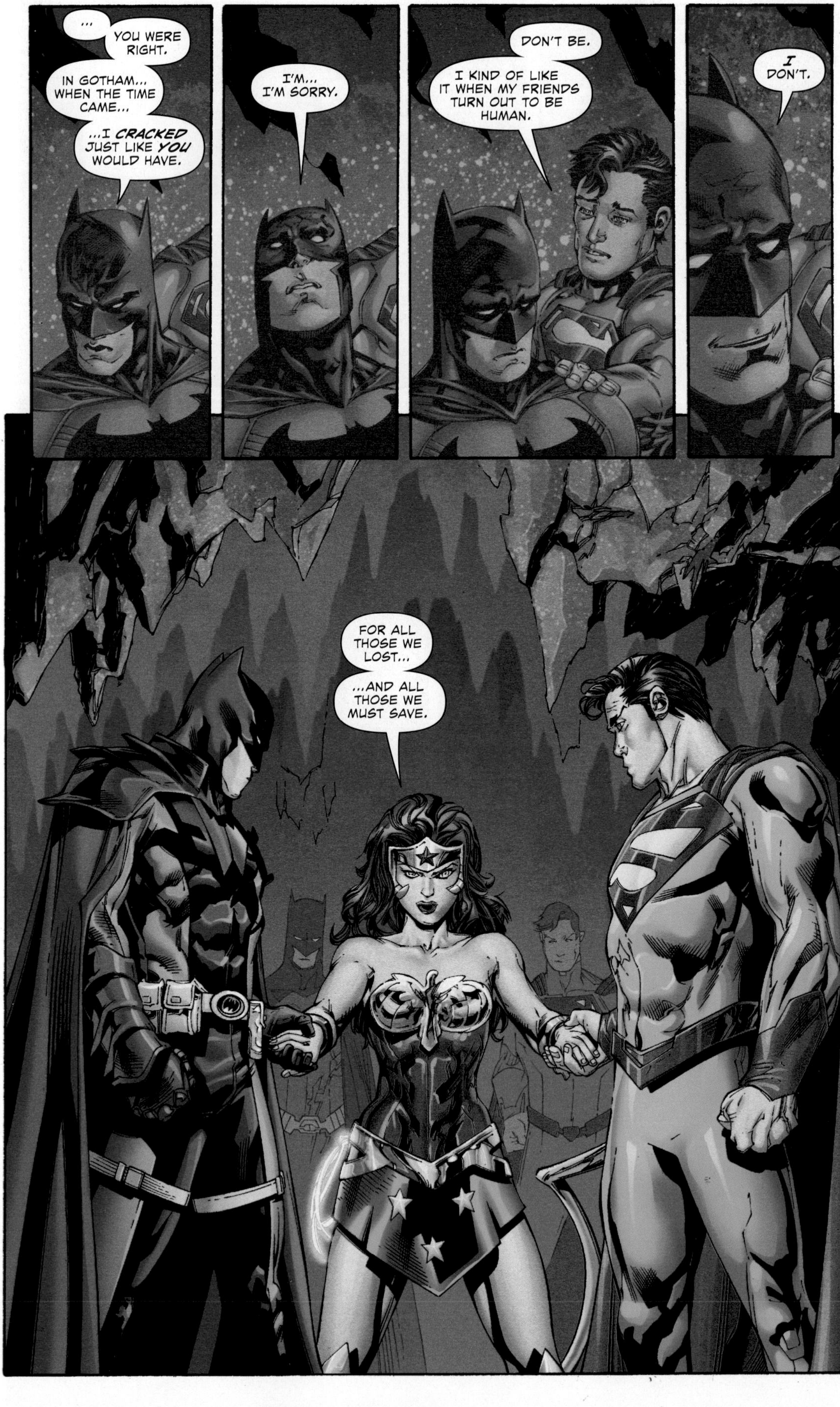
...
YOU WERE RIGHT.
IN GOTHAM... WHEN THE TIME CAME...
...I CRACKED JUST LIKE YOU WOULD HAVE.
I'M... I'M SORRY.
DON'T BE.
I KIND OF LIKE IT WHEN MY FRIENDS TURN OUT TO BE HUMAN.
I DON'T.
FOR ALL THOSE WE LOST...
...AND ALL THOSE WE MUST SAVE.

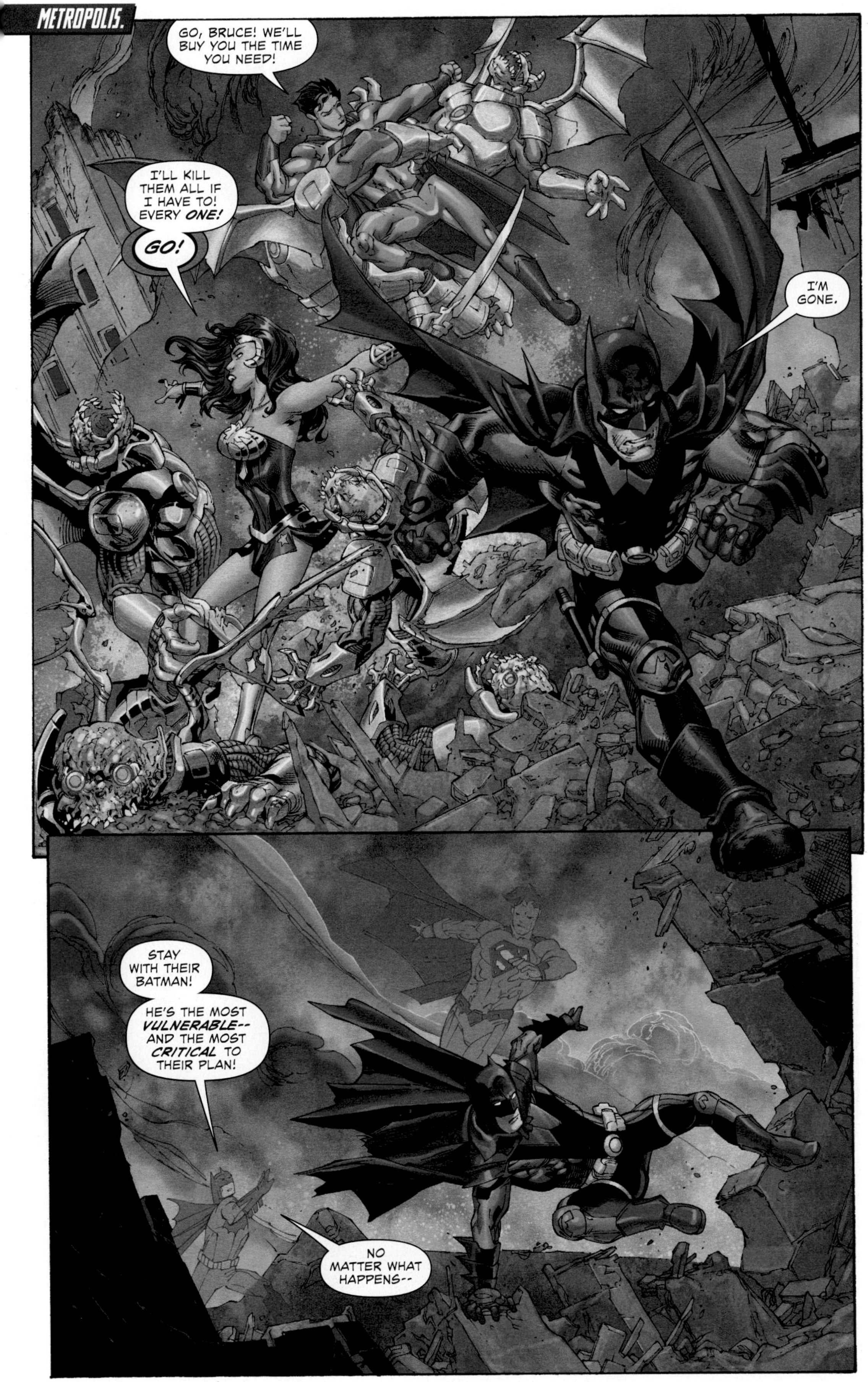
METROPOLIS.
GO, BRUCE! WE'LL BUY YOU THE TIME YOU NEED!
I'LL KILL THEM ALL IF I HAVE TO! EVERY ONE!
GO!
I'M GONE.
STAY WITH THEIR BATMAN!
HE'S THE MOST VULNERABLE-- AND THE MOST CRITICAL TO THEIR PLAN!
NO MATTER WHAT HAPPENS--

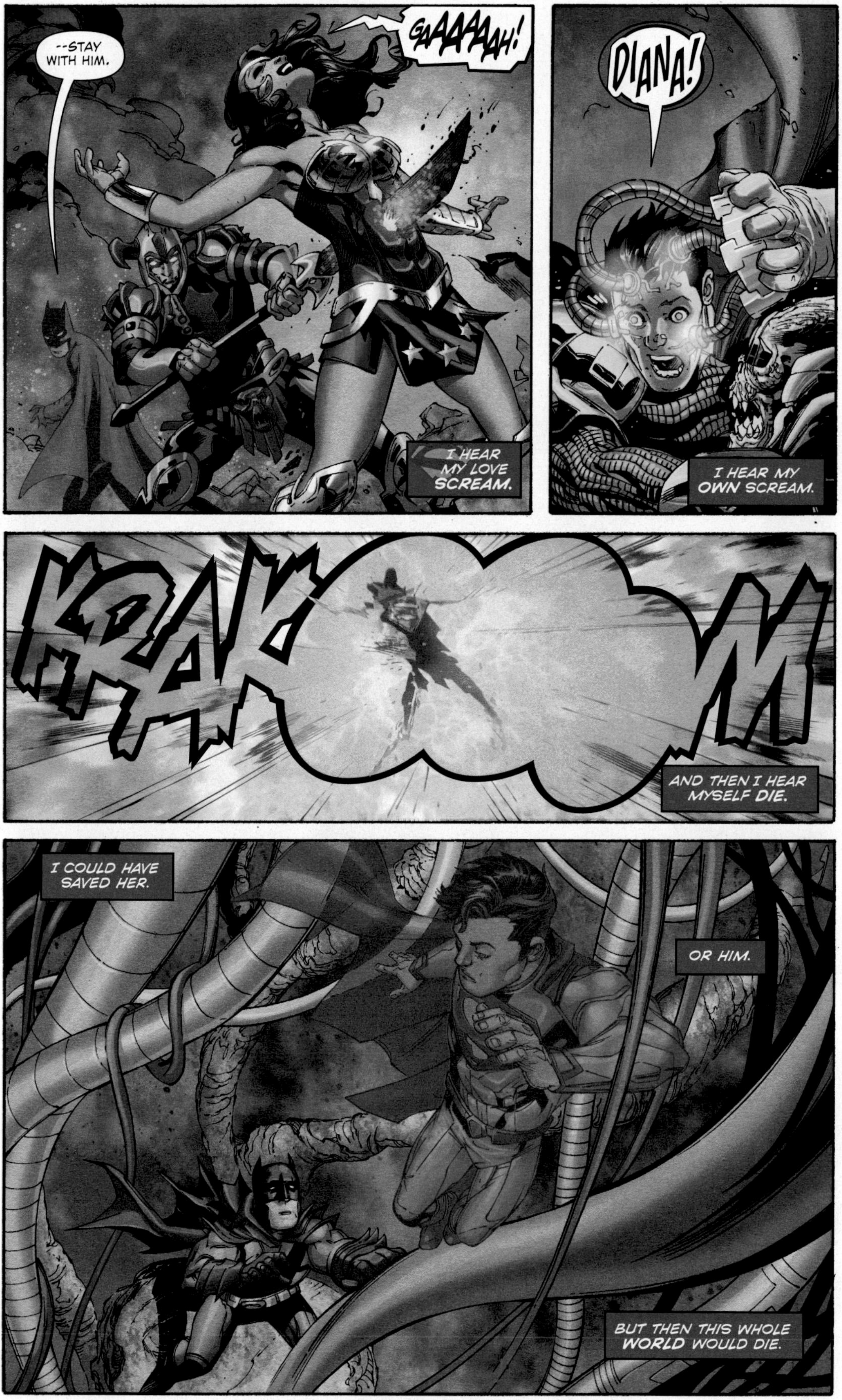
--STAY WITH HIM.
GAAAAAAH!
I HEAR MY LOVE SCREAM.
DIANA!
I HEAR MY OWN SCREAM.
KRAKOOOM
AND THEN I HEAR MYSELF DIE.
I COULD HAVE SAVED HER.
OR HIM.
BUT THEN THIS WHOLE WORLD WOULD DIE.

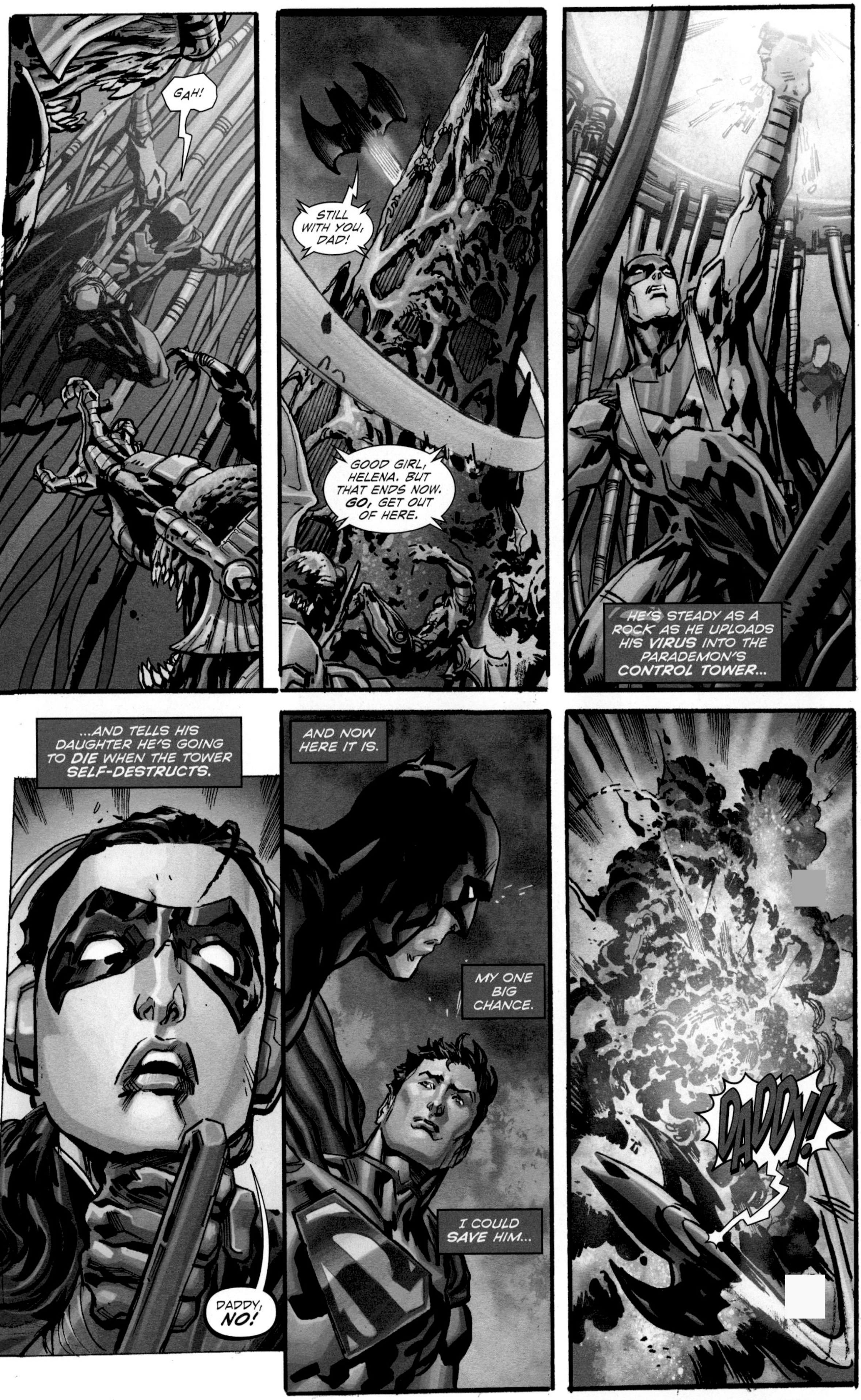
GAH!
STILL WITH YOU, DAD!
GOOD GIRL, HELENA. BUT THAT ENDS NOW. GO, GET OUT OF HERE.
HE'S STEADY AS A ROCK AS HE UPLOADS HIS VIRUS INTO THE PARADEMON'S CONTROL TOWER...
...AND TELLS HIS DAUGHTER HE'S GOING TO DIE WHEN THE TOWER SELF-DESTRUCTS.
DADDY, NO!
AND NOW HERE IT IS.
MY ONE BIG CHANCE.
I COULD SAVE HIM...
DADDY!

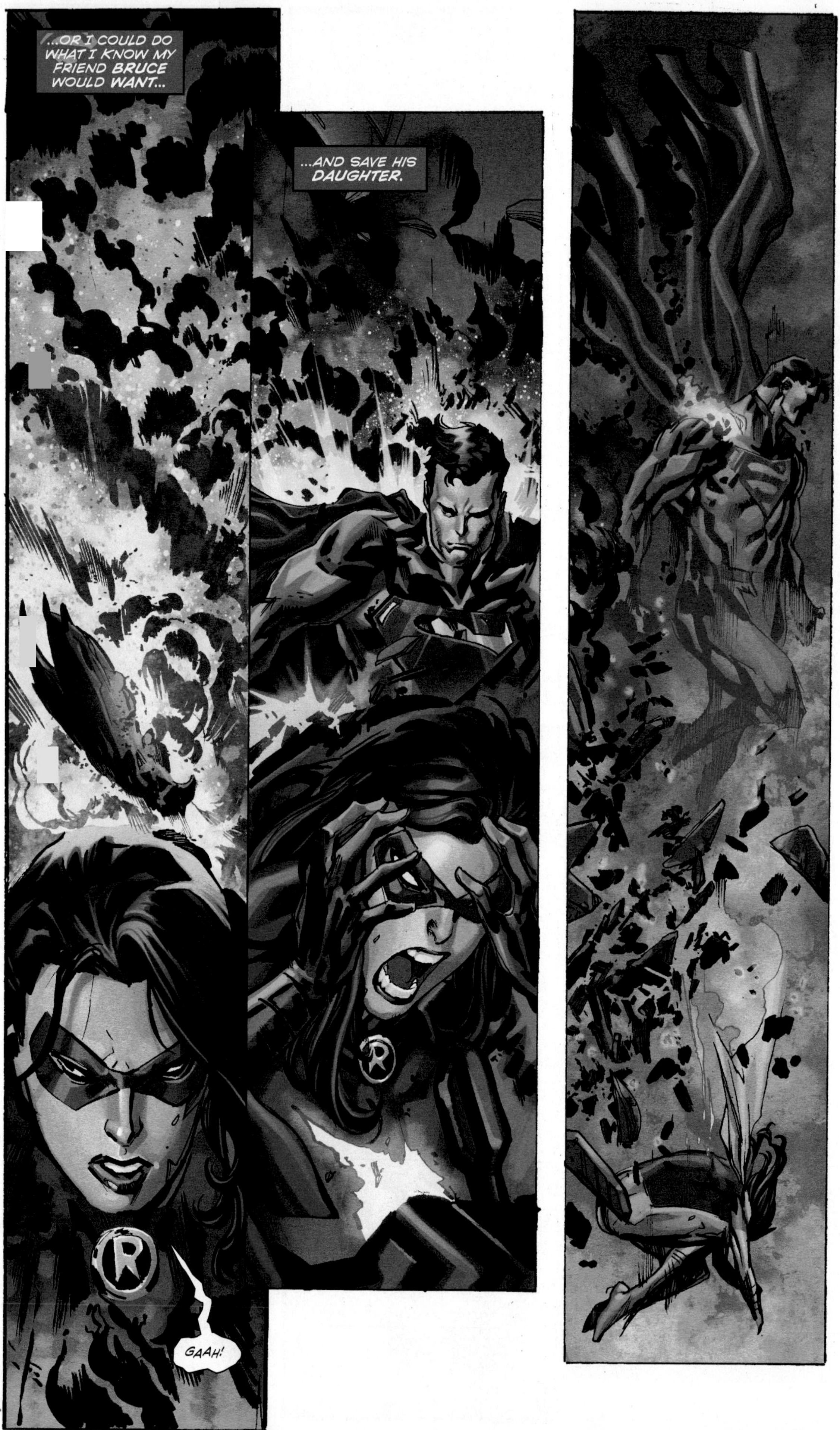
...OR I COULD DO WHAT I KNOW MY FRIEND BRUCE WOULD WANT...
...AND SAVE HIS DAUGHTER.
GAAH!

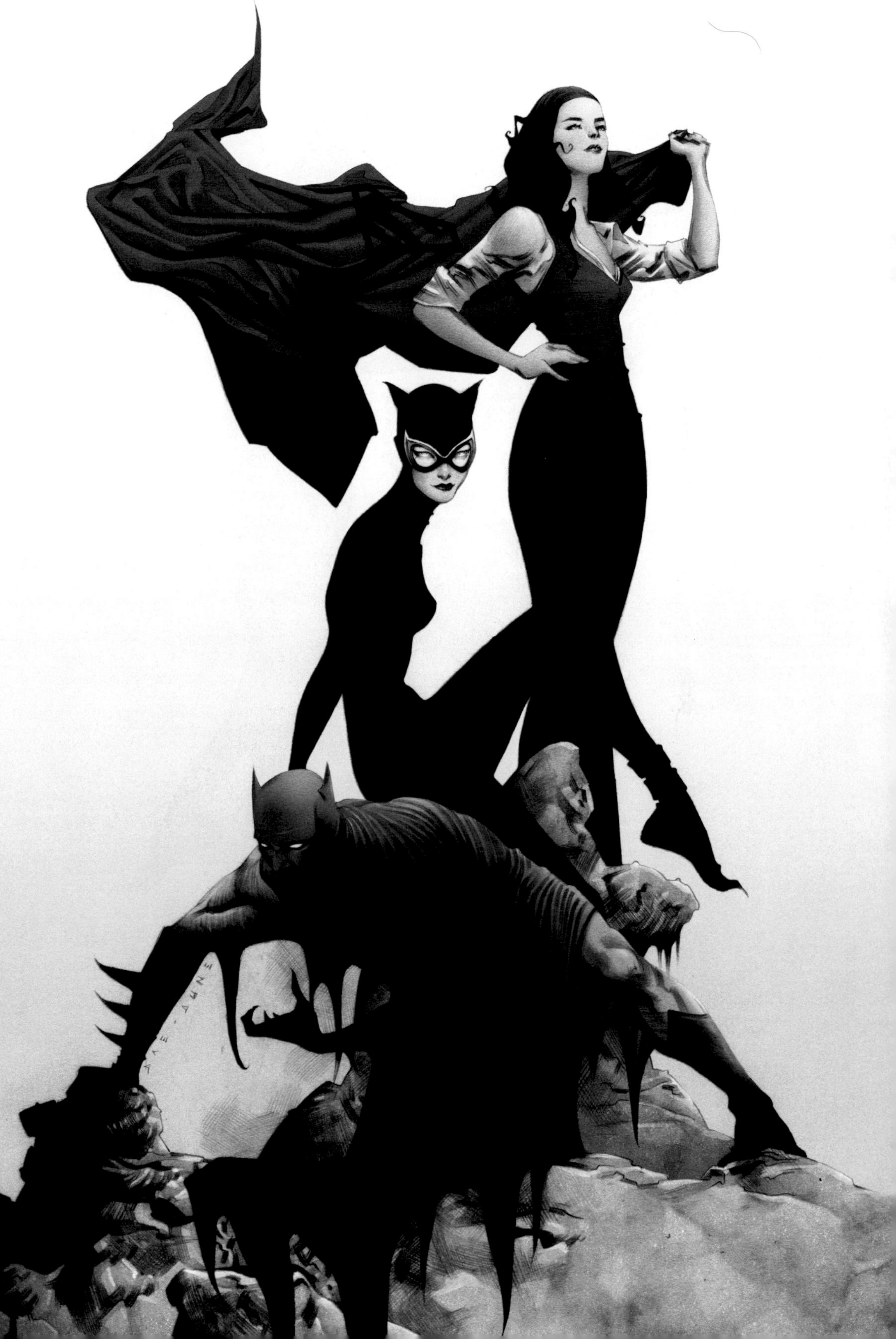

EYE OF SATANUS

GREG PAK writer **JAE LEE** artist **JUNE CHUNG** colorist **ROB LEIGH** letterer cover by **JAE LEE** with **JUNE CHUNG**

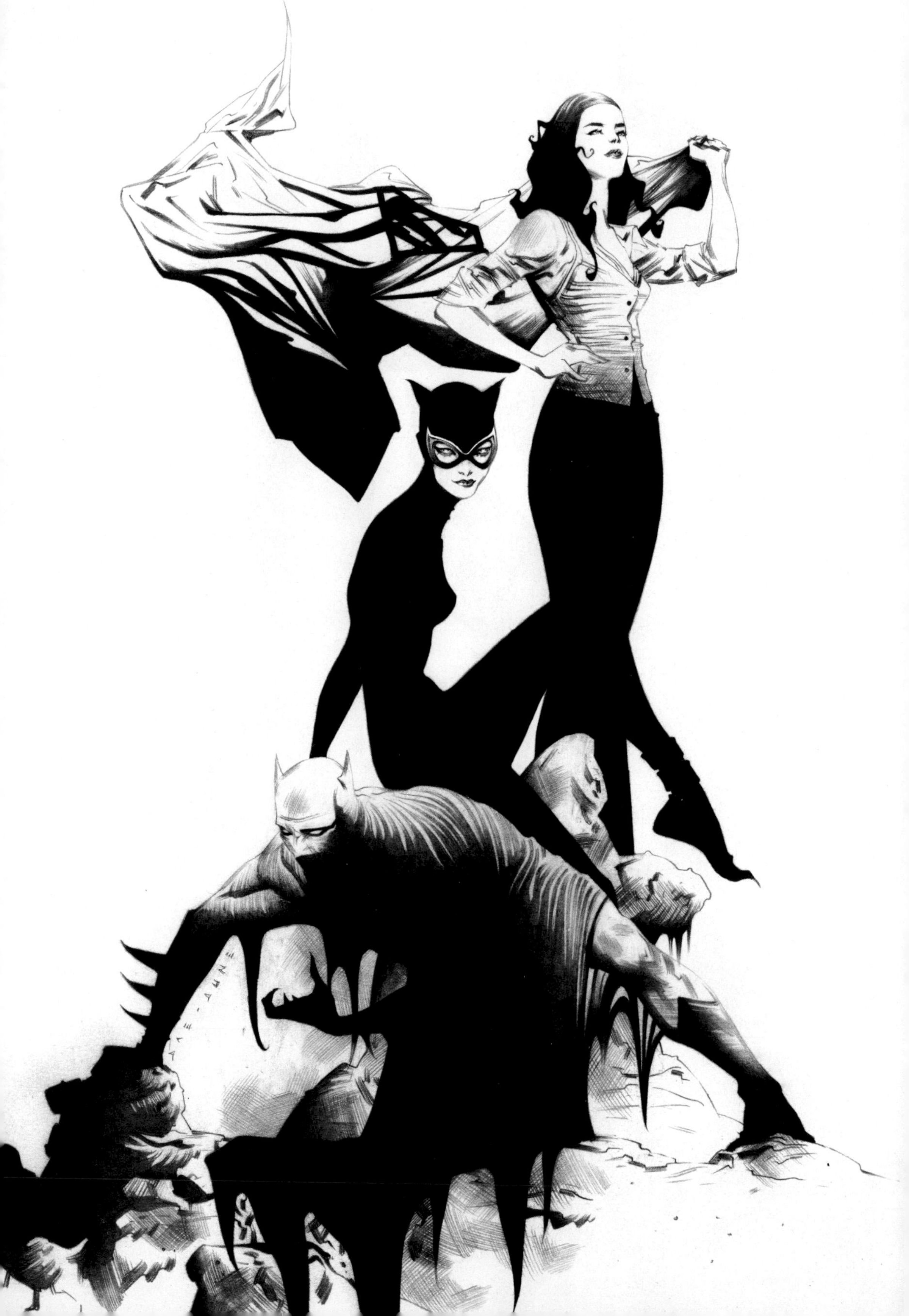

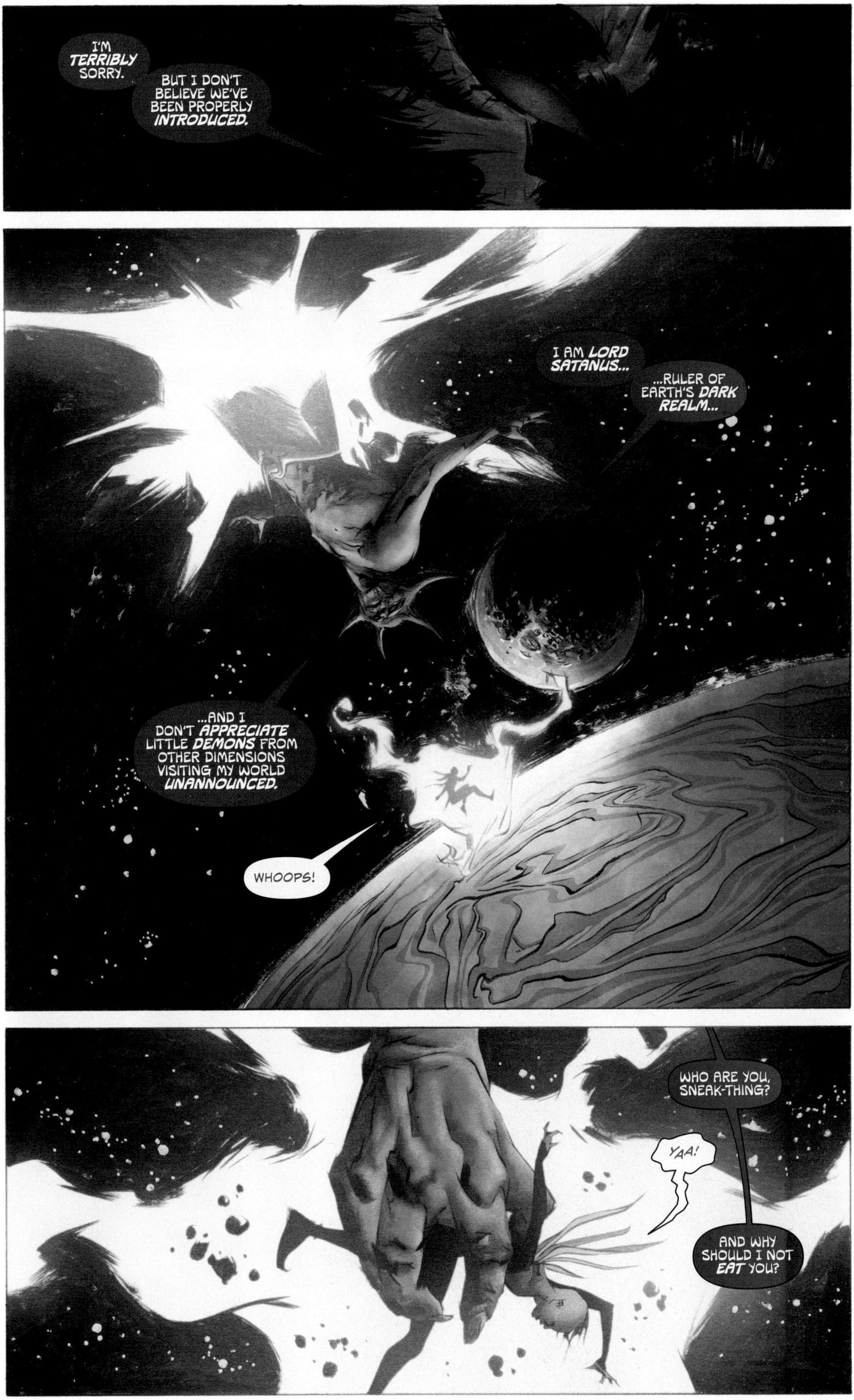
I'M TERRIBLY SORRY.
BUT I DON'T BELIEVE WE'VE BEEN PROPERLY INTRODUCED.
I AM LORD SATANUS...
...RULER OF EARTH'S DARK REALM...
...AND I DON'T APPRECIATE LITTLE DEMONS FROM OTHER DIMENSIONS VISITING MY WORLD UNANNOUNCED.
WHOOPS!
WHO ARE YOU, SNEAK-THING?
YAA!
AND WHY SHOULD I NOT EAT YOU?

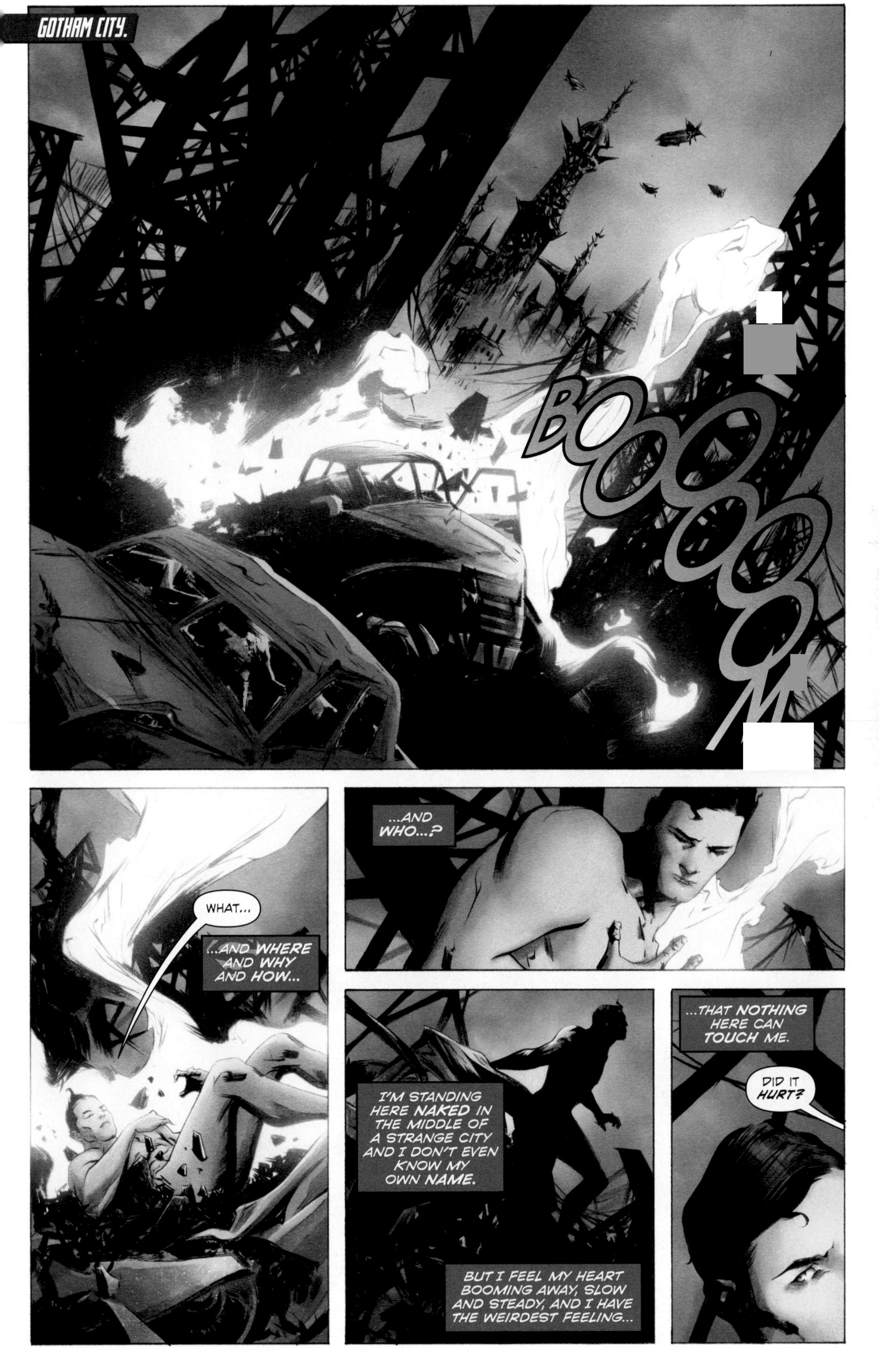
GOTHAM CITY.
BOOOOOOM
WHAT...
...AND WHERE AND WHY AND HOW...
...AND WHO...?
I'M STANDING HERE NAKED IN THE MIDDLE OF A STRANGE CITY AND I DON'T EVEN KNOW MY OWN NAME.
BUT I FEEL MY HEART BOOMING AWAY, SLOW AND STEADY, AND I HAVE THE WEIRDEST FEELING...
...THAT NOTHING HERE CAN TOUCH ME.
DID IT HURT?

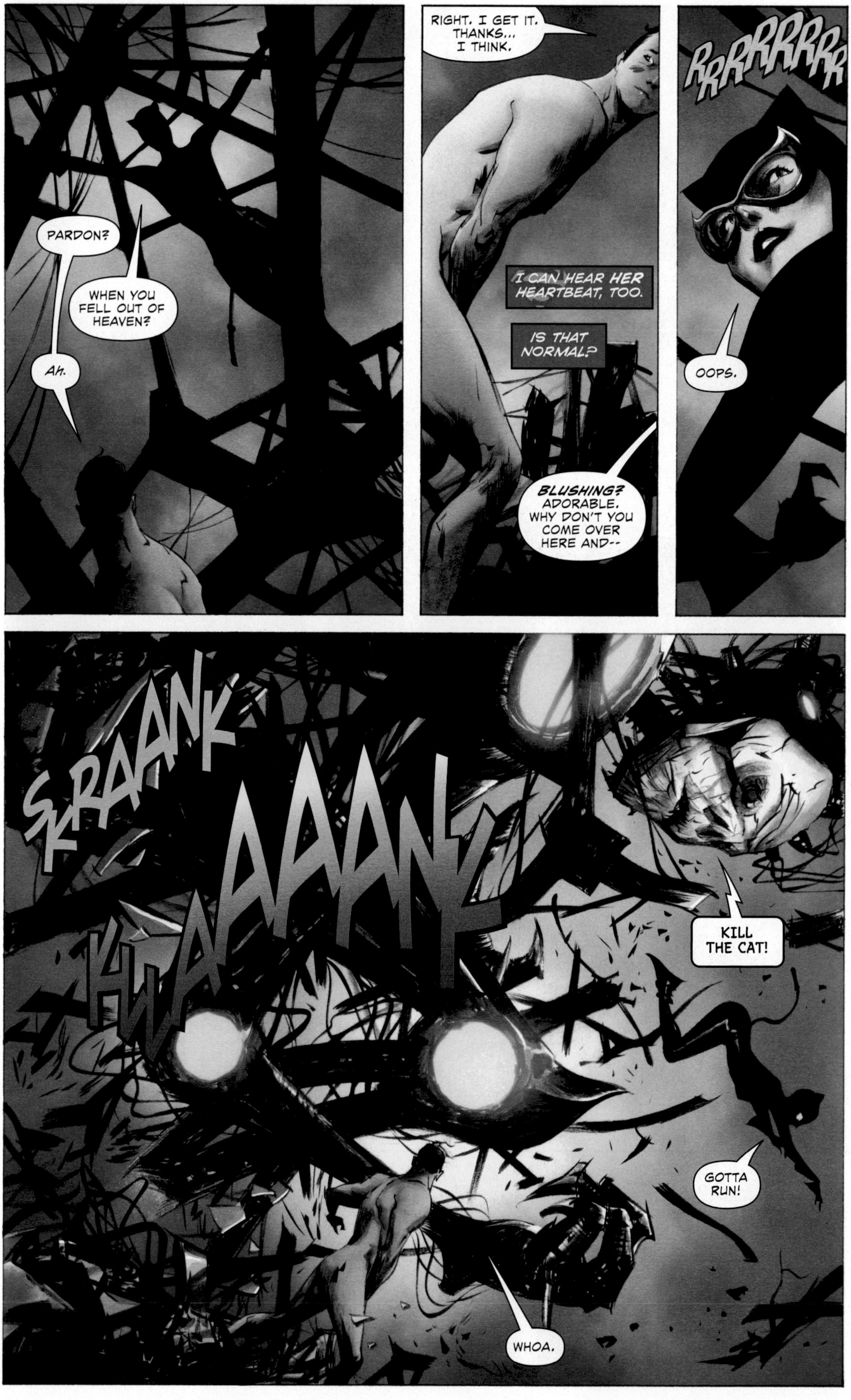
PARDON?
WHEN YOU FELL OUT OF HEAVEN?
Ah.
RIGHT. I GET IT. THANKS... I THINK.
I CAN HEAR HER HEARTBEAT, TOO.
IS THAT NORMAL?
BLUSHING? ADORABLE. WHY DON'T YOU COME OVER HERE AND--
RRRRRRRRR
OOPS.
SKRAANK
KWAAAANK
KILL THE CAT!
GOTTA RUN!
WHOA.

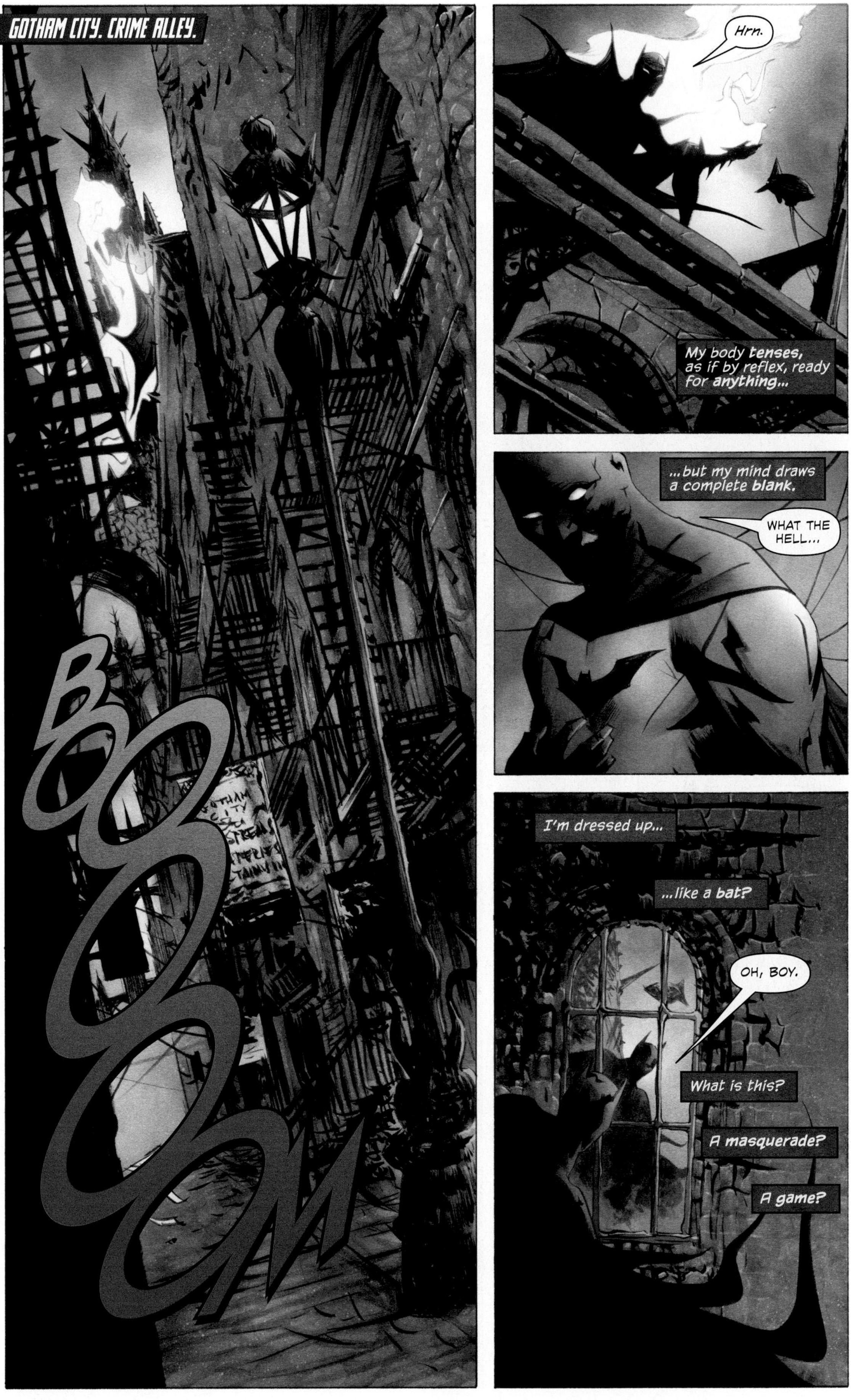
GOTHAM CITY. CRIME ALLEY.
BOOOOM
Hrn.
My body tenses, as if by reflex, ready for anything...
...but my mind draws a complete blank.
WHAT THE HELL...
I'm dressed up...
...like a bat?
OH, BOY.
What is this?
A masquerade?
A game?

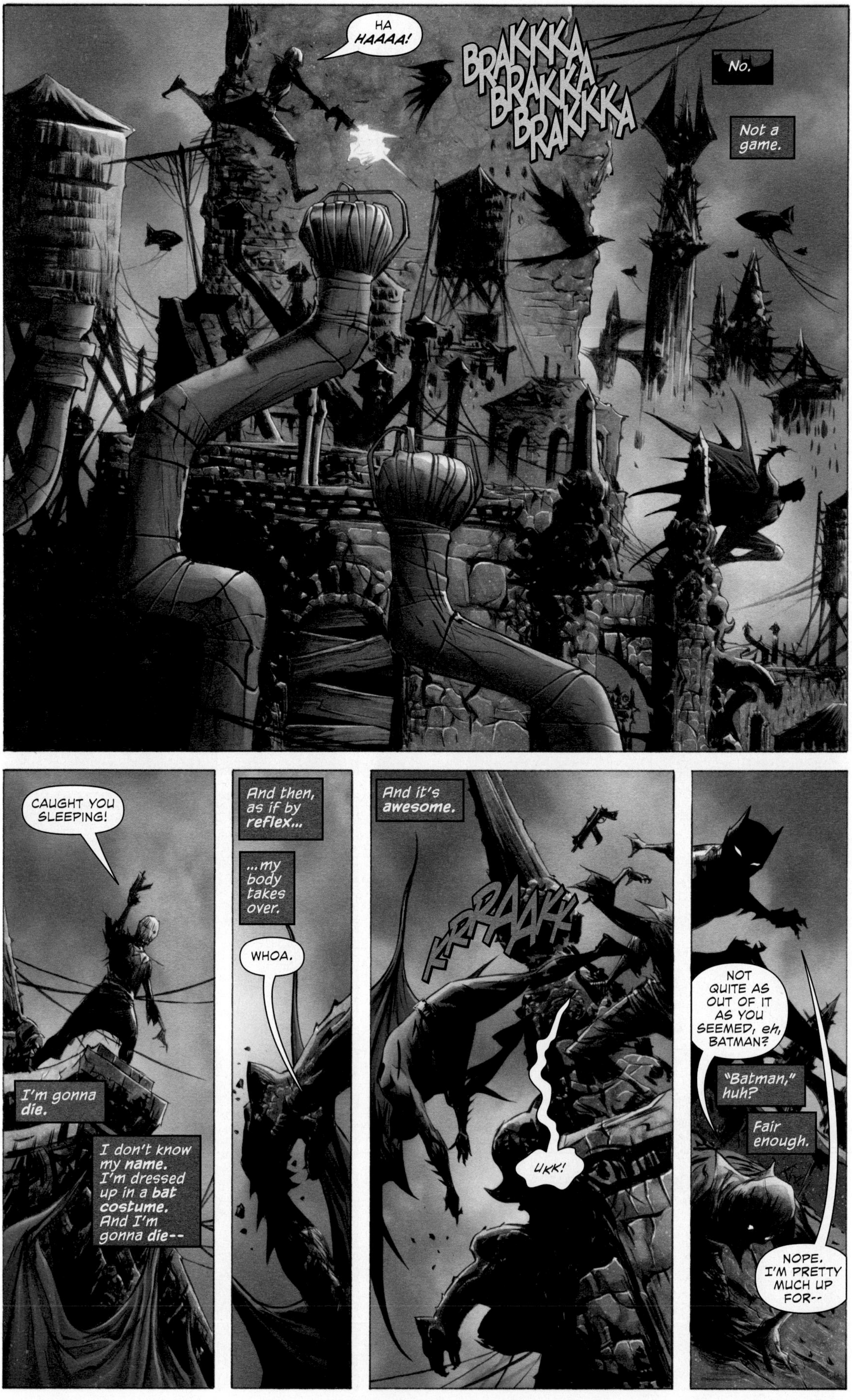

HA HAAAA!
BRAKKKA BRAKKKA BRAKKKA
No.
Not a game.
CAUGHT YOU SLEEPING!
I'm gonna die.
I don't know my name. I'm dressed up in a bat costume. And I'm gonna die--
And then, as if by reflex...
...my body takes over.
WHOA.
And it's awesome.
UKK!
NOT QUITE AS OUT OF IT AS YOU SEEMED, eh, BATMAN?
"Batman," huh?
Fair enough.
NOPE. I'M PRETTY MUCH UP FOR--

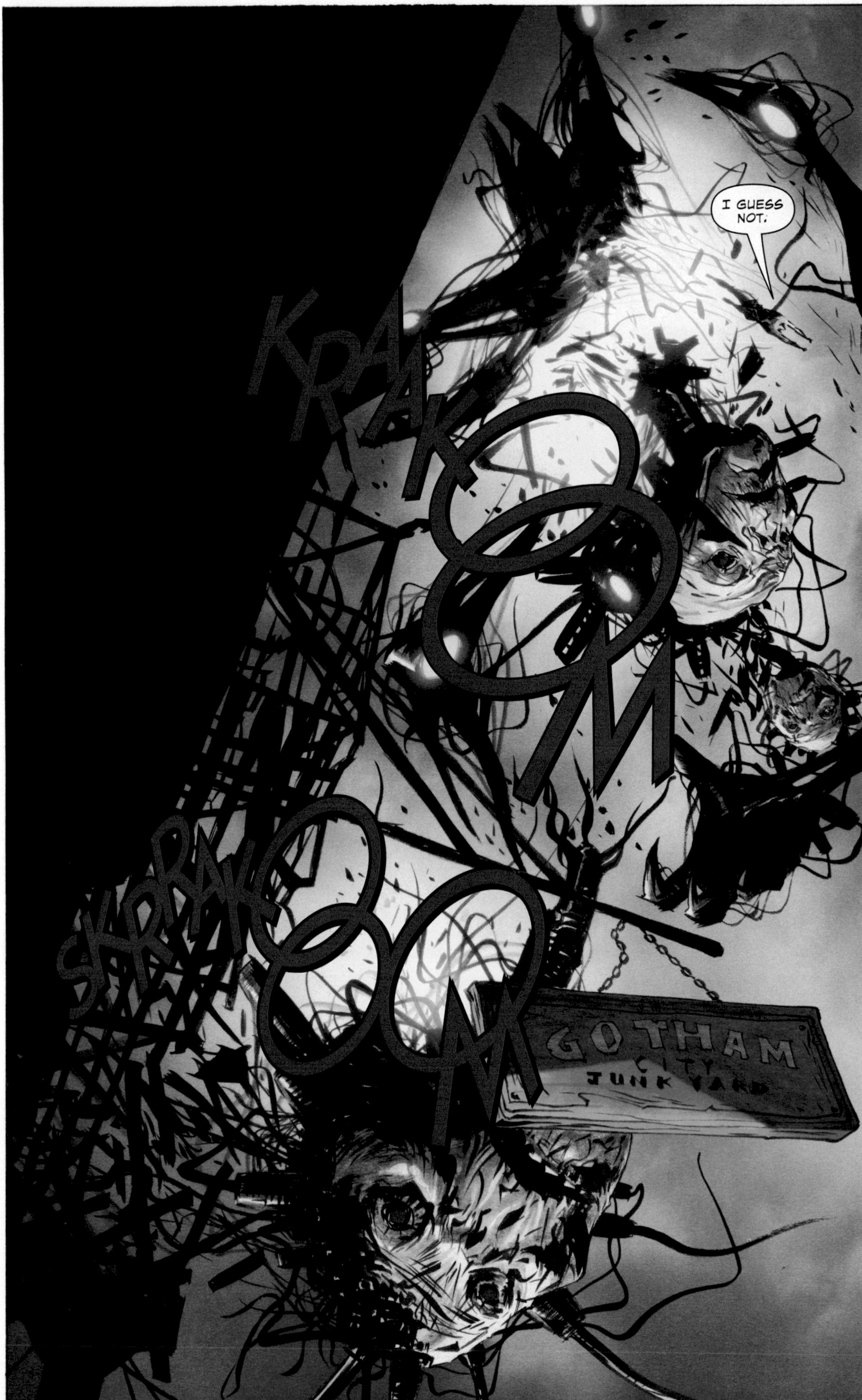
I GUESS NOT.
KRAAKOOM
SKRRAKOOM
GOTHAM CITY JUNK YARD

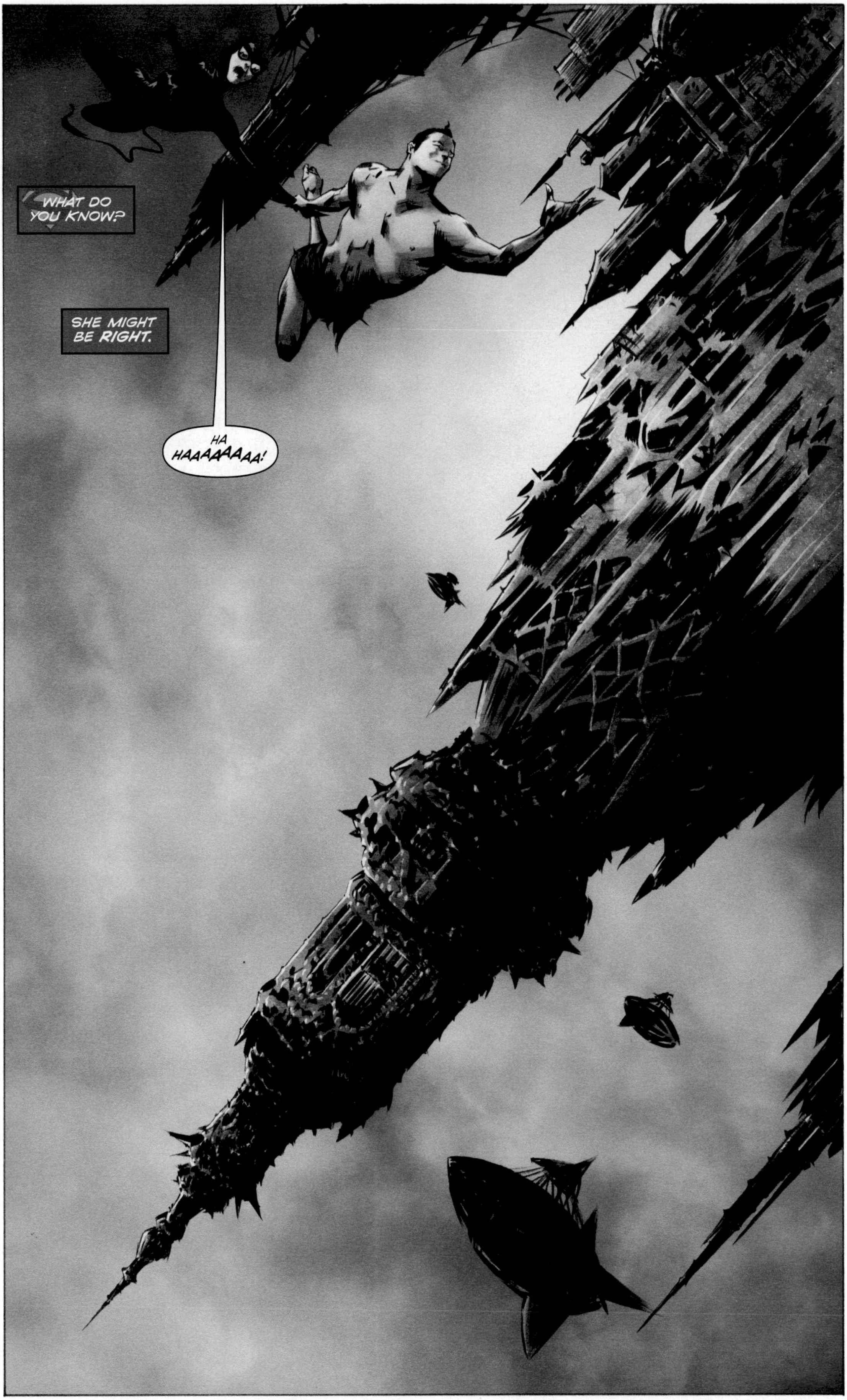
WHAT DO YOU KNOW?
SHE MIGHT BE RIGHT.
HA HAAAAAAAA!

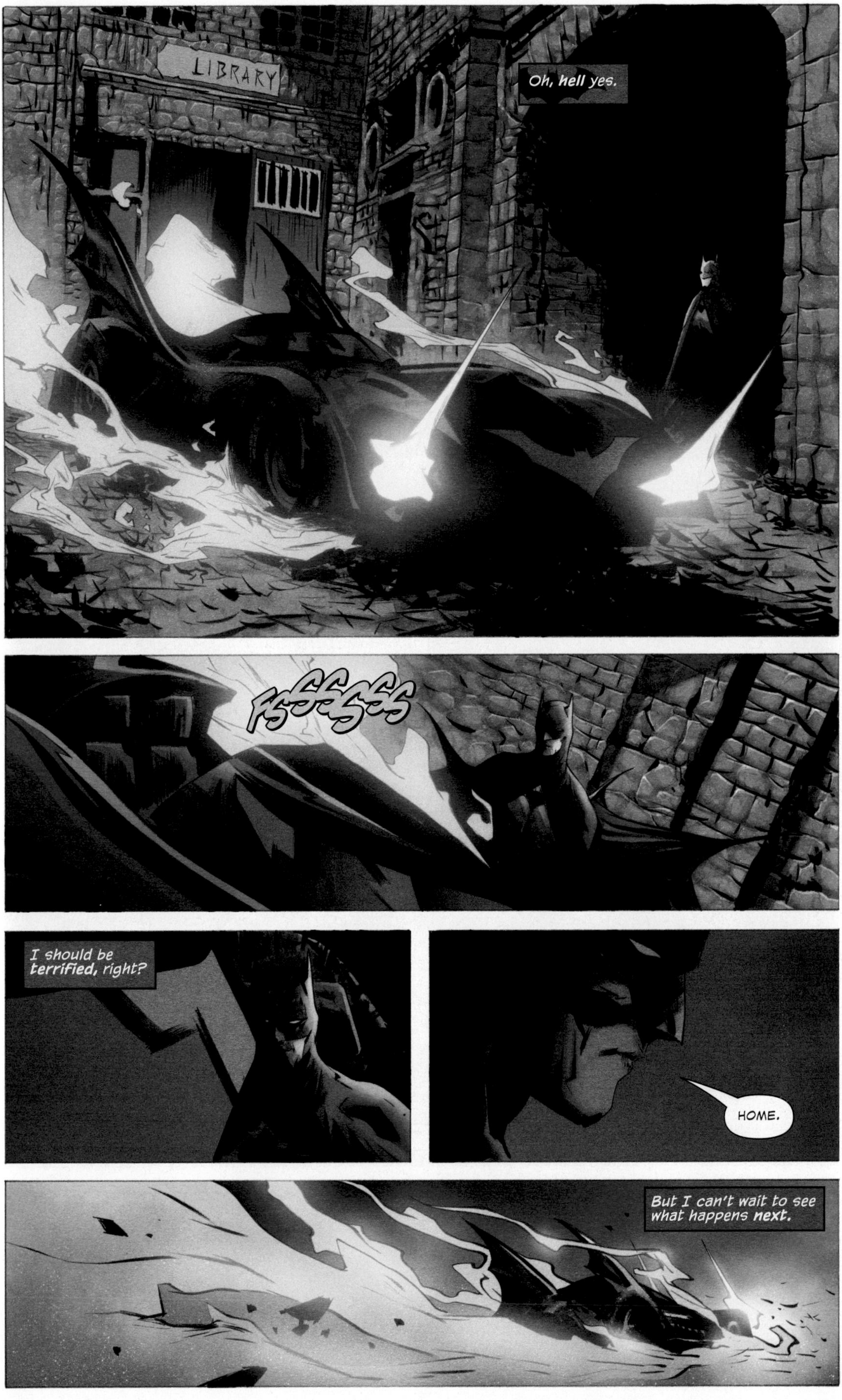
LIBRARY
Oh, hell yes.
FSSSSSS
I should be terrified, right?
HOME.
But I can't wait to see what happens next.

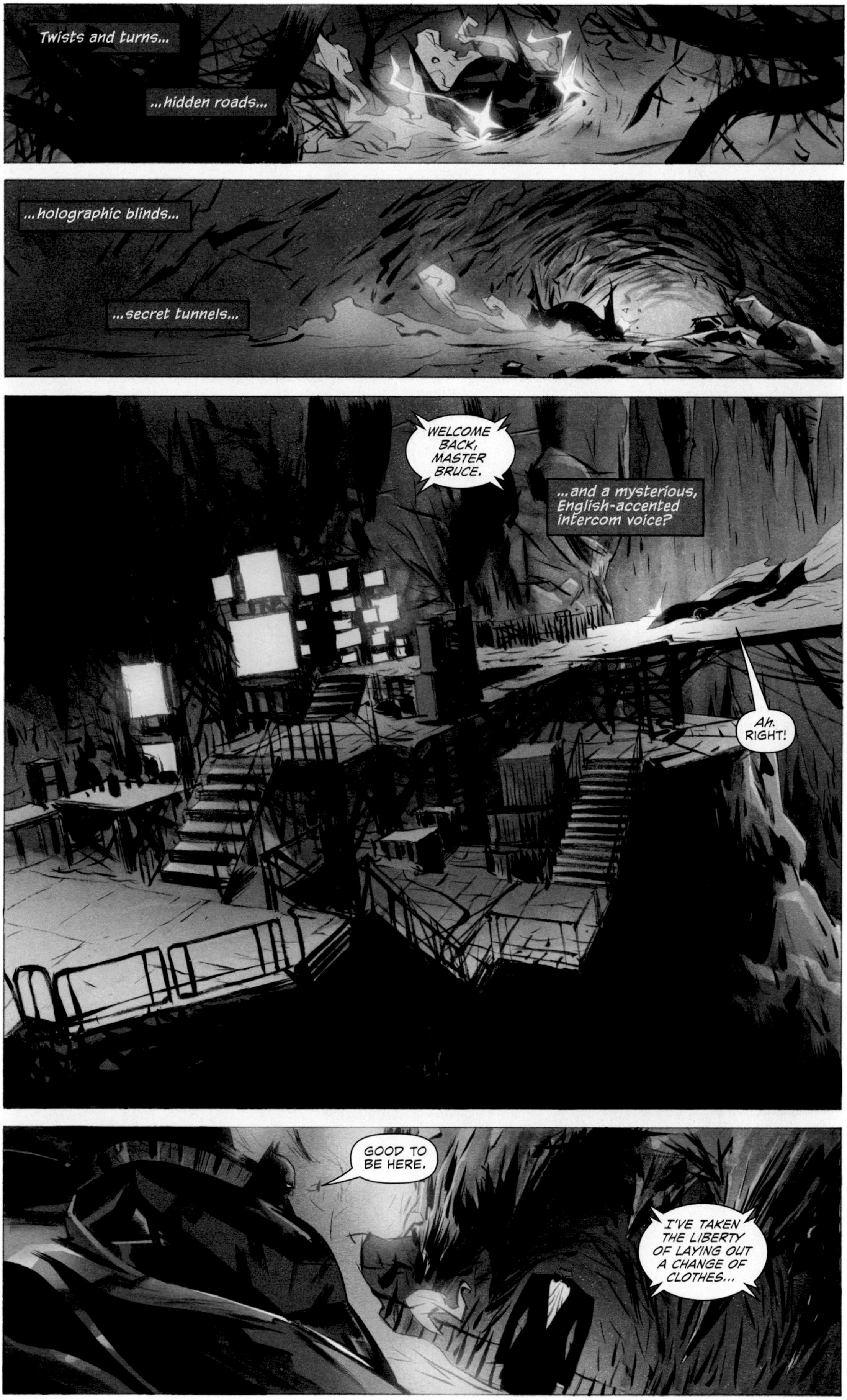
Twists and turns...
...hidden roads...
...holographic blinds...
...secret tunnels...
WELCOME BACK, MASTER BRUCE.
...and a mysterious, English-accented intercom voice?
Ah. RIGHT!
GOOD TO BE HERE.
I'VE TAKEN THE LIBERTY OF LAYING OUT A CHANGE OF CLOTHES...

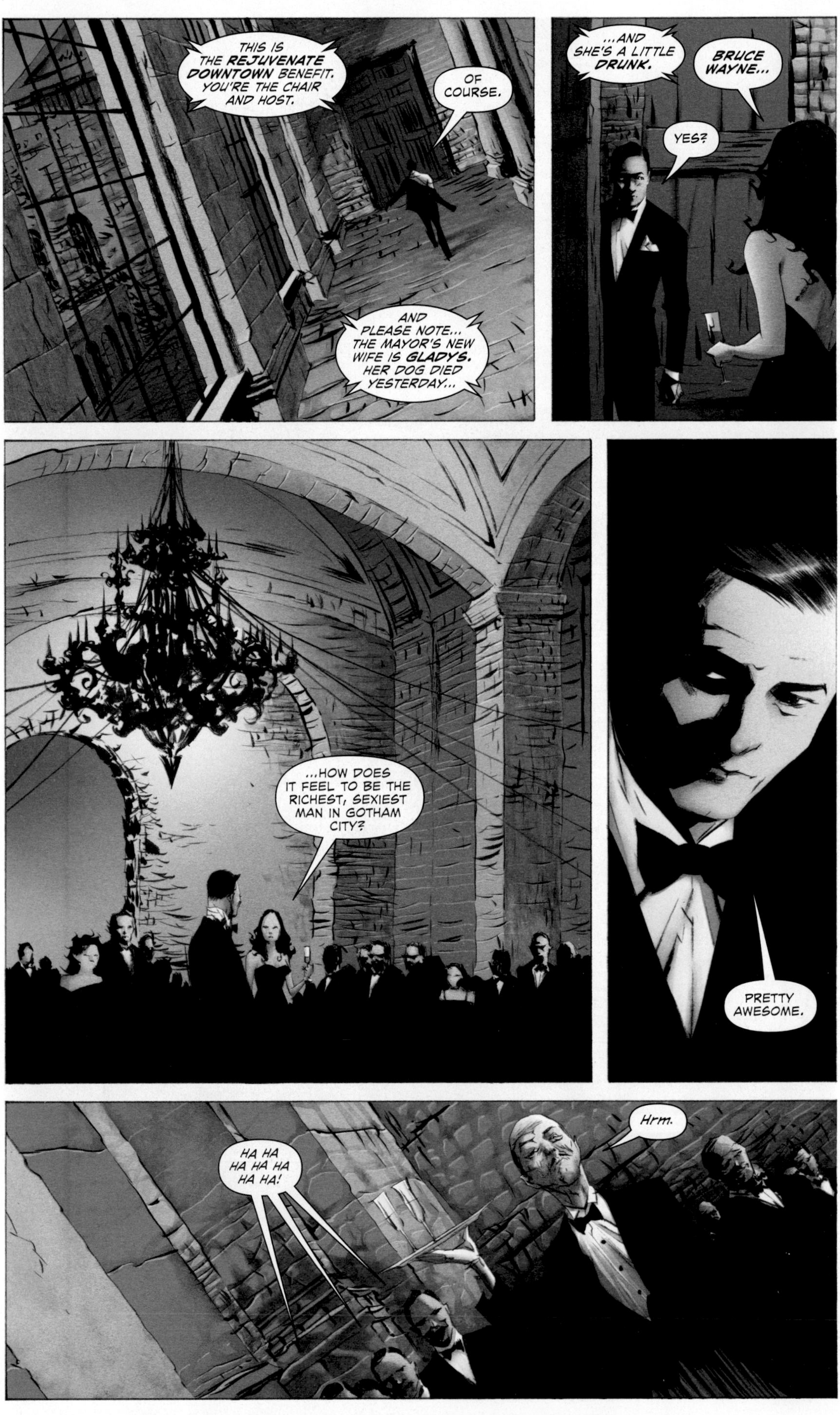
THIS IS THE REJUVENATE DOWNTOWN BENEFIT. YOU'RE THE CHAIR AND HOST.
OF COURSE.
AND PLEASE NOTE... THE MAYOR'S NEW WIFE IS GLADYS. HER DOG DIED YESTERDAY...
...AND SHE'S A LITTLE DRUNK.
BRUCE WAYNE...
YES?
...HOW DOES IT FEEL TO BE THE RICHEST, SEXIEST MAN IN GOTHAM CITY?
PRETTY AWESOME.
Hrm.
HA HA HA HA HA HA HA!

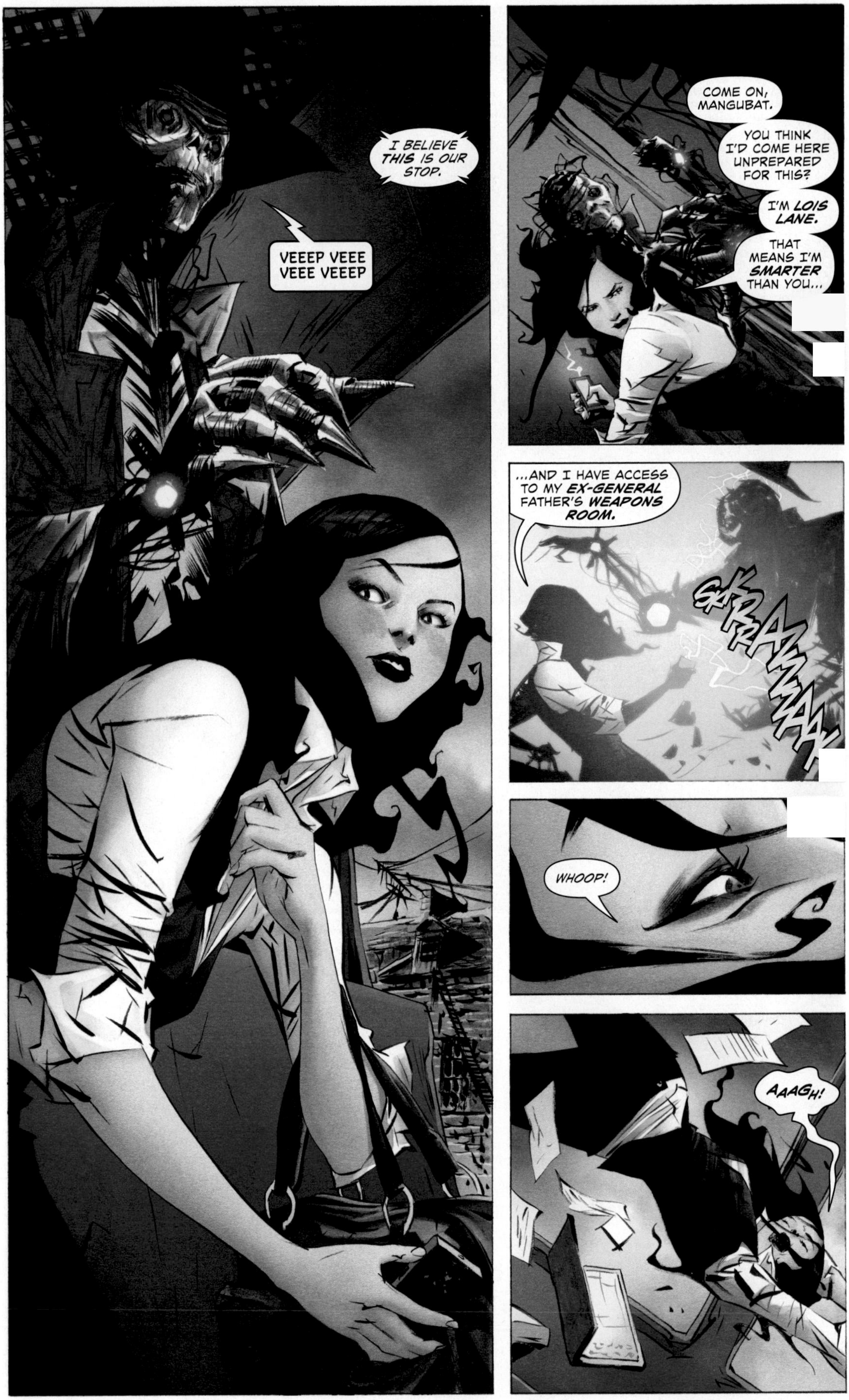
I BELIEVE THIS IS OUR STOP.
VEEEP VEEE VEEE VEEEP
COME ON, MANGUBAT.
YOU THINK I'D COME HERE UNPREPARED FOR THIS?
I'M LOIS LANE.
THAT MEANS I'M SMARTER THAN YOU...
...AND I HAVE ACCESS TO MY EX-GENERAL FATHER'S WEAPONS ROOM.
SKKRRAAWAAK
WHOOP!
AAAGH!

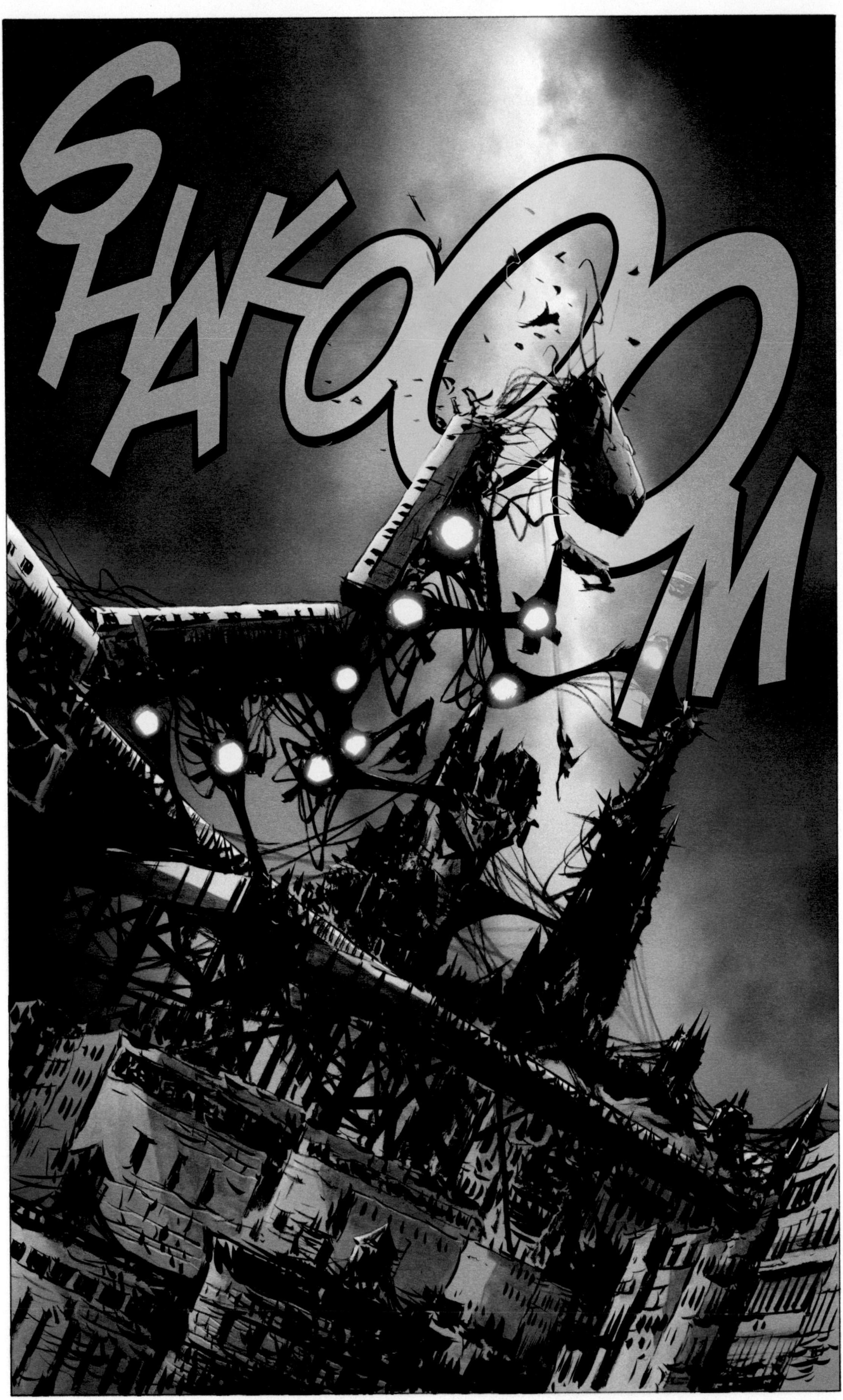
SHAKOOOM

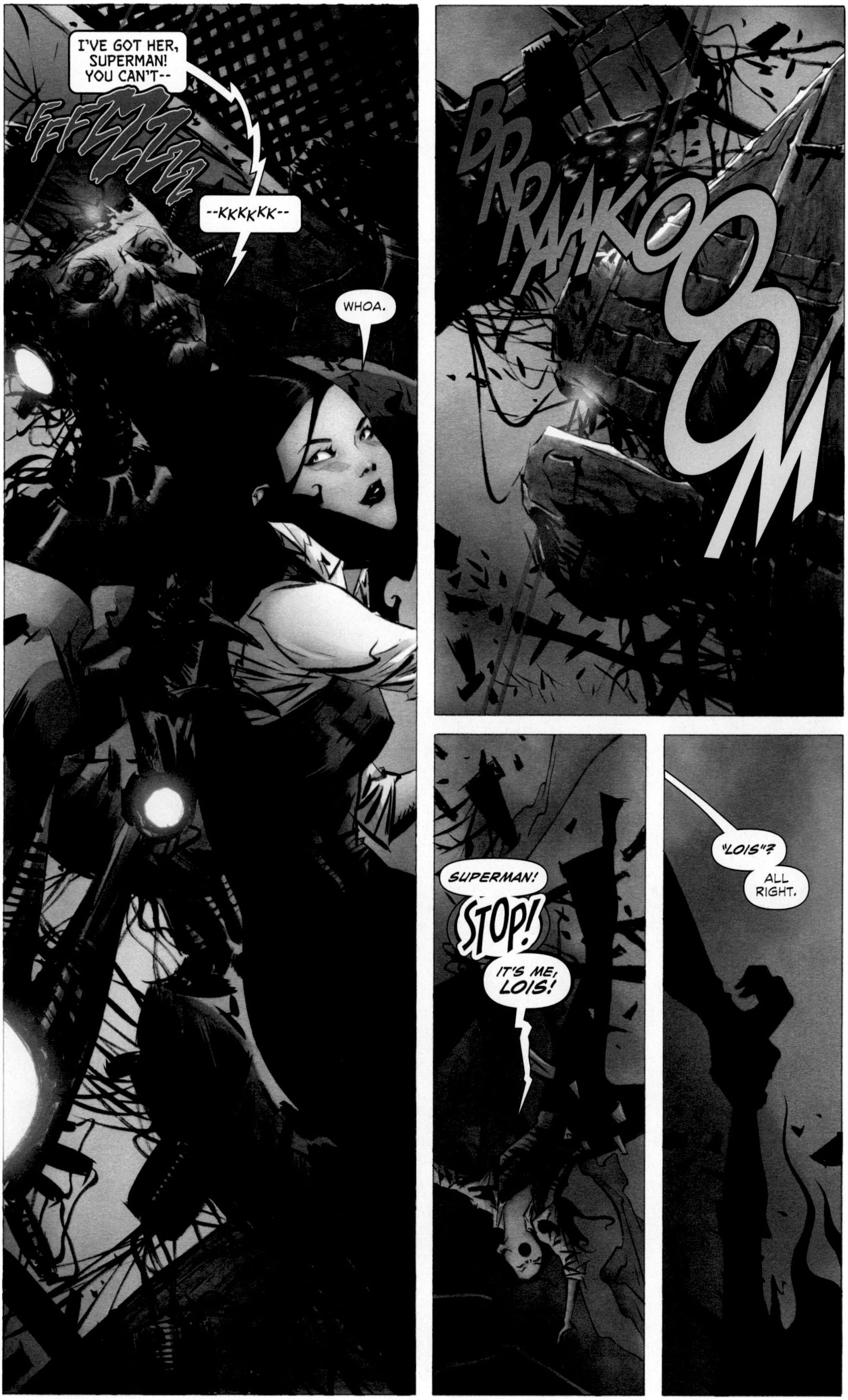
I'VE GOT HER, SUPERMAN! YOU CAN'T--
FFFZZZZZ
--KKKKKK--
WHOA.
BRRAAKOOOM
SUPERMAN!
STOP!
IT'S ME, LOIS!
"LOIS"?
ALL RIGHT.

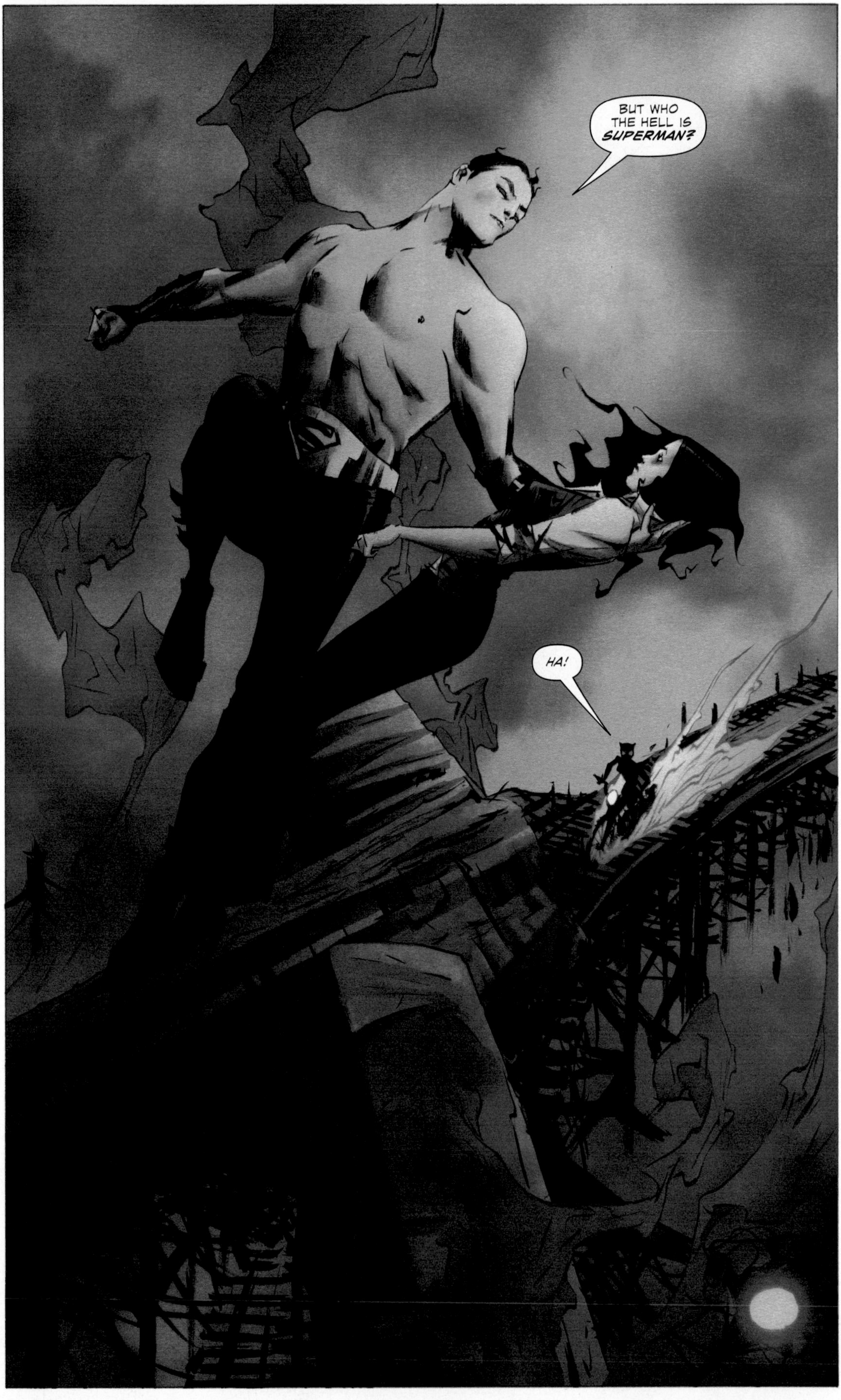
BUT WHO THE HELL IS SUPERMAN?
HA!

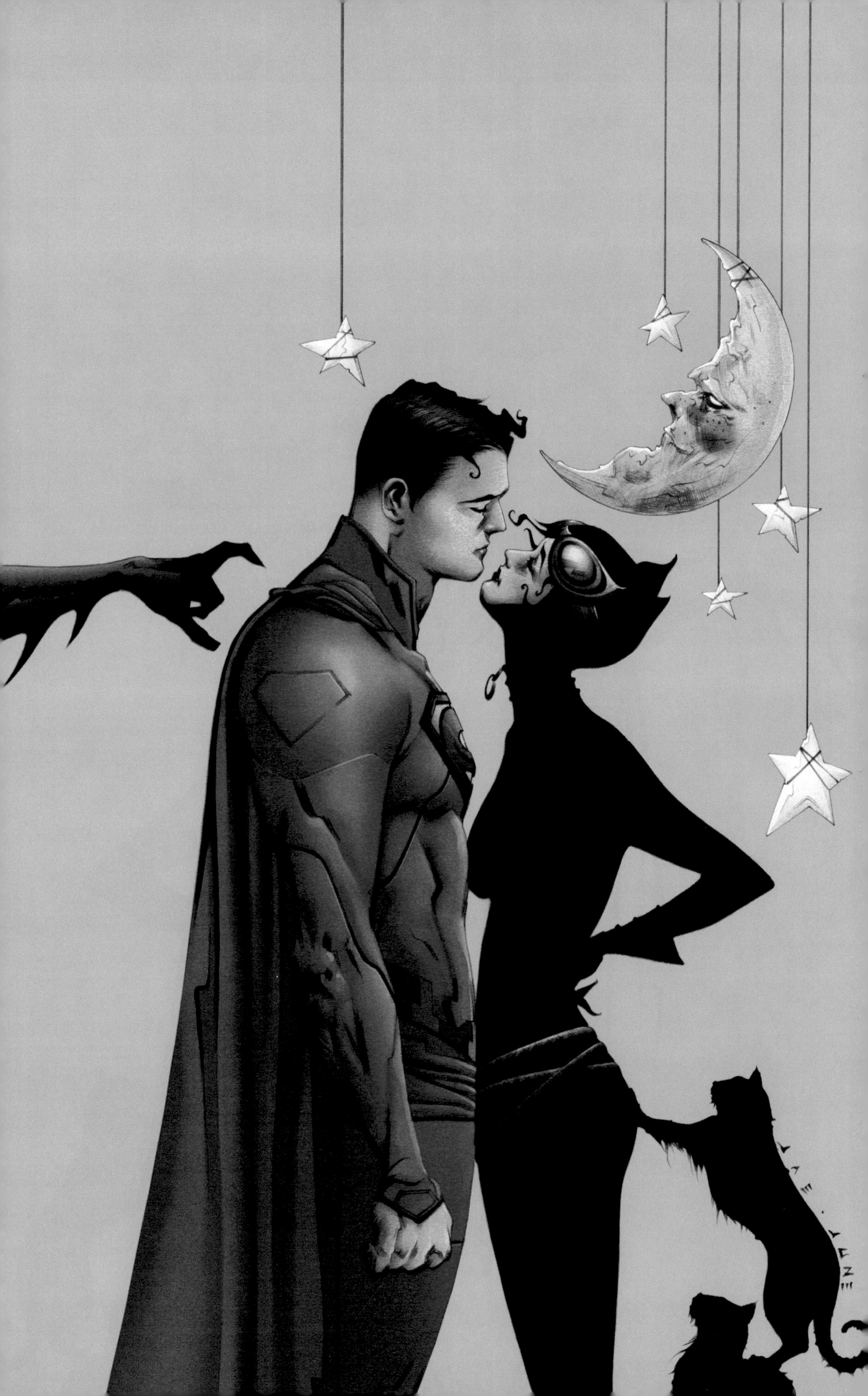

BLANK SLATE

GREG PAK writer **DIOGENES NEVES MARC DEERING** artists **JUNE CHUNG** colorist **ROB LEIGH** letterer cover by **JAE LEE** with **JUNE CHUNG**

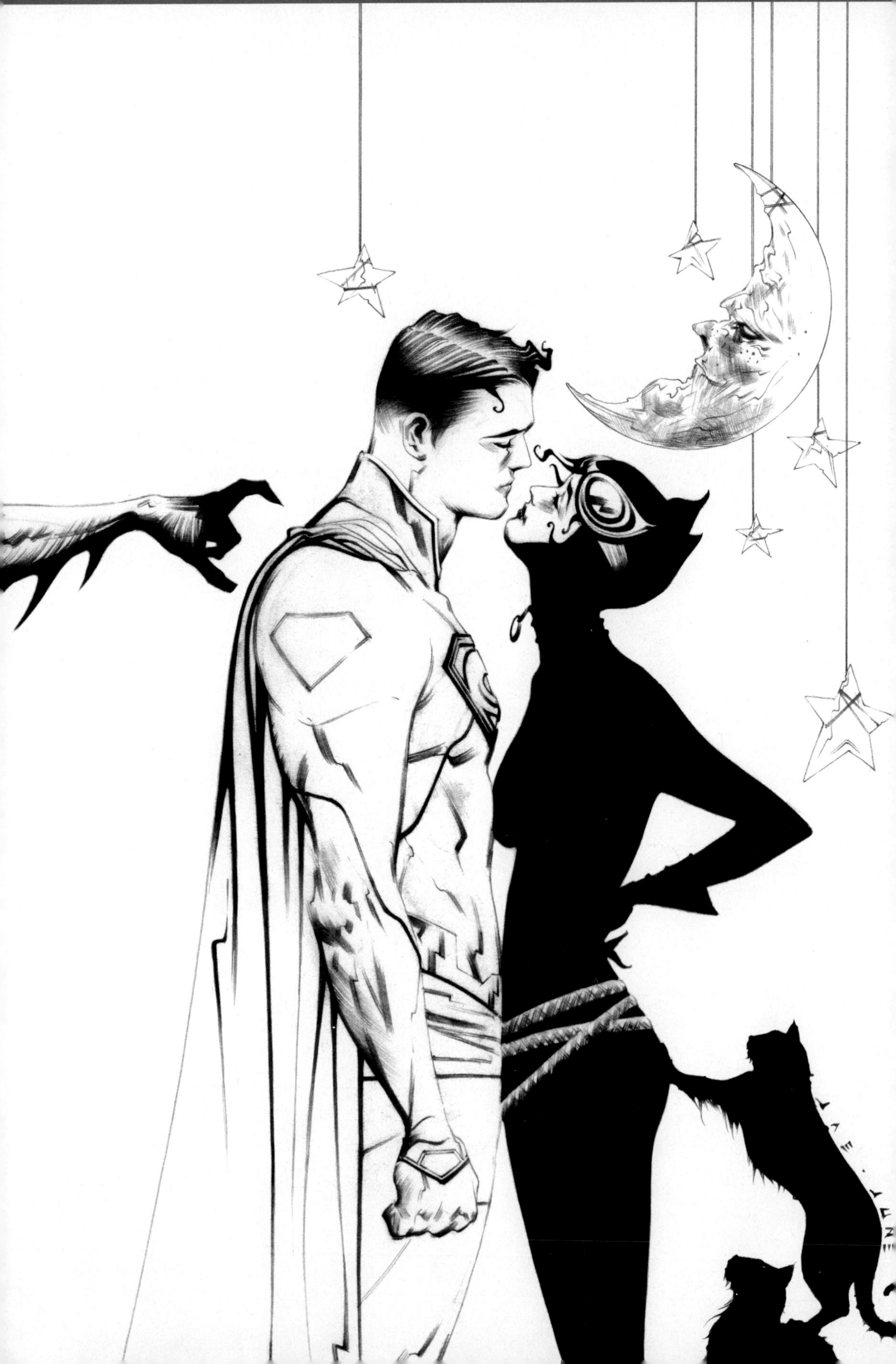

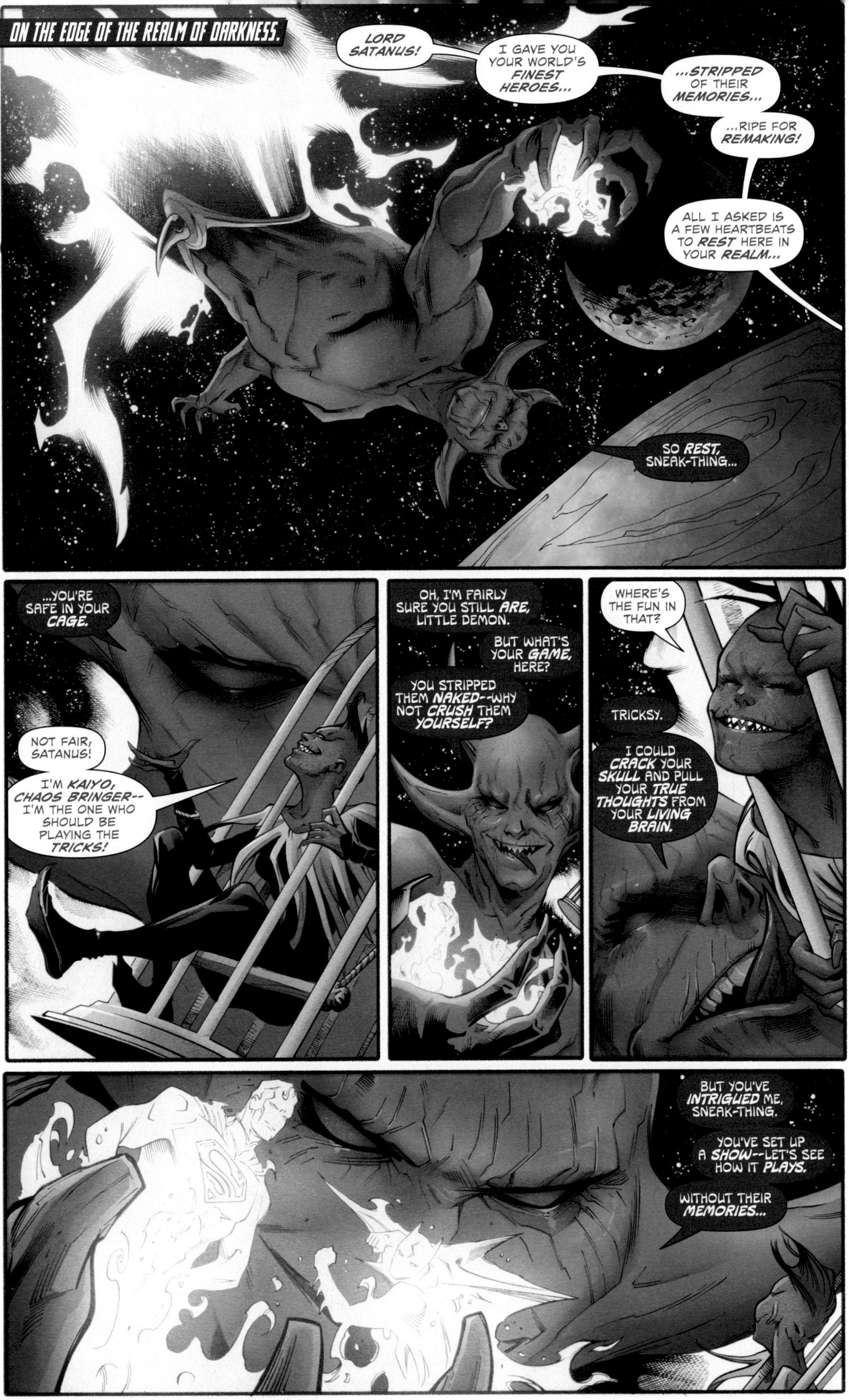
ON THE EDGE OF THE REALM OF DARKNESS.
LORD SATANUS!
I GAVE YOU YOUR WORLD'S FINEST HEROES...
...STRIPPED OF THEIR MEMORIES...
...RIPE FOR REMAKING!
ALL I ASKED IS A FEW HEARTBEATS TO REST HERE IN YOUR REALM...
SO REST, SNEAK-THING...
...YOU'RE SAFE IN YOUR CAGE.
NOT FAIR, SATANUS!
I'M KAIYO, CHAOS BRINGER--I'M THE ONE WHO SHOULD BE PLAYING THE TRICKS!
OH, I'M FAIRLY SURE YOU STILL ARE, LITTLE DEMON.
BUT WHAT'S YOUR GAME, HERE?
YOU STRIPPED THEM NAKED--WHY NOT CRUSH THEM YOURSELF?
WHERE'S THE FUN IN THAT?
TRICKSY.
I COULD CRACK YOUR SKULL AND PULL YOUR TRUE THOUGHTS FROM YOUR LIVING BRAIN.
BUT YOU'VE INTRIGUED ME, SNEAK-THING.
YOU'VE SET UP A SHOW--LET'S SEE HOW IT PLAYS.
WITHOUT THEIR MEMORIES...

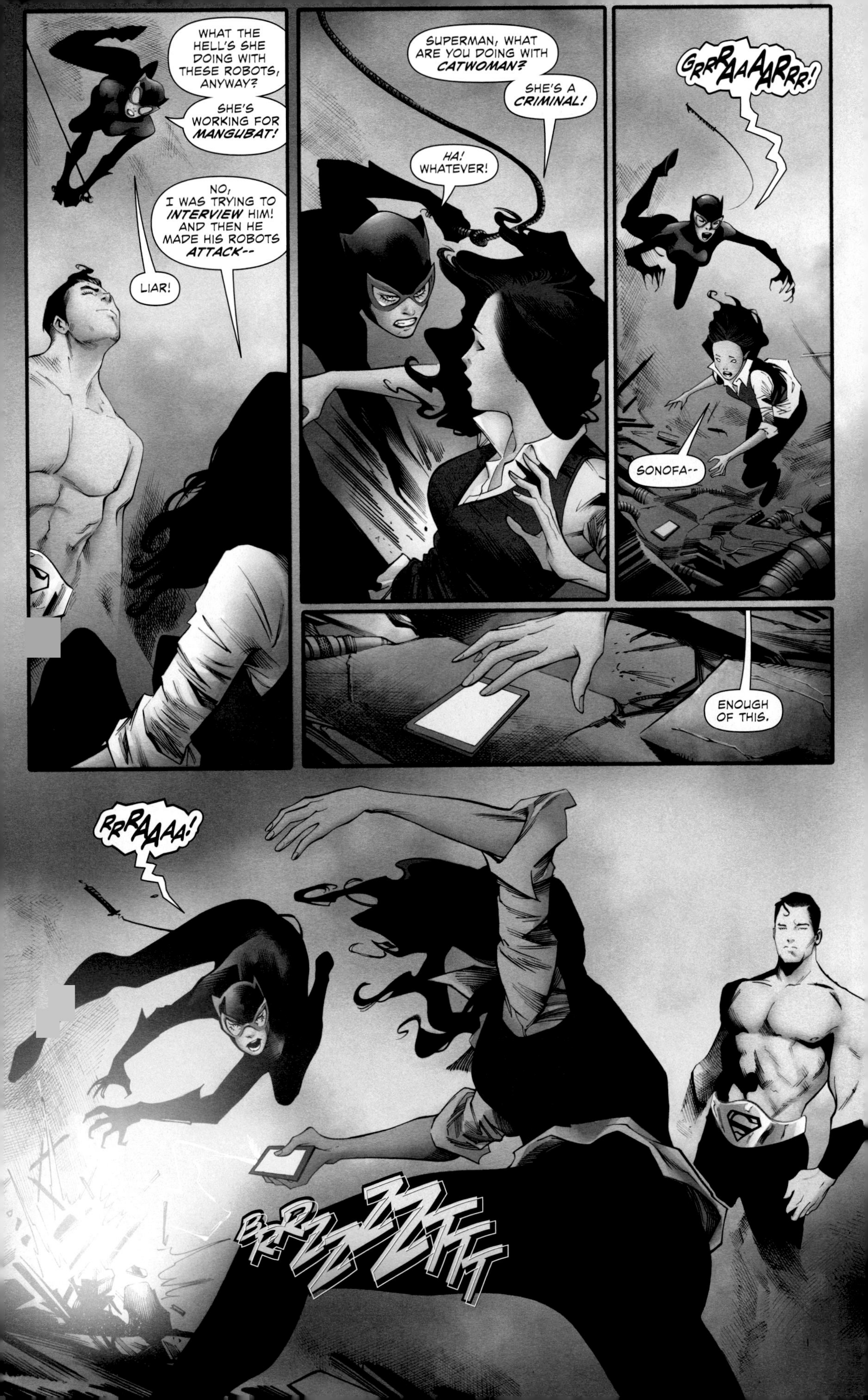
WHAT THE HELL'S SHE DOING WITH THESE ROBOTS, ANYWAY?
SHE'S WORKING FOR MANGUBAT!
NO, I WAS TRYING TO INTERVIEW HIM! AND THEN HE MADE HIS ROBOTS ATTACK--
LIAR!
SUPERMAN, WHAT ARE YOU DOING WITH CATWOMAN?
SHE'S A CRIMINAL!
HA! WHATEVER!
GRRRAAAARRR!
SONOFA--
ENOUGH OF THIS.
RRRAAAA!
BRRRZZZZZTTT

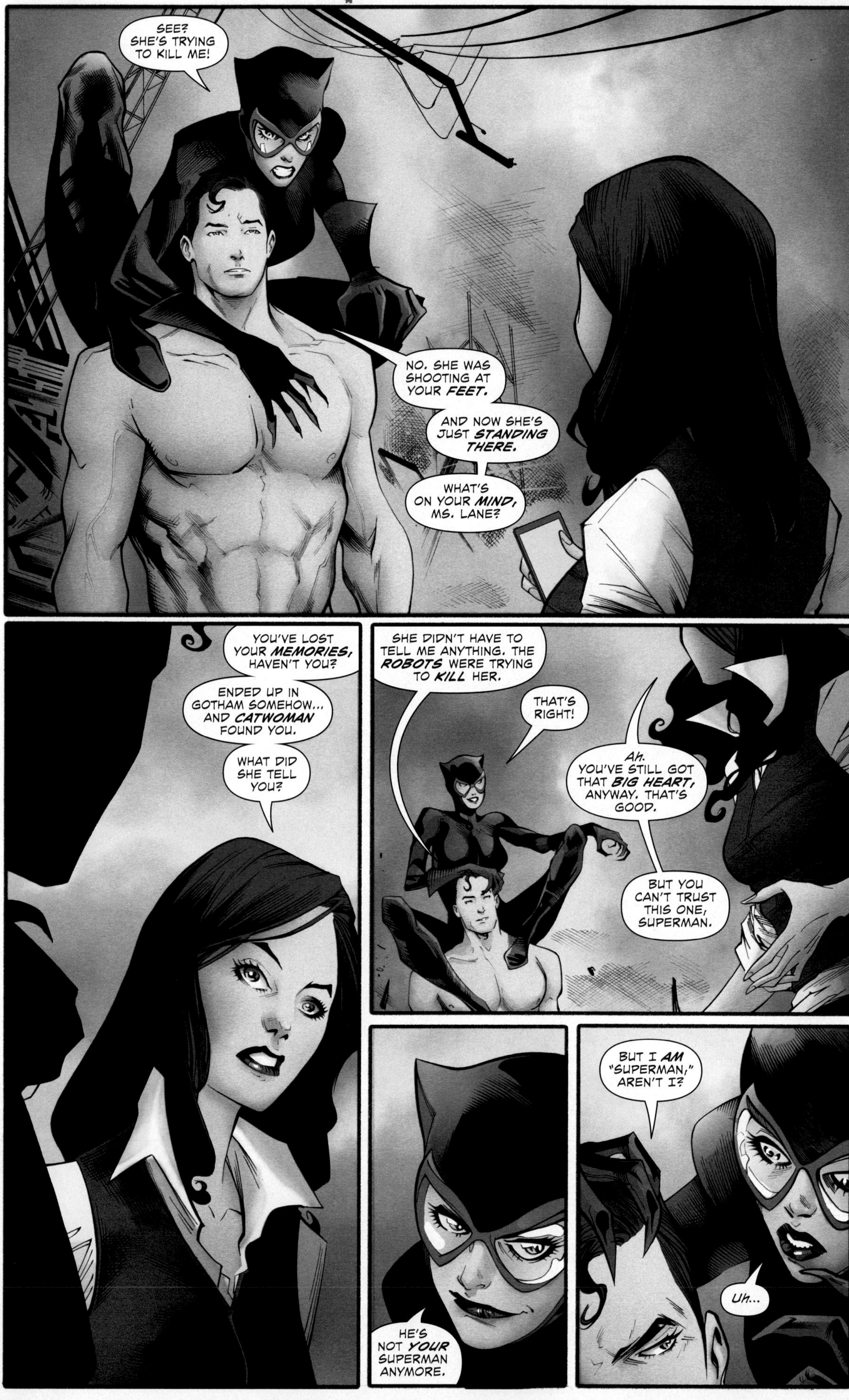
SEE? SHE'S TRYING TO KILL ME!
NO. SHE WAS SHOOTING AT YOUR *FEET.*
AND NOW SHE'S JUST *STANDING THERE.*
WHAT'S ON YOUR *MIND,* MS. LANE?
YOU'VE LOST YOUR *MEMORIES,* HAVEN'T YOU?
ENDED UP IN GOTHAM SOMEHOW... AND *CATWOMAN* FOUND YOU.
WHAT DID SHE TELL YOU?
SHE DIDN'T HAVE TO TELL ME ANYTHING. THE *ROBOTS* WERE TRYING TO *KILL* HER.
THAT'S RIGHT!
Ah. YOU'VE STILL GOT THAT *BIG HEART,* ANYWAY. THAT'S GOOD.
BUT YOU CAN'T TRUST THIS ONE, SUPERMAN.
HE'S NOT *YOUR* SUPERMAN ANYMORE.
BUT I *AM* "SUPERMAN," AREN'T I?
Uh...

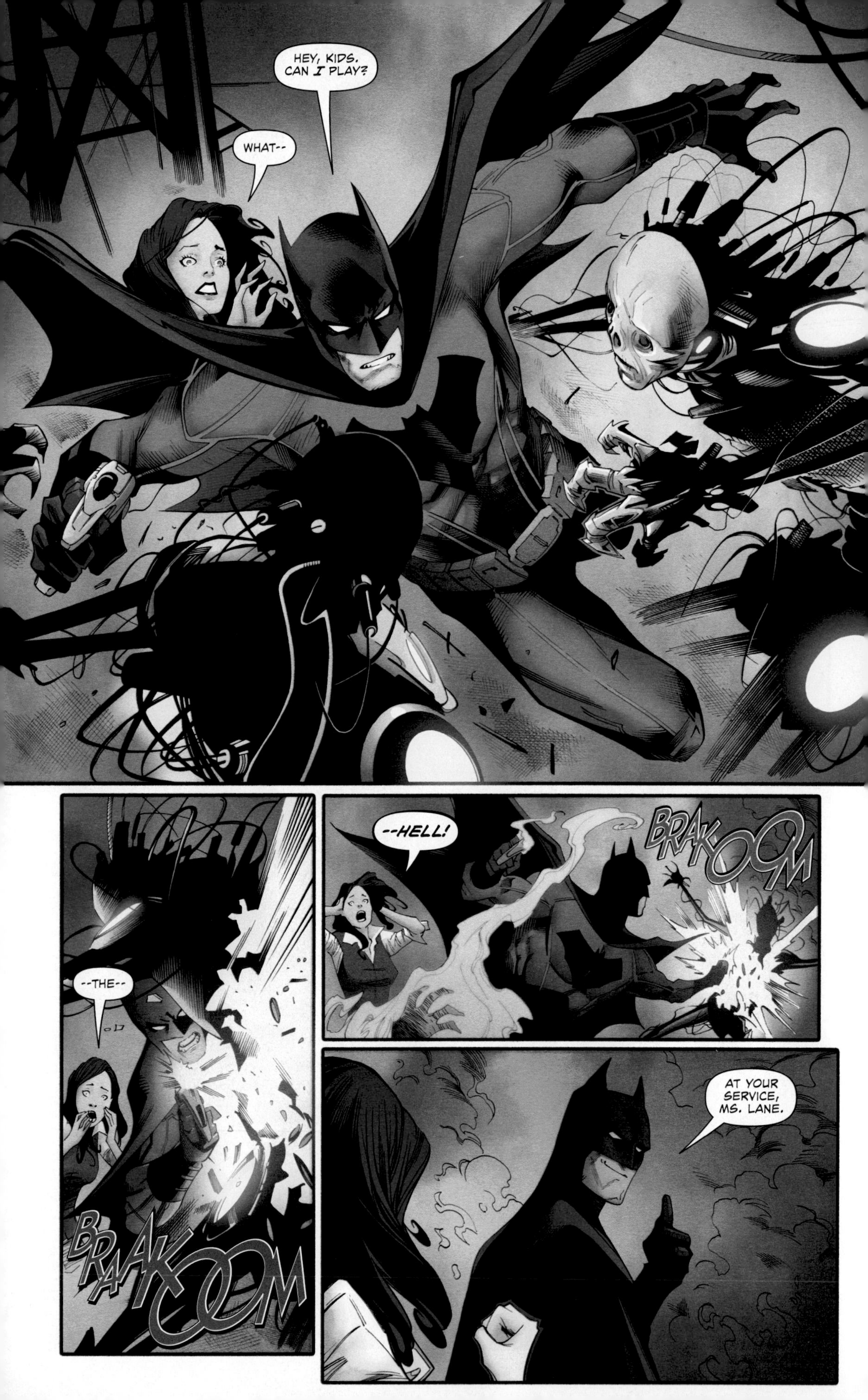
HEY, KIDS. CAN I PLAY?
WHAT--
--THE--
BRAAKOOM
--HELL!
BRAKOOM
AT YOUR SERVICE, MS. LANE.

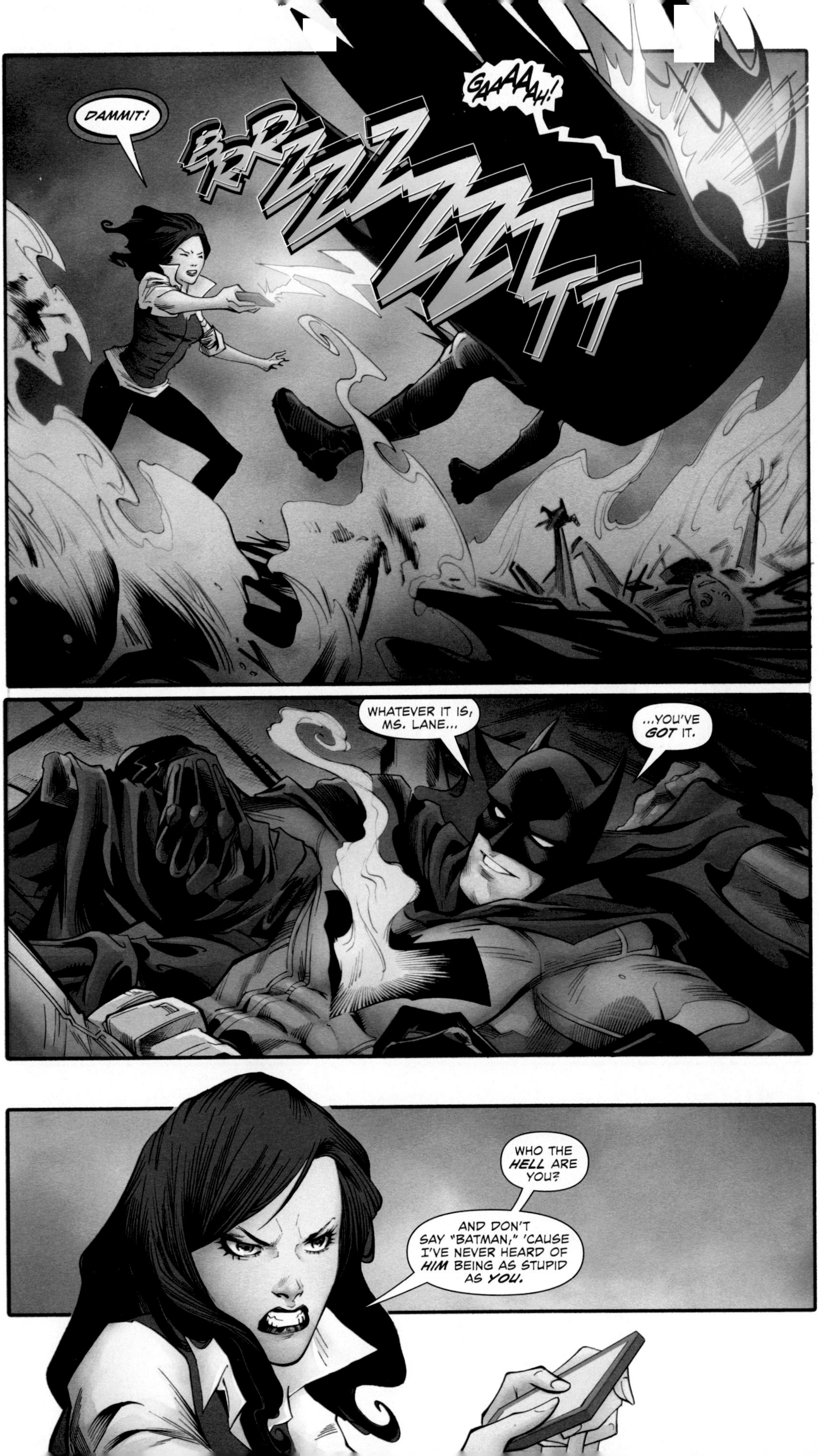

DAMMIT!
GAAAAAH!
WHATEVER IT IS, MS. LANE...
...YOU'VE *GOT* IT.
WHO THE *HELL* ARE YOU?
AND DON'T SAY "BATMAN," 'CAUSE I'VE NEVER HEARD OF *HIM* BEING AS STUPID AS *YOU.*

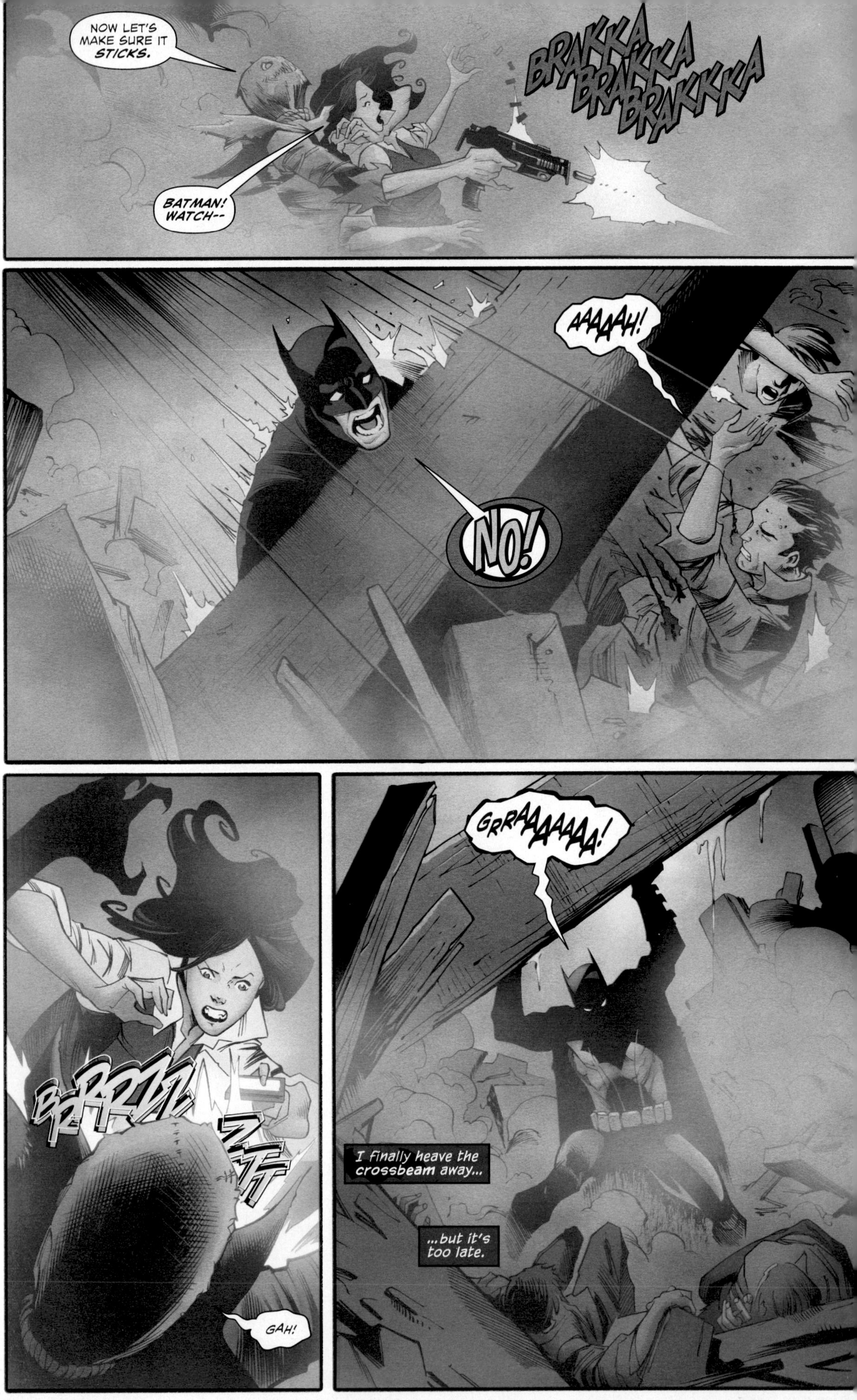
NOW LET'S MAKE SURE IT STICKS.
BRAKKA BRAKKKA BRABRAKKKA
BATMAN! WATCH--
AAAAAH!
NO!
BRRRT
ZZFFT
GAH!
GRRAAAAAAA!
I finally heave the crossbeam away...
...but it's too late.

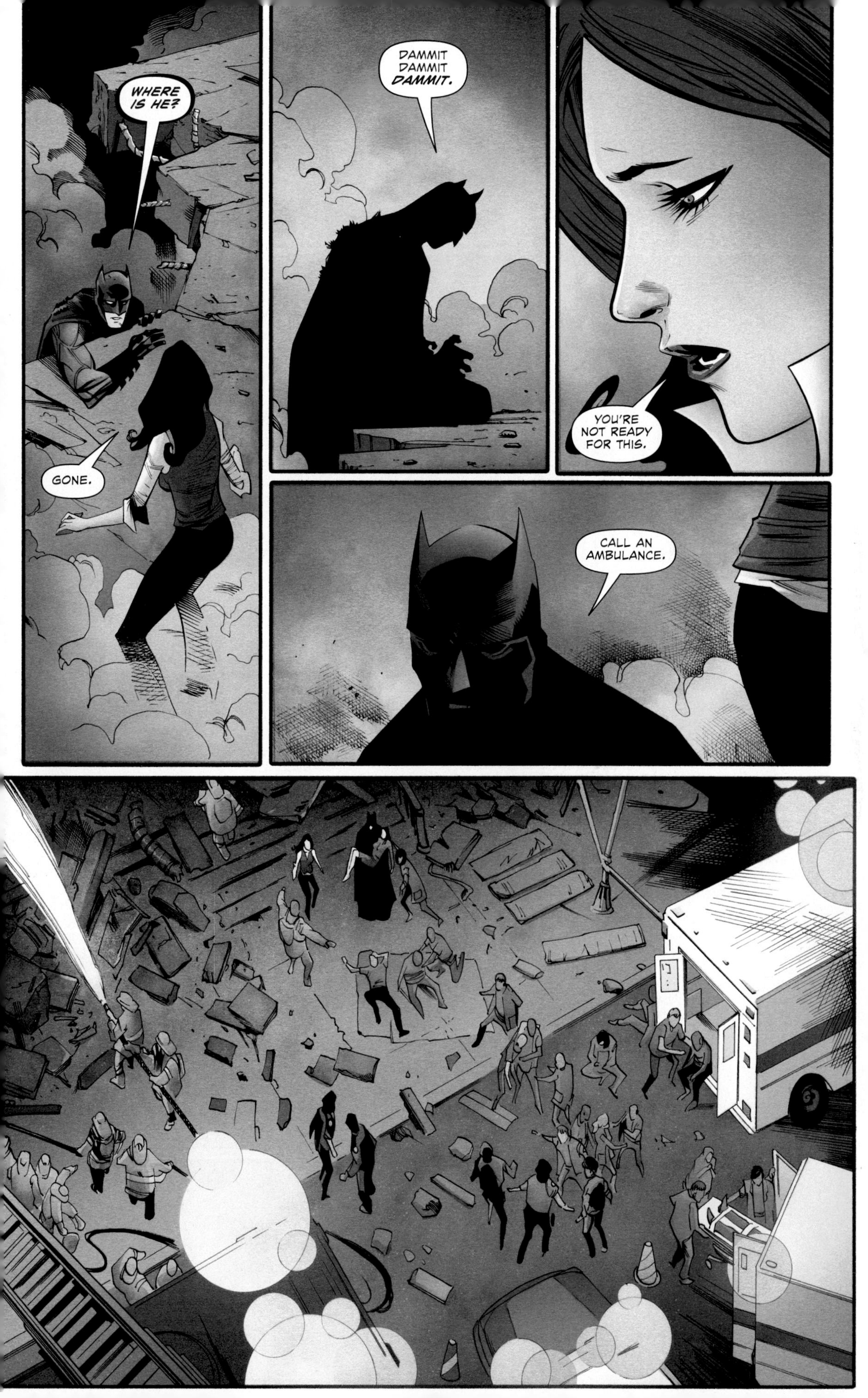
WHERE IS HE?
GONE.
DAMMIT DAMMIT DAMMIT.
YOU'RE NOT READY FOR THIS.
CALL AN AMBULANCE.

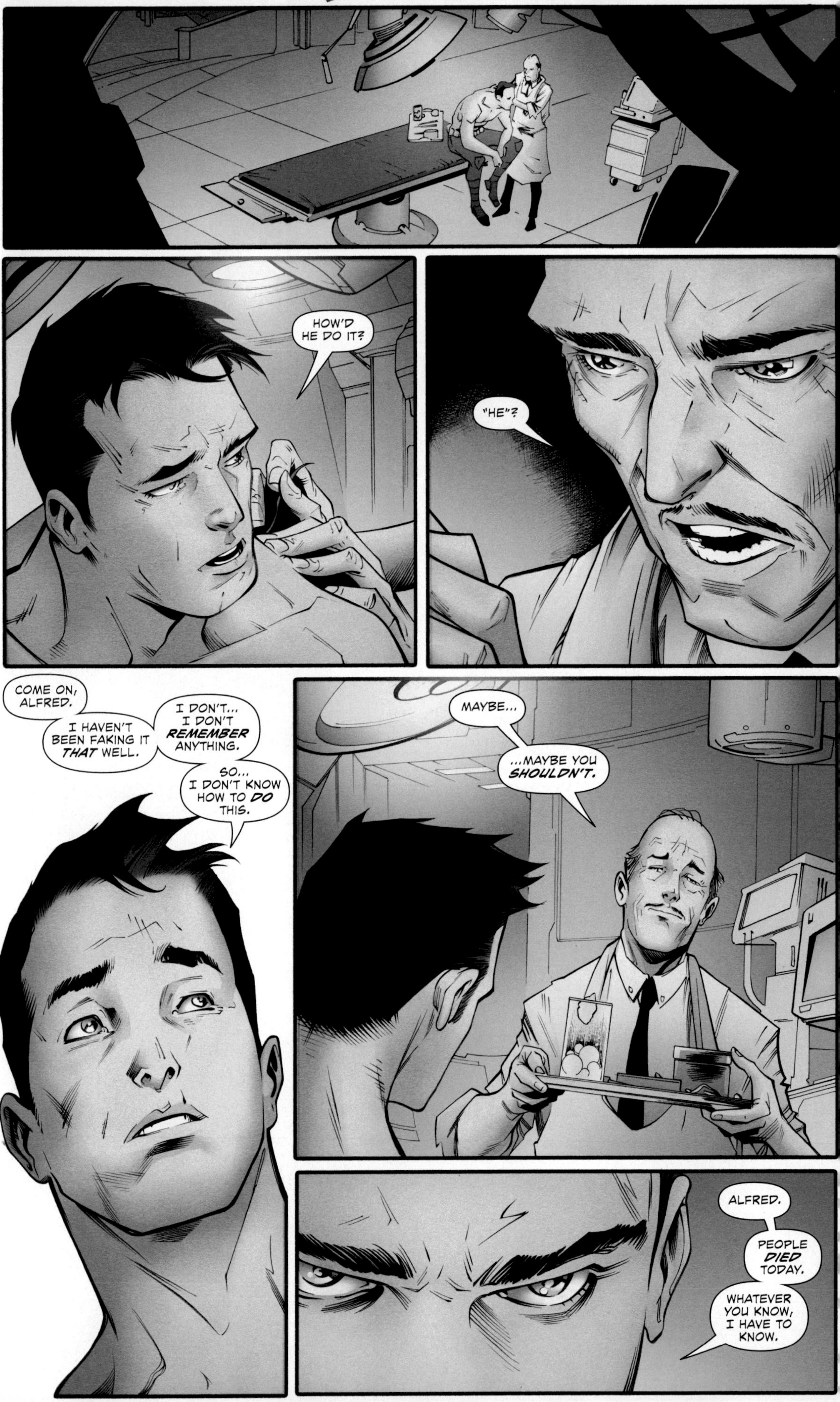
HOW'D HE DO IT?
"HE"?
COME ON, ALFRED.
I HAVEN'T BEEN FAKING IT *THAT* WELL.
I DON'T... I DON'T *REMEMBER* ANYTHING.
SO... I DON'T KNOW HOW TO *DO* THIS.
MAYBE...
...MAYBE YOU *SHOULDN'T.*
ALFRED.
PEOPLE *DIED* TODAY.
WHATEVER YOU KNOW, I HAVE TO KNOW.

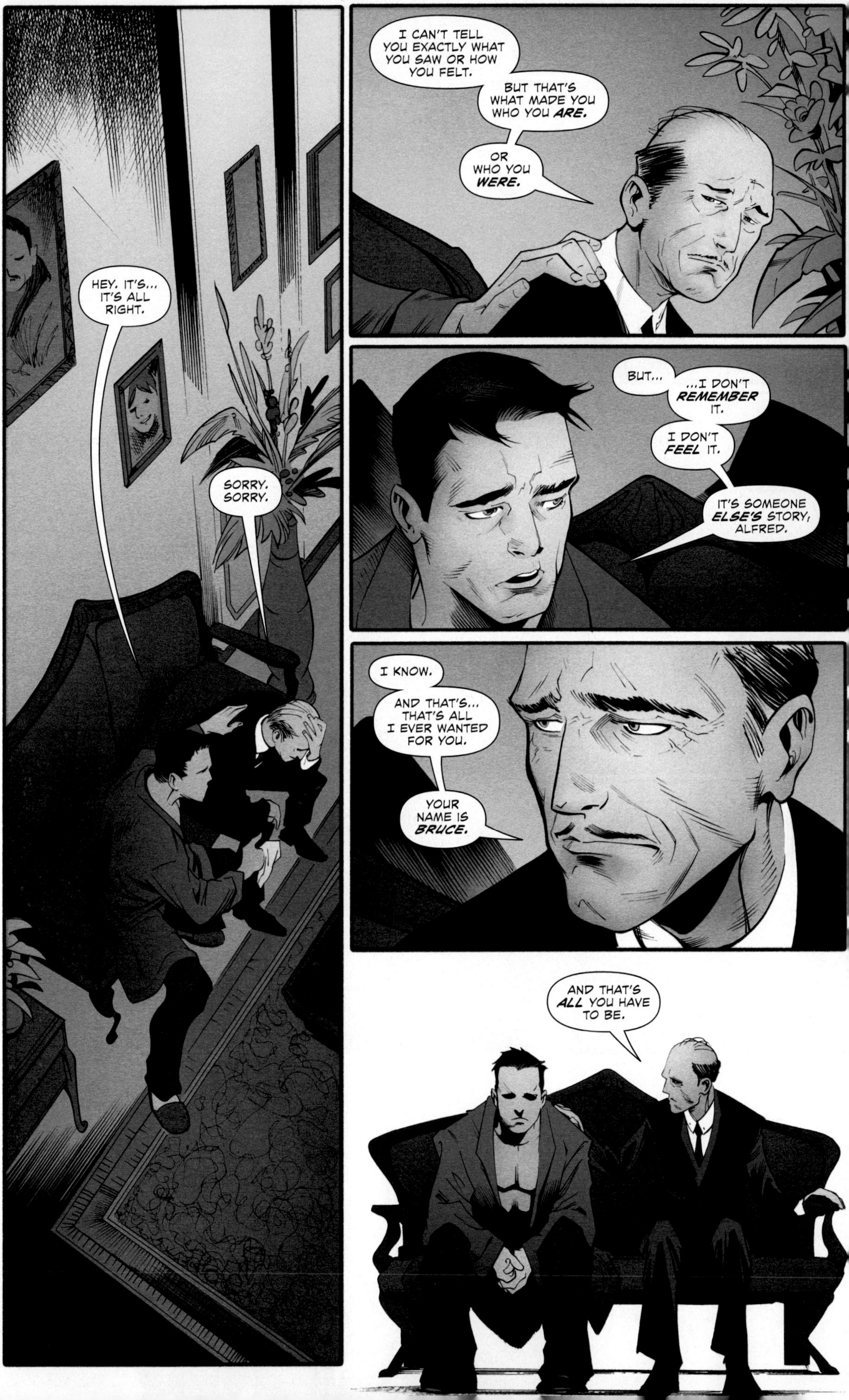
HEY. IT'S... IT'S ALL RIGHT.
SORRY. SORRY.
I CAN'T TELL YOU EXACTLY WHAT YOU SAW OR HOW YOU FELT.
BUT THAT'S WHAT MADE YOU WHO YOU *ARE.*
OR WHO YOU *WERE.*
BUT...
...I DON'T *REMEMBER* IT.
I DON'T *FEEL* IT.
IT'S SOMEONE *ELSE'S* STORY, ALFRED.
I KNOW.
AND THAT'S... THAT'S ALL I EVER WANTED FOR YOU.
YOUR NAME IS *BRUCE.*
AND THAT'S *ALL* YOU HAVE TO BE.

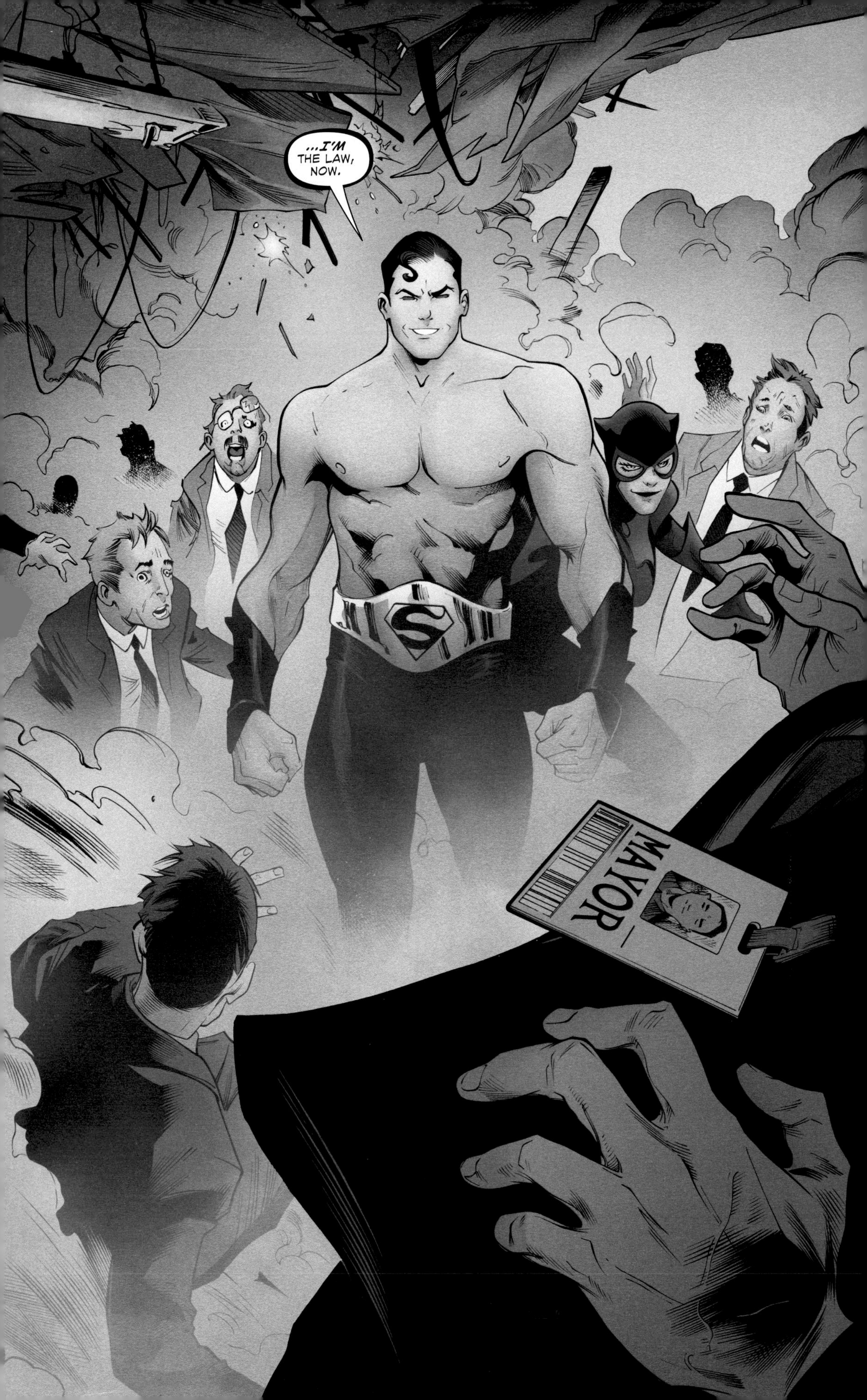
...I'M THE LAW, NOW.
MAYOR

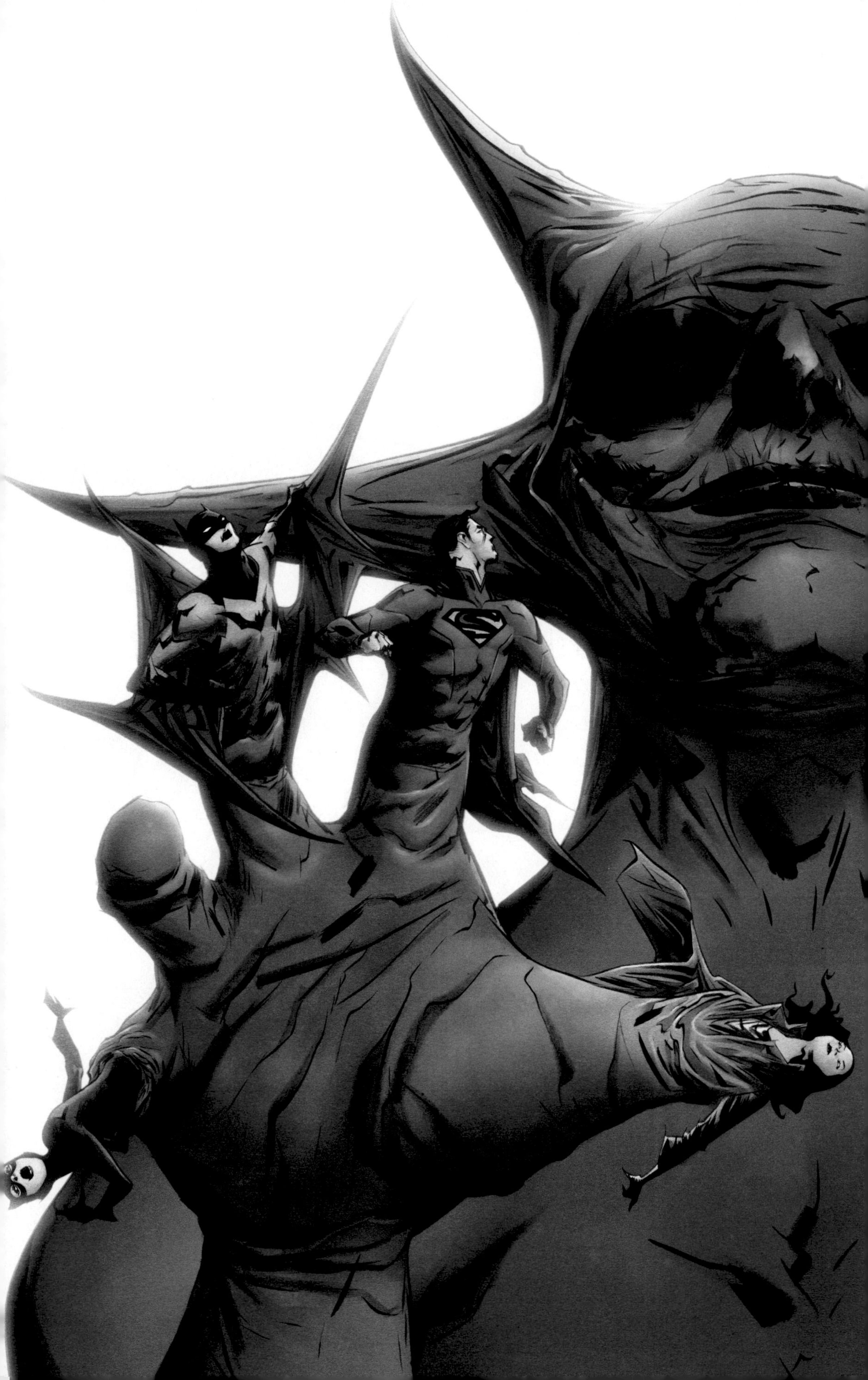

FORGET-ME-NOT

GREG PAK writer **PASCAL ALIXE DIOGENES NEVES MARC DEERING CLIFF RICHARDS** artists **ULISES ARREOLA** colorist **ROB LEIGH** letterer
cover by **JAE LEE** with **JUNE CHUNG**

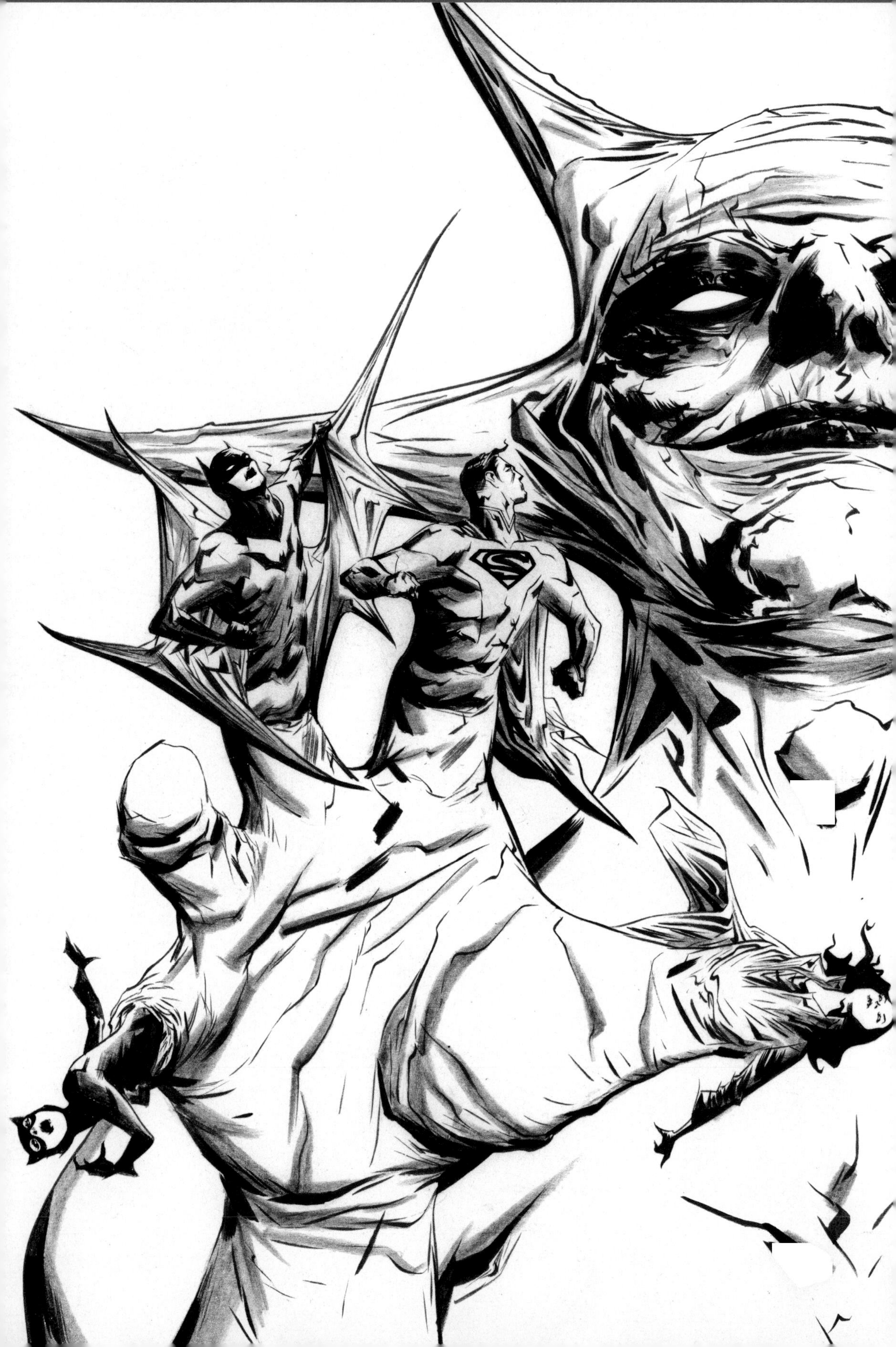

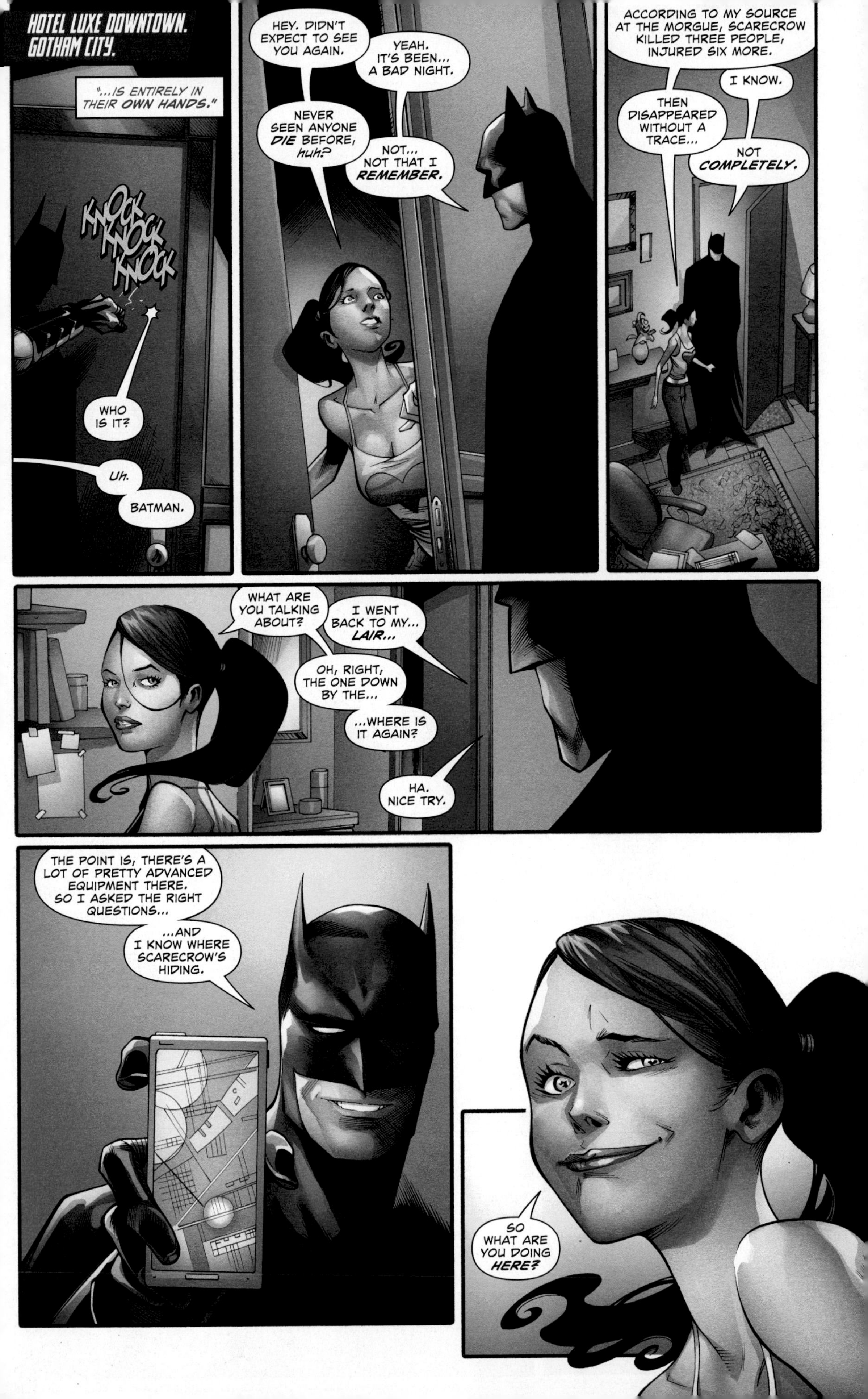
HOTEL LUXE DOWNTOWN. GOTHAM CITY.
"...IS ENTIRELY IN THEIR OWN HANDS."
KNOCK KNOCK KNOCK
WHO IS IT?
Uh.
BATMAN.
HEY. DIDN'T EXPECT TO SEE YOU AGAIN.
YEAH. IT'S BEEN... A BAD NIGHT.
NEVER SEEN ANYONE DIE BEFORE, huh?
NOT... NOT THAT I REMEMBER.
ACCORDING TO MY SOURCE AT THE MORGUE, SCARECROW KILLED THREE PEOPLE, INJURED SIX MORE.
I KNOW.
THEN DISAPPEARED WITHOUT A TRACE...
NOT COMPLETELY.
WHAT ARE YOU TALKING ABOUT?
I WENT BACK TO MY... LAIR...
OH, RIGHT, THE ONE DOWN BY THE...
...WHERE IS IT AGAIN?
HA. NICE TRY.
THE POINT IS, THERE'S A LOT OF PRETTY ADVANCED EQUIPMENT THERE. SO I ASKED THE RIGHT QUESTIONS...
...AND I KNOW WHERE SCARECROW'S HIDING.
SO WHAT ARE YOU DOING HERE?

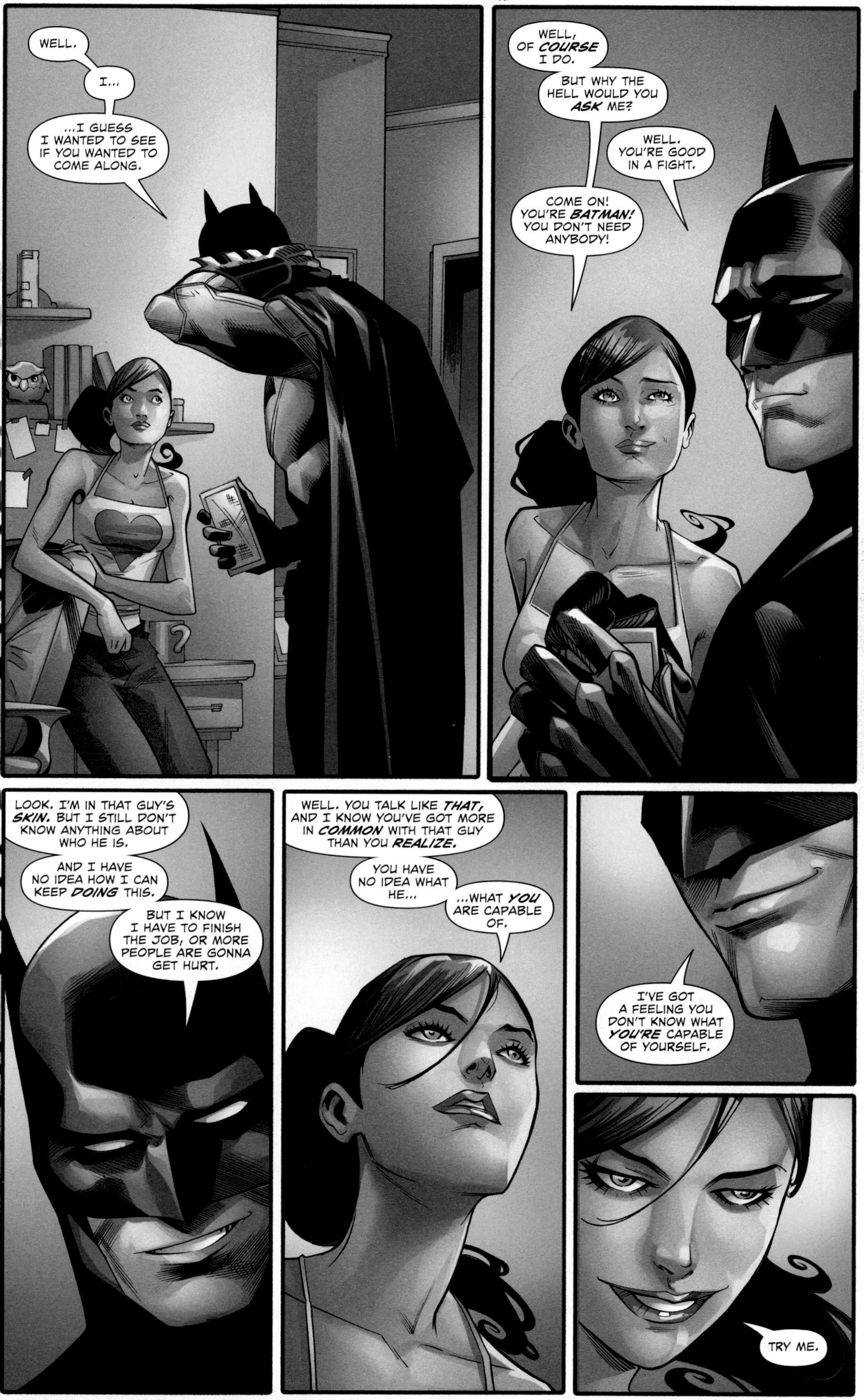
WELL.
I...
...I GUESS I WANTED TO SEE IF YOU WANTED TO COME ALONG.
WELL, OF COURSE I DO.
BUT WHY THE HELL WOULD YOU ASK ME?
COME ON! YOU'RE BATMAN! YOU DON'T NEED ANYBODY!
WELL. YOU'RE GOOD IN A FIGHT.
LOOK. I'M IN THAT GUY'S SKIN. BUT I STILL DON'T KNOW ANYTHING ABOUT WHO HE IS.
AND I HAVE NO IDEA HOW I CAN KEEP DOING THIS.
BUT I KNOW I HAVE TO FINISH THE JOB, OR MORE PEOPLE ARE GONNA GET HURT.
WELL. YOU TALK LIKE THAT, AND I KNOW YOU'VE GOT MORE IN COMMON WITH THAT GUY THAN YOU REALIZE.
YOU HAVE NO IDEA WHAT HE...
...WHAT YOU ARE CAPABLE OF.
I'VE GOT A FEELING YOU DON'T KNOW WHAT YOU'RE CAPABLE OF YOURSELF.
TRY ME.

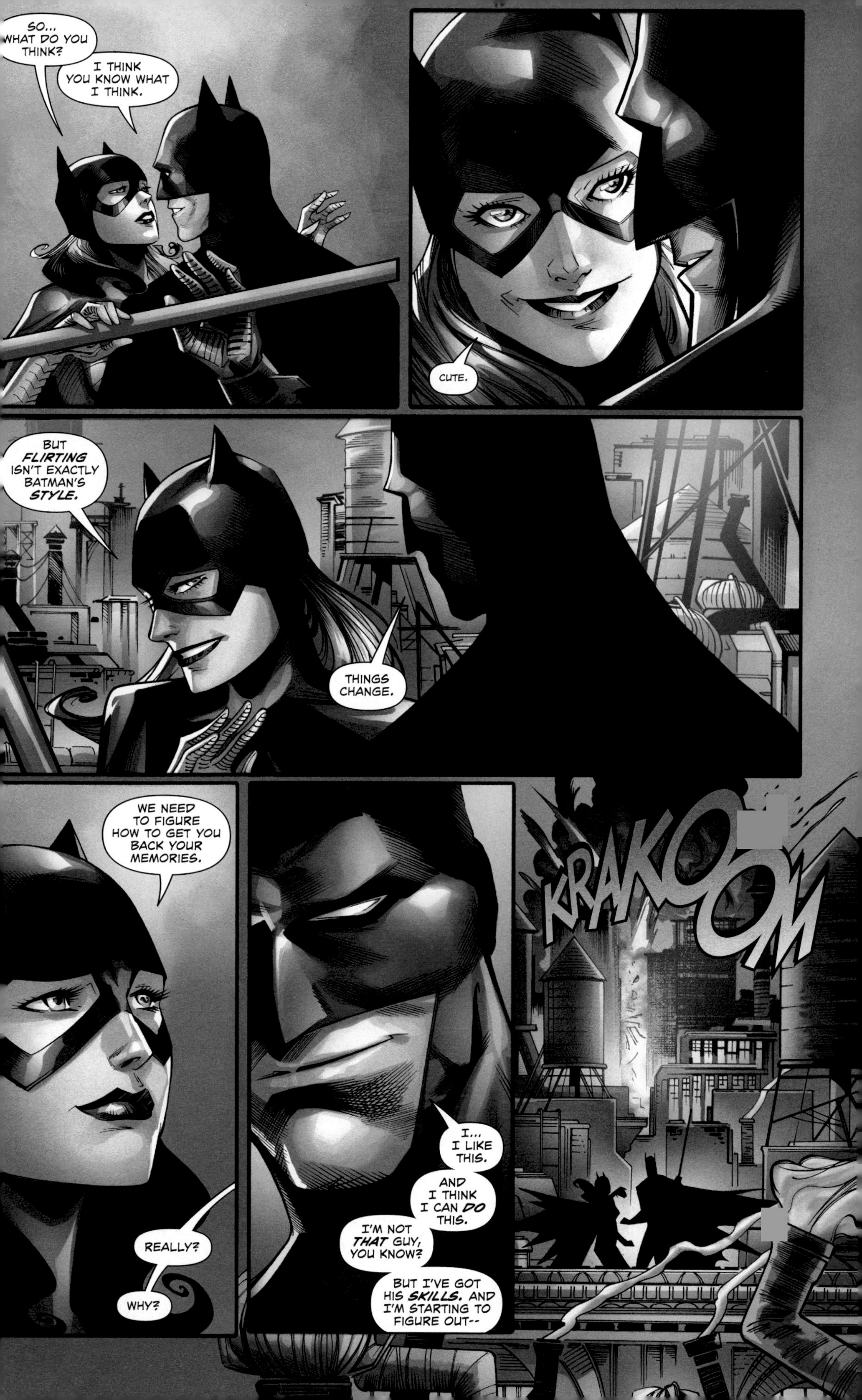
SO... WHAT DO YOU THINK?
I THINK YOU KNOW WHAT I THINK.
CUTE.
BUT *FLIRTING* ISN'T EXACTLY BATMAN'S *STYLE.*
THINGS CHANGE.
WE NEED TO FIGURE HOW TO GET YOU BACK YOUR MEMORIES.
REALLY?
WHY?
I... I LIKE THIS.
AND I THINK I CAN *DO* THIS.
I'M NOT *THAT* GUY, YOU KNOW?
BUT I'VE GOT HIS *SKILLS.* AND I'M STARTING TO FIGURE OUT--
KRAKOOOM

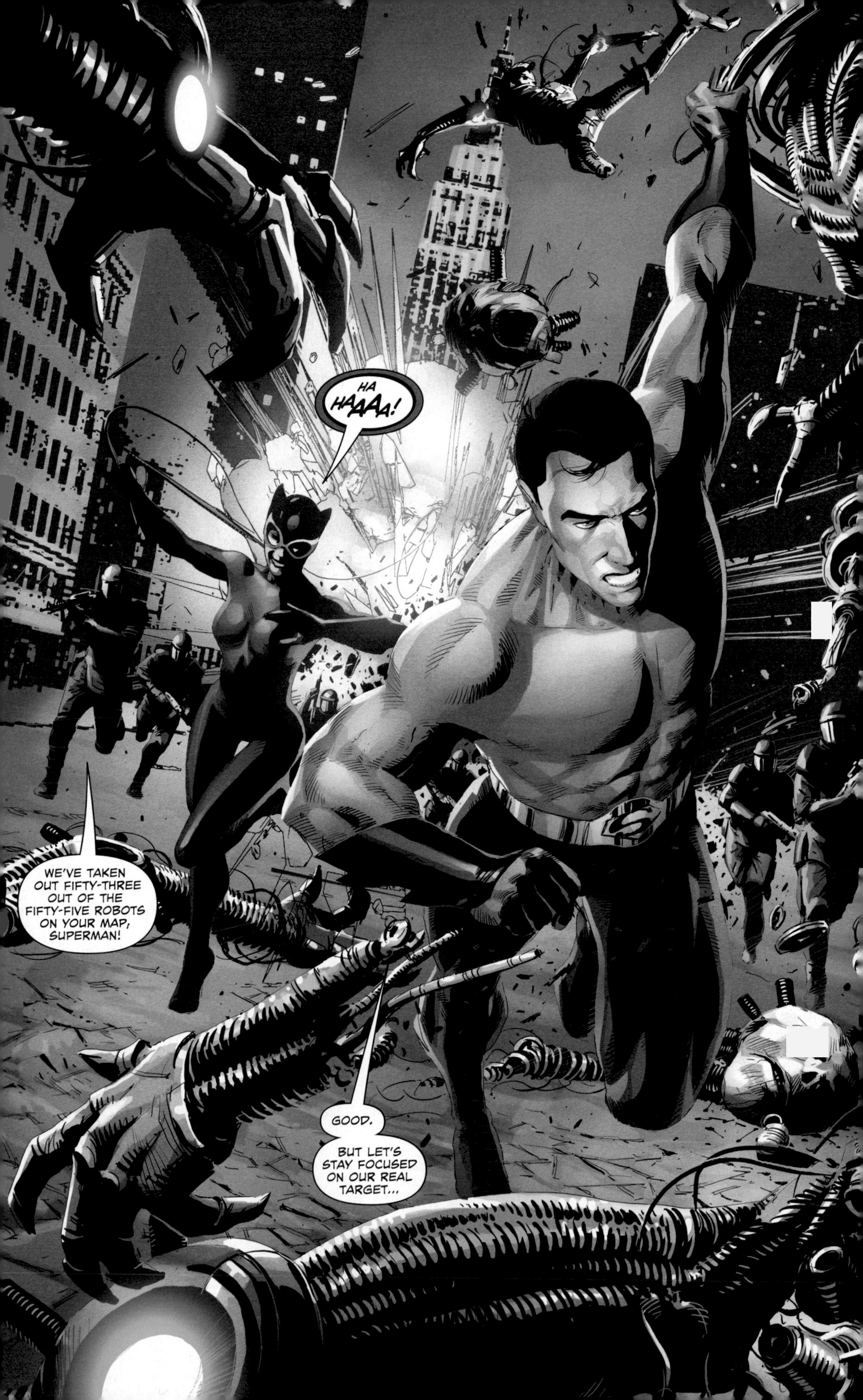
HA HAAAA!
WE'VE TAKEN OUT FIFTY-THREE OUT OF THE FIFTY-FIVE ROBOTS ON YOUR MAP, SUPERMAN!
GOOD.
BUT LET'S STAY FOCUSED ON OUR REAL TARGET...

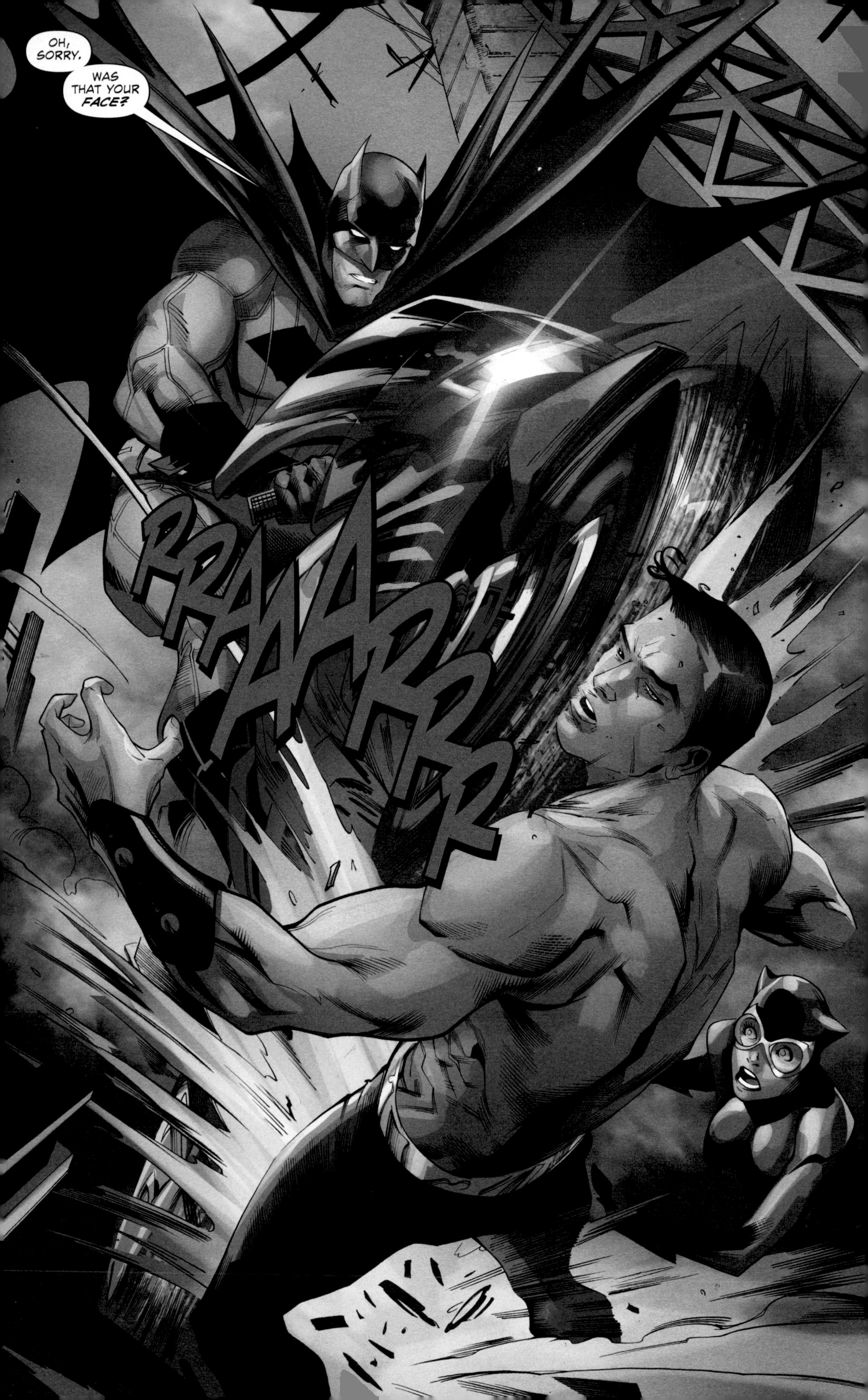
OH, SORRY.
WAS THAT YOUR *FACE?*
RRAAARRR

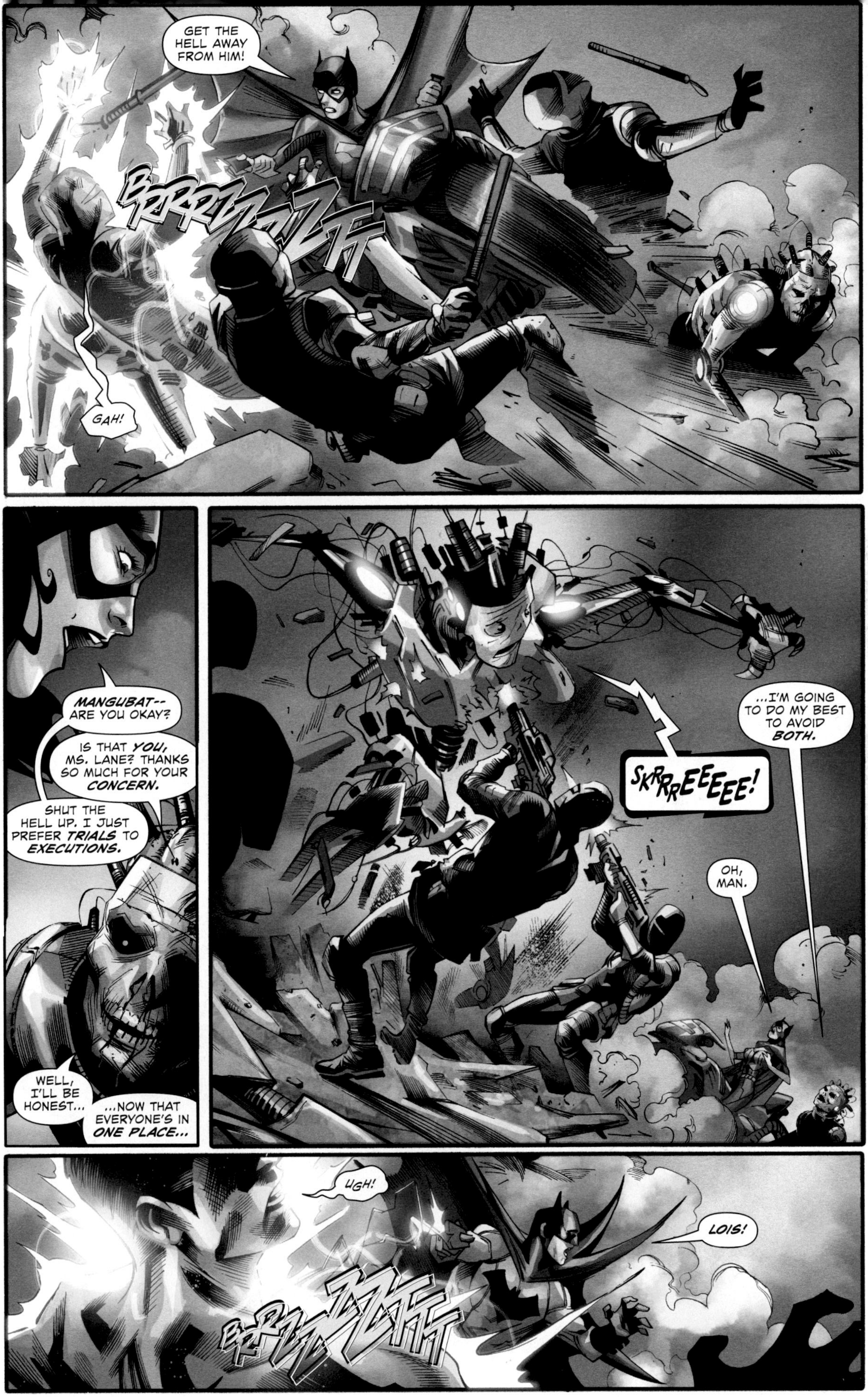
GET THE HELL AWAY FROM HIM!
BRRRZZZZZTT
GAH!
MANGUBAT-- ARE YOU OKAY?
IS THAT YOU, MS. LANE? THANKS SO MUCH FOR YOUR CONCERN.
SHUT THE HELL UP. I JUST PREFER TRIALS TO EXECUTIONS.
WELL, I'LL BE HONEST...
...NOW THAT EVERYONE'S IN ONE PLACE...
...I'M GOING TO DO MY BEST TO AVOID BOTH.
SKRRREEEEEE!
OH, MAN.
UGH!
LOIS!
BRRZZZZZZZTTT

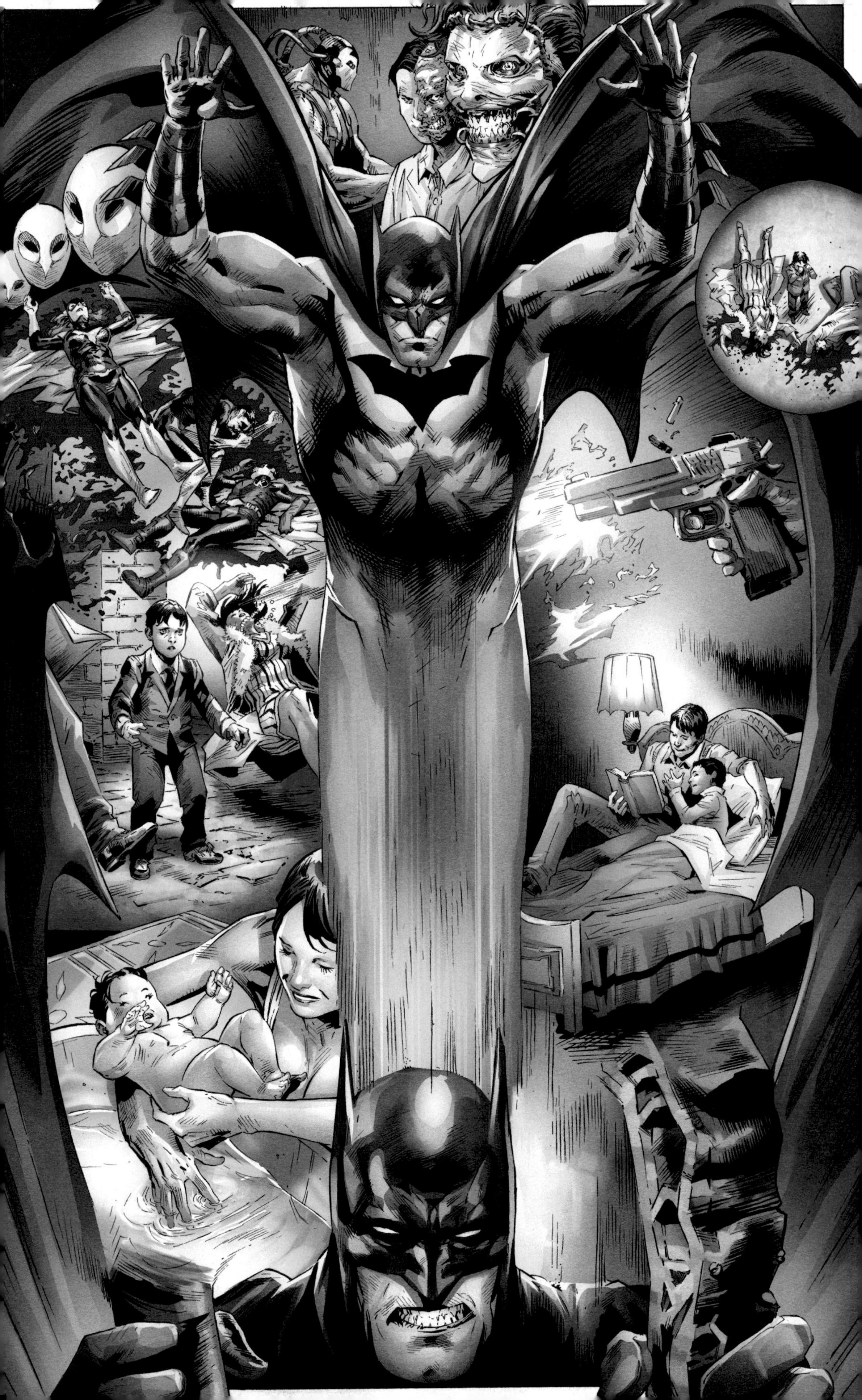

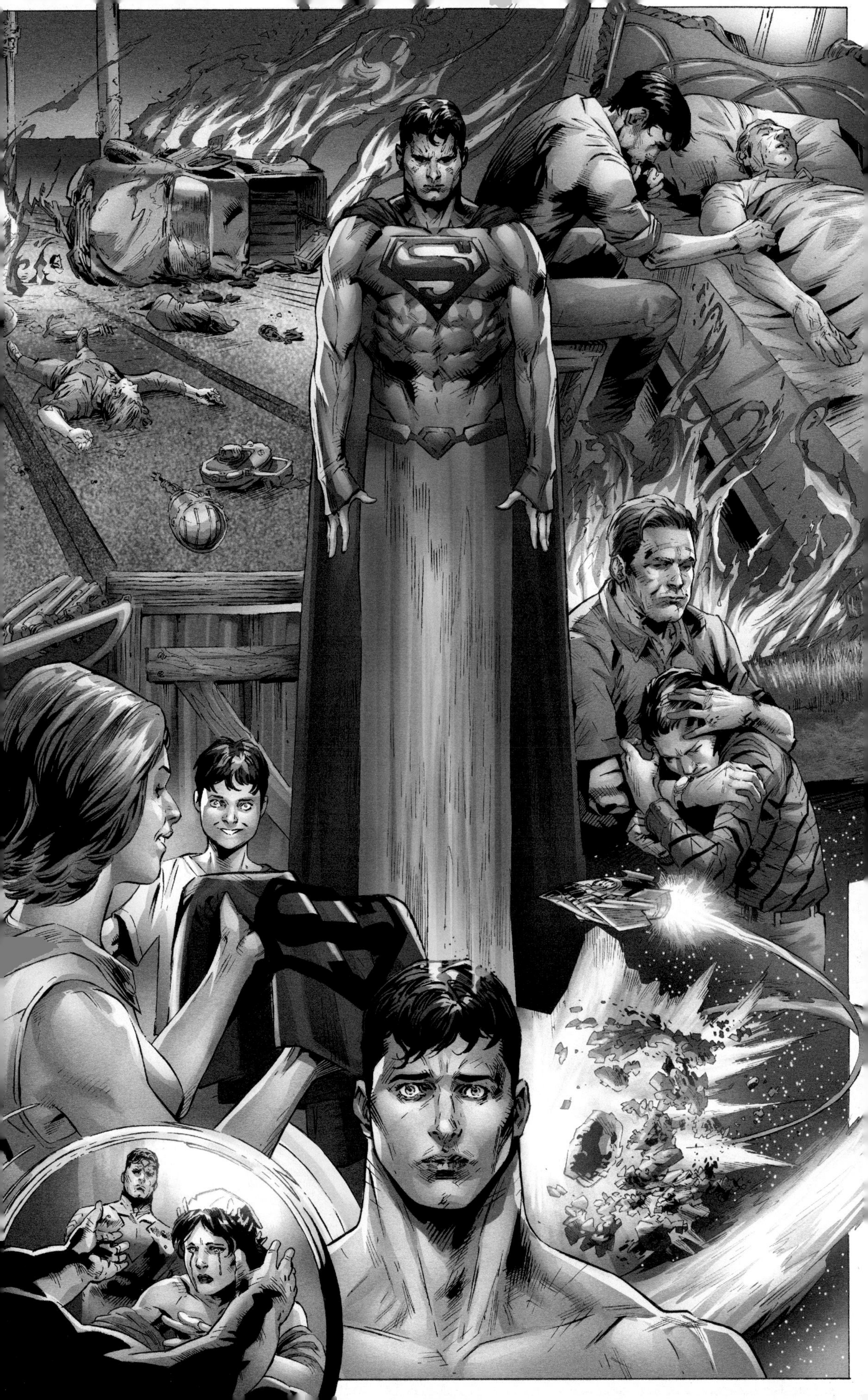

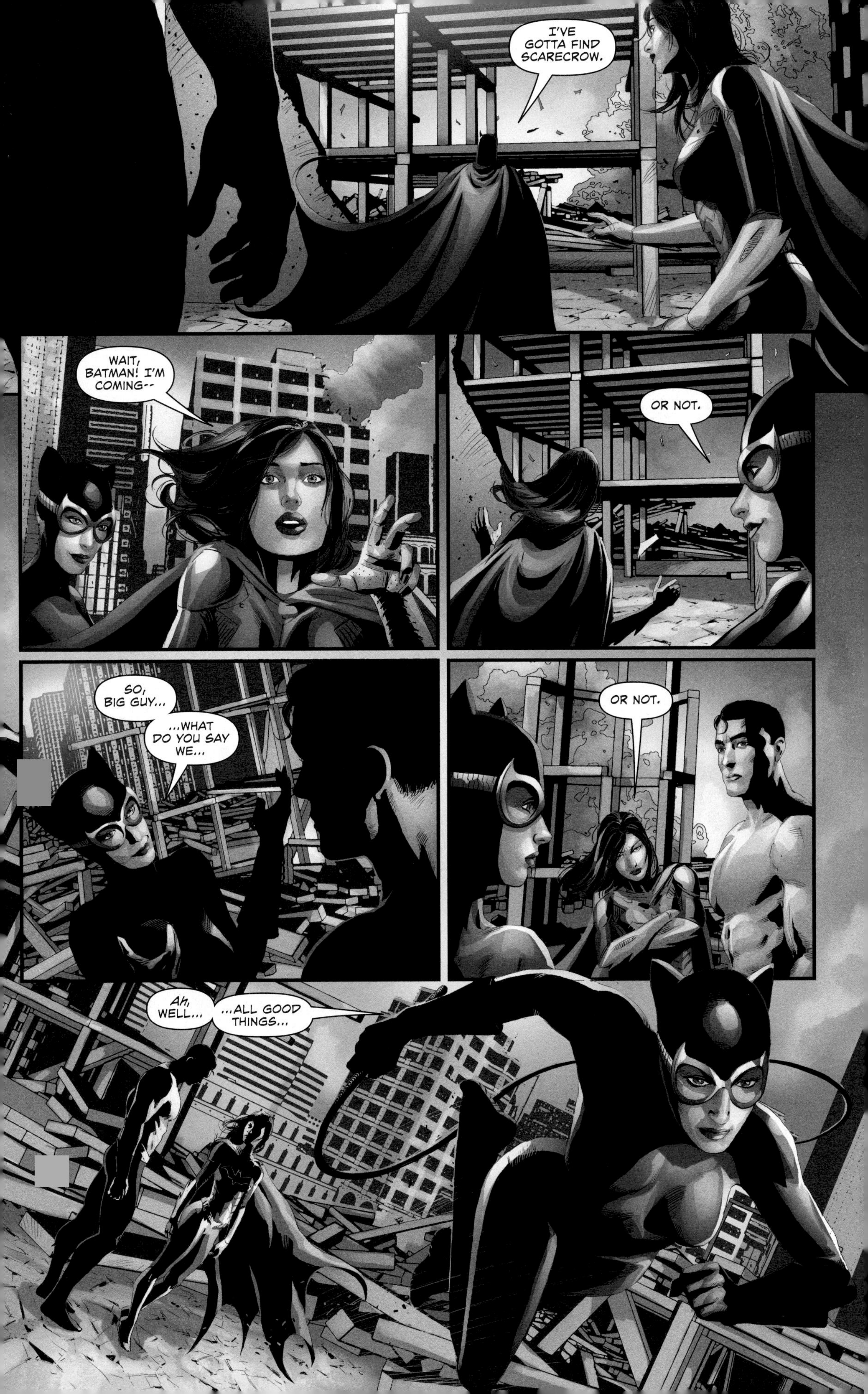
I'VE GOTTA FIND SCARECROW.
WAIT, BATMAN! I'M COMING--
OR NOT.
SO, BIG GUY...
...WHAT DO YOU SAY WE...
OR NOT.
Ah, WELL...
...ALL GOOD THINGS...

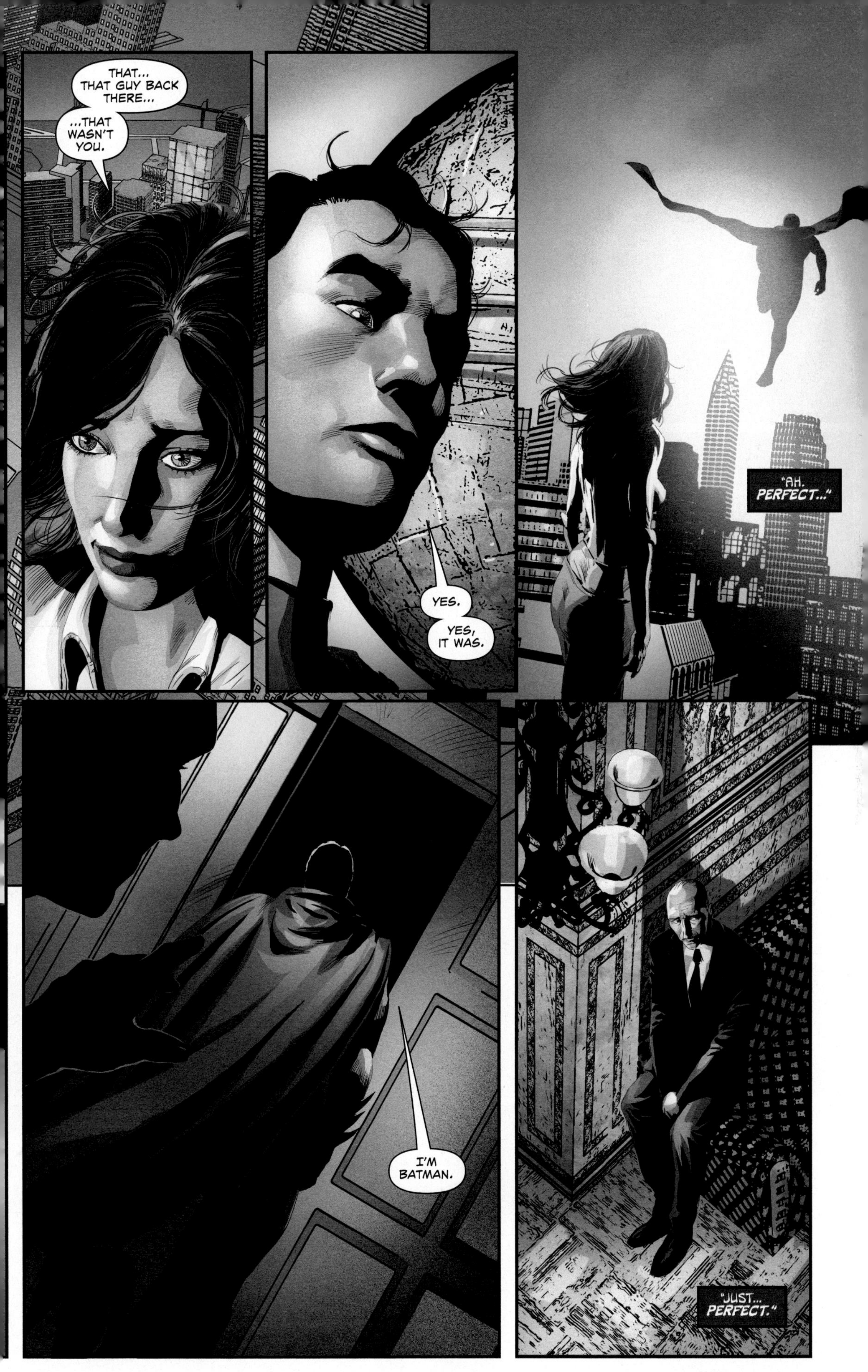
THAT... THAT GUY BACK THERE...
...THAT WASN'T YOU.
YES.
YES, IT WAS.
"AH. PERFECT..."
I'M BATMAN.
"JUST... PERFECT."

BATMAN/SUPERMAN 11
BATMAN '66 variant by Mike and Laura Allred

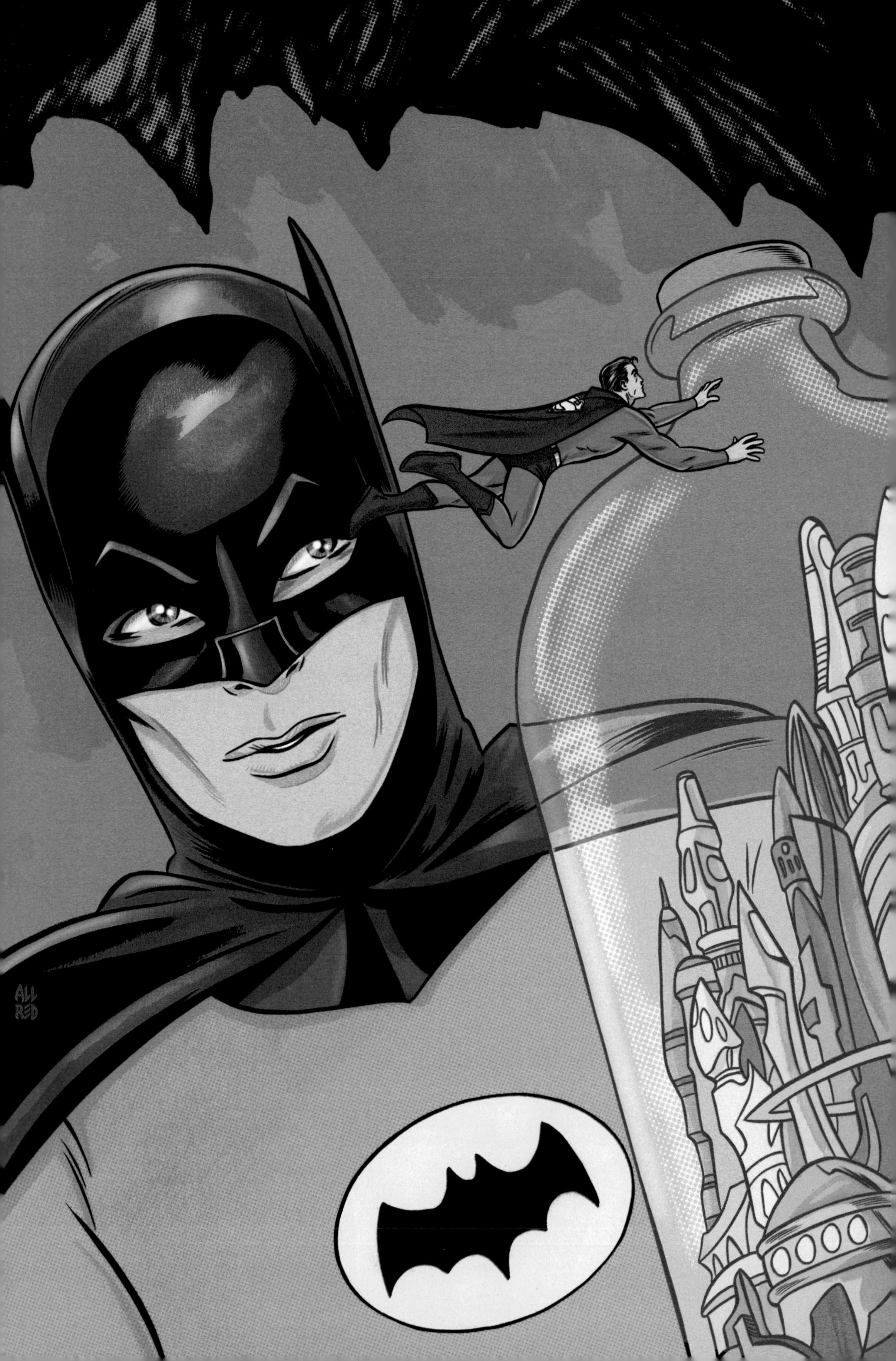

BATMAN/SUPERMAN 12
Variant by Emanuela Lupacchino with Fabio Mantovani

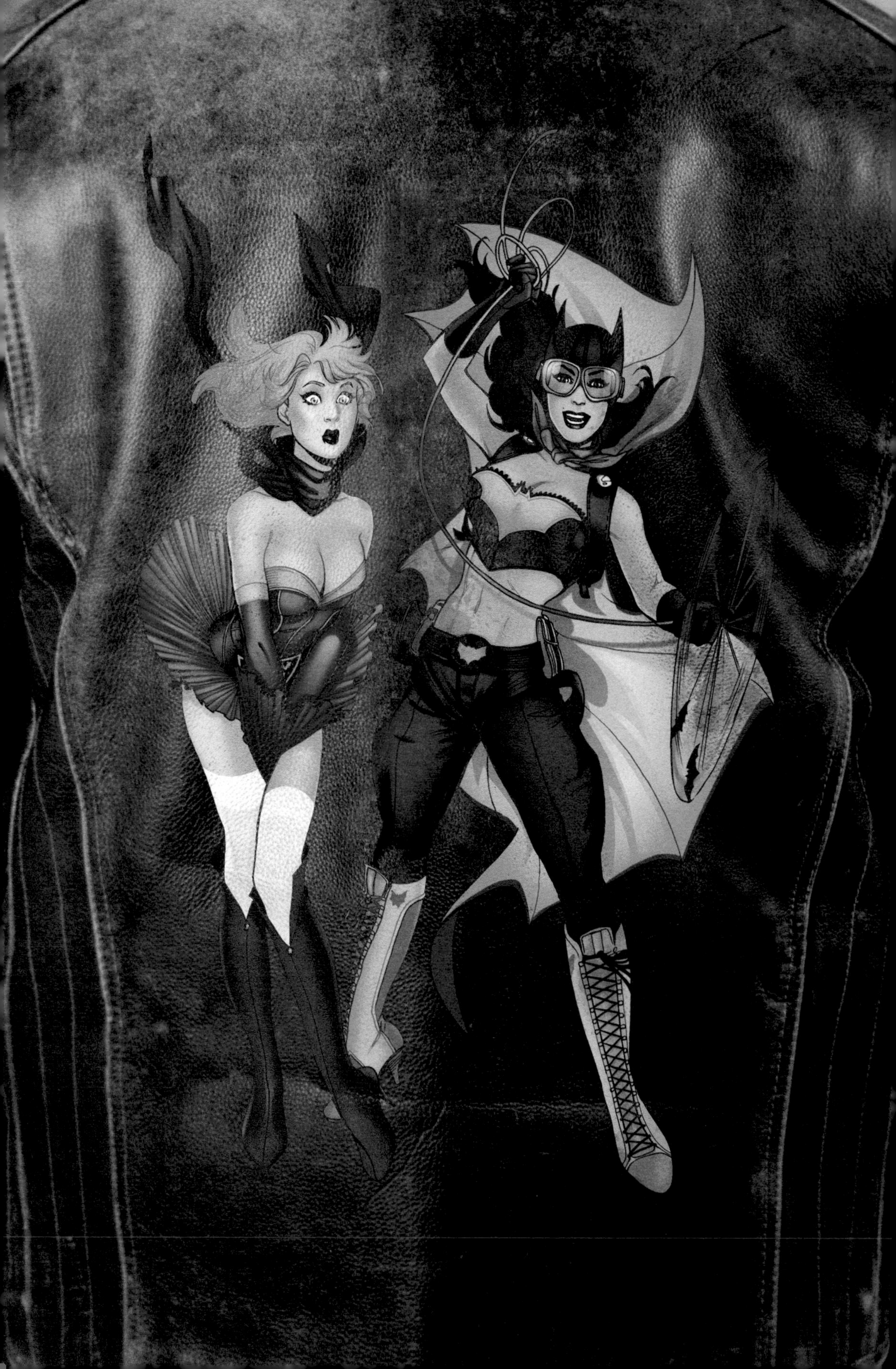

BATMAN/SUPERMAN 13
Variant by Ben Oliver

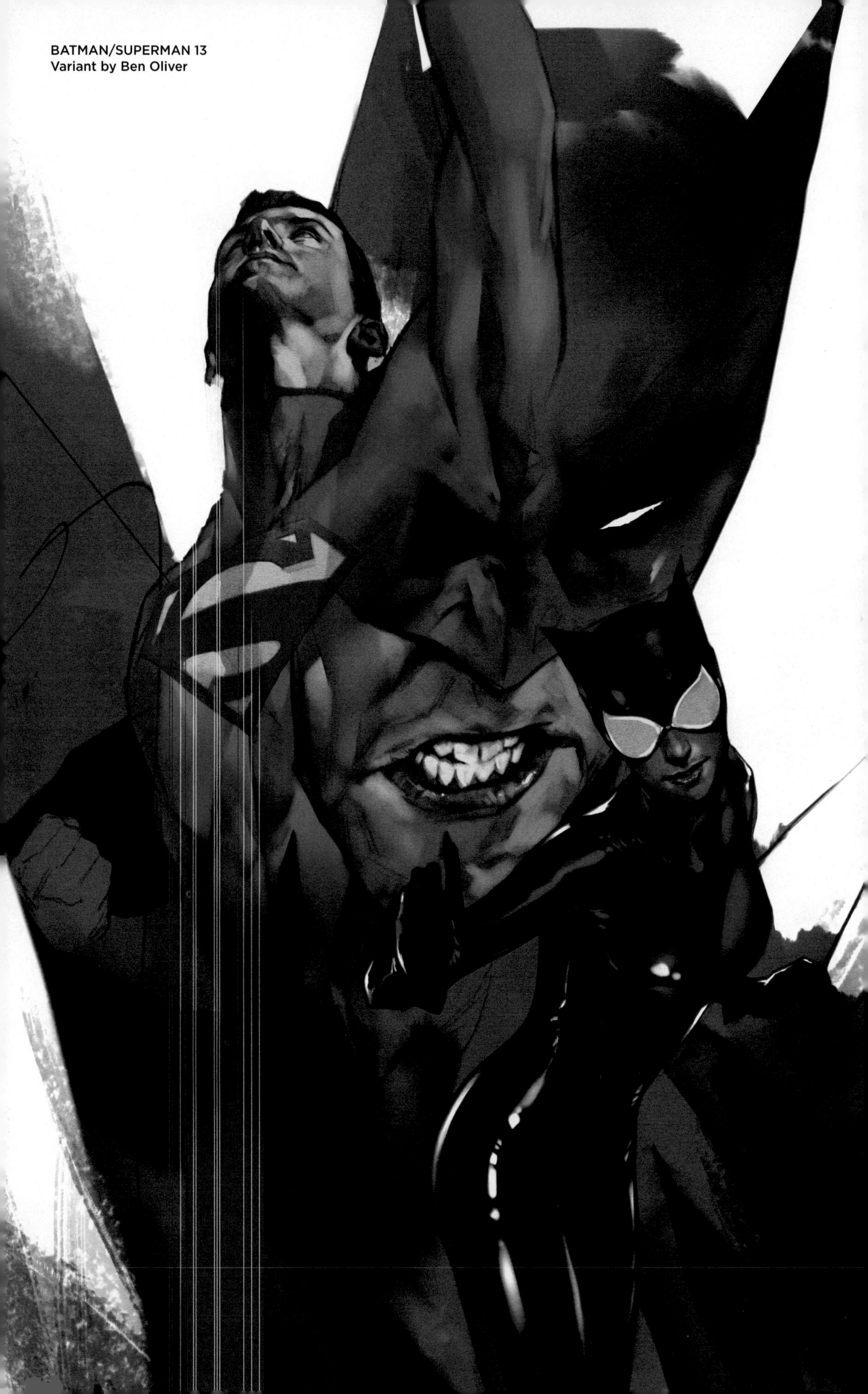

BATMAN/SUPERMAN 14
Variant by Paulo Siqueira

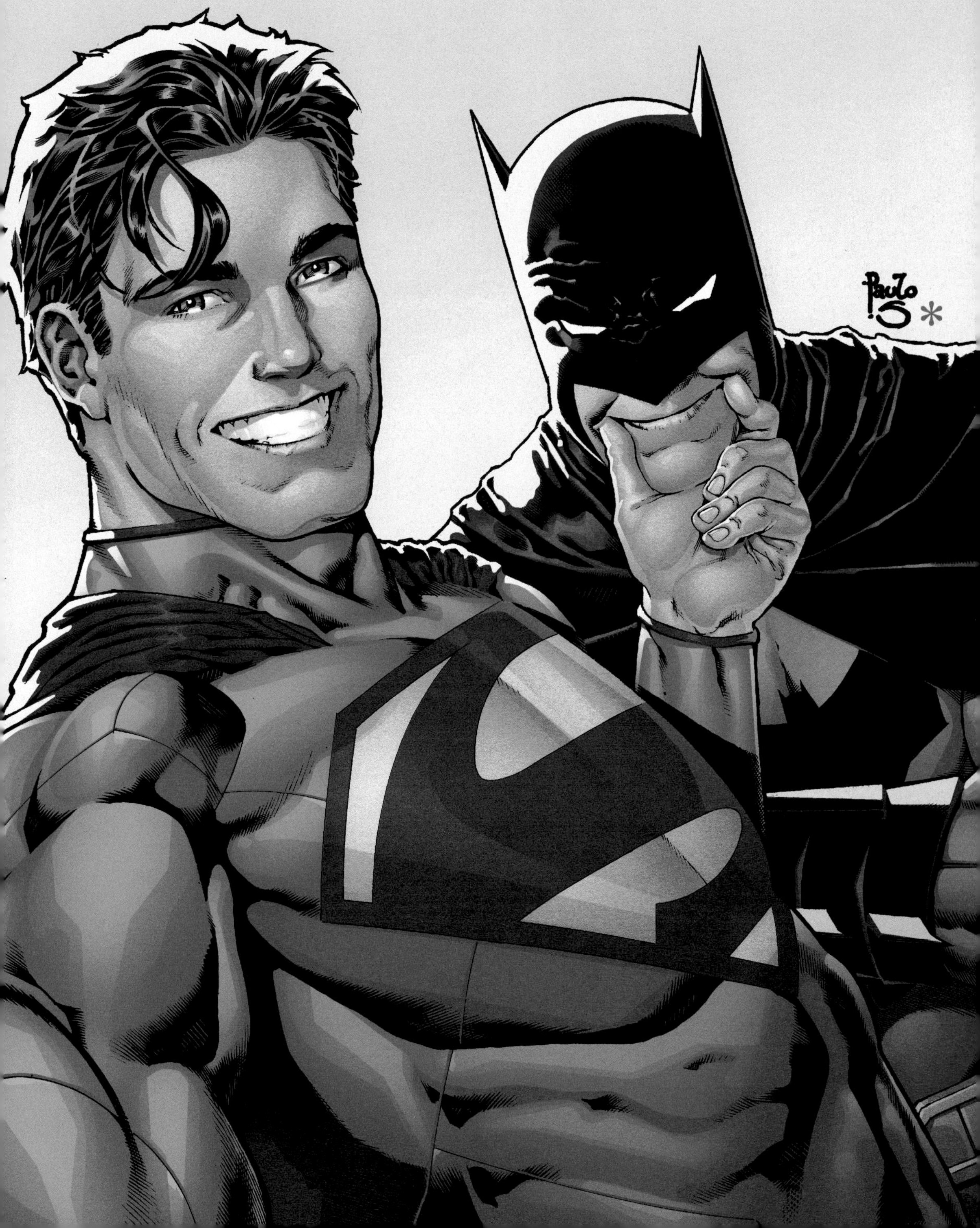

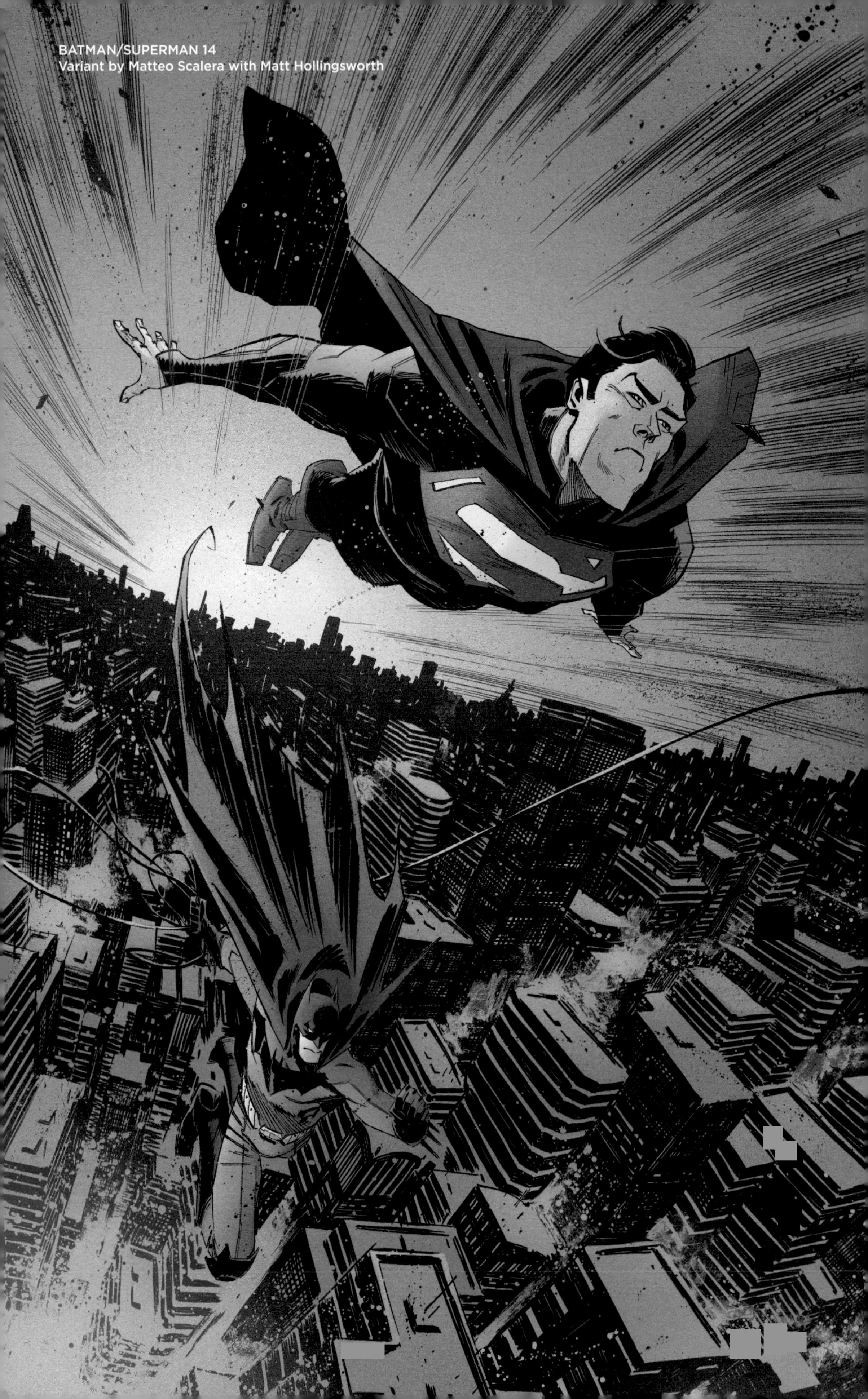

BATMAN/SUPERMAN 14
Variant by Matteo Scalera with Matt Hollingsworth

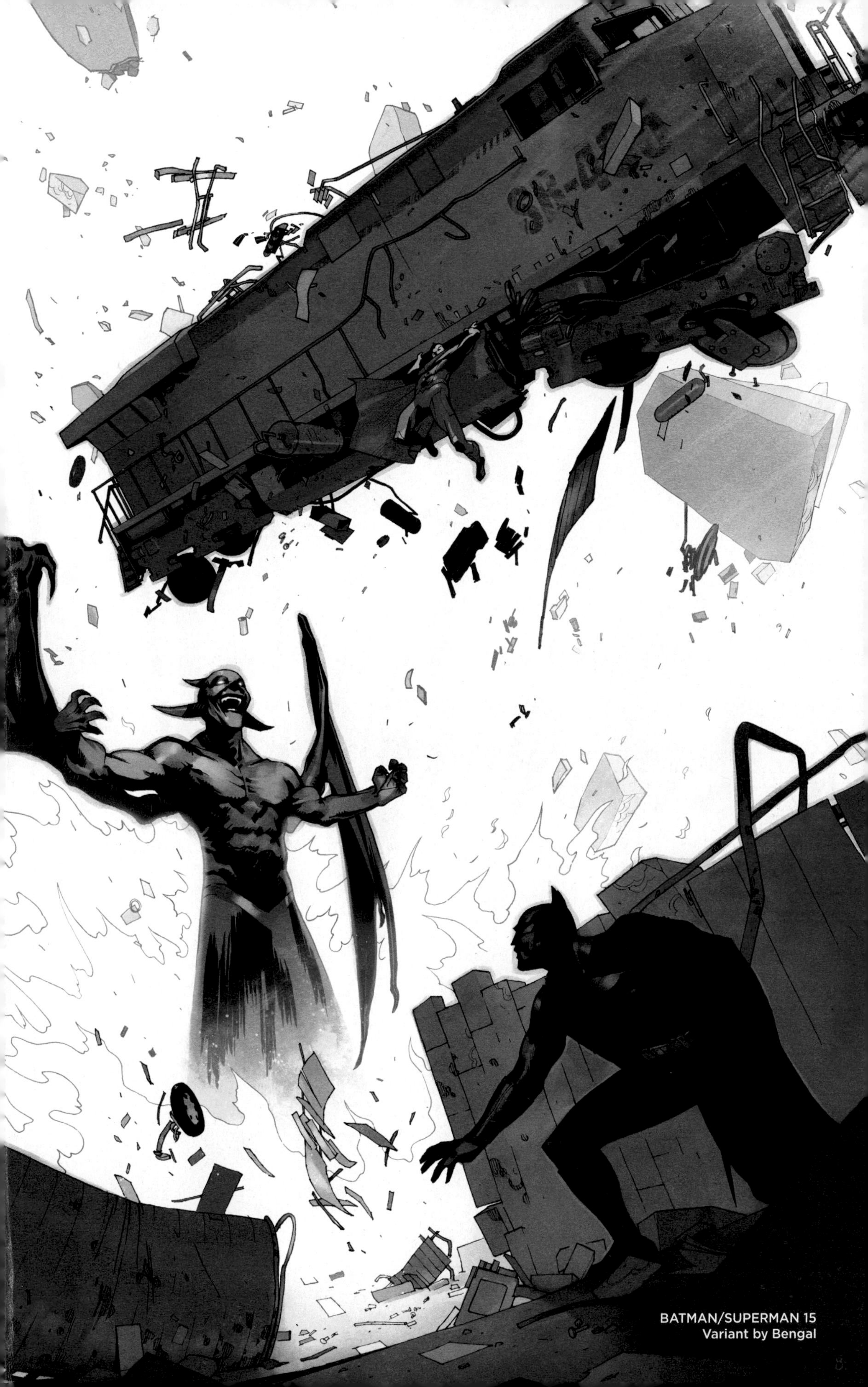

BATMAN/SUPERMAN 15
Variant by Bengal

BATMAN/SUPERMAN 15
Variant by Jon Bogdanove

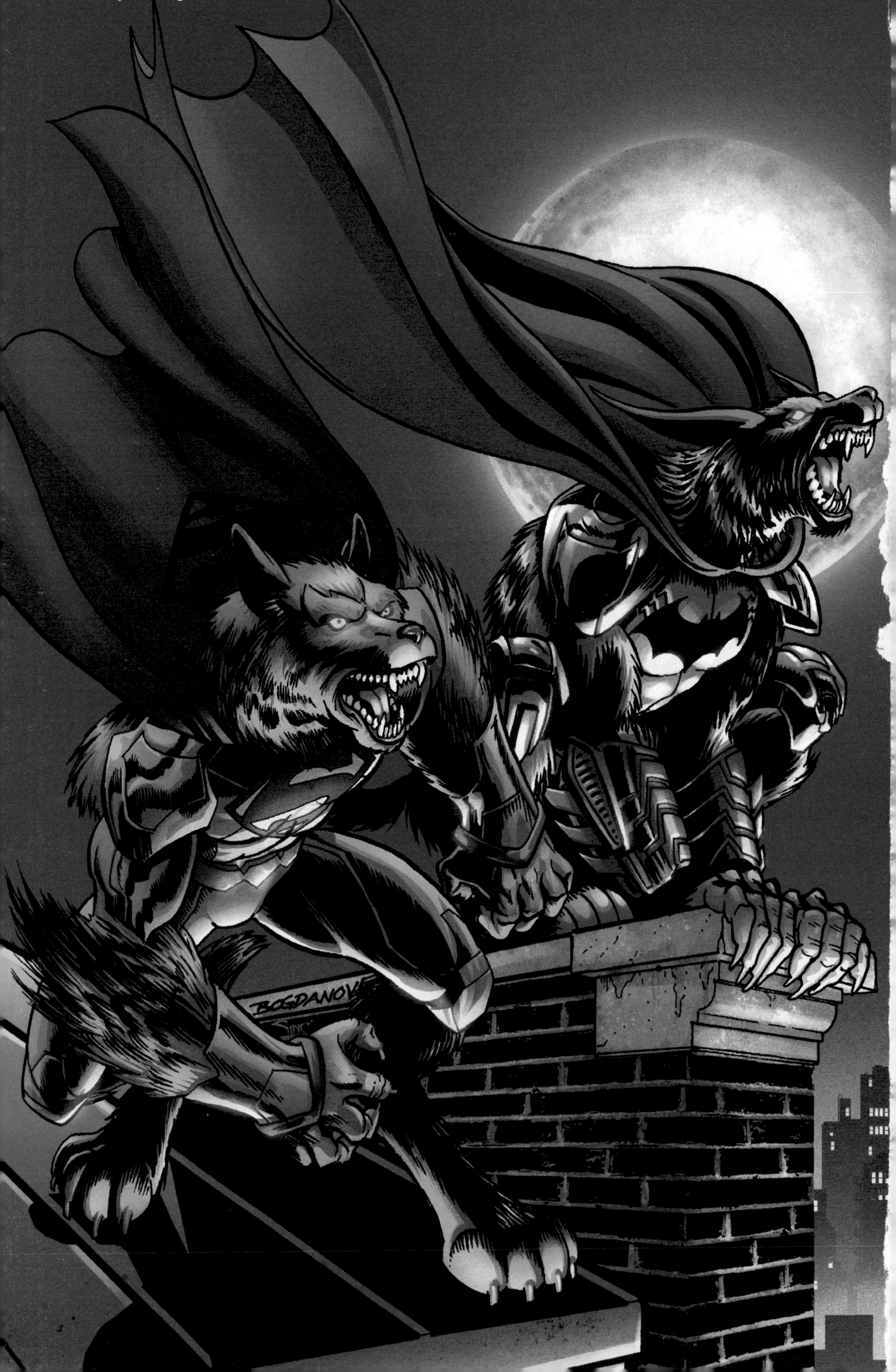
BOGDANOVE